CECIL C. KU

MW01010395

A Litigator's Guide to

Building Your Best Argument

SECOND EDITION

AMERICAN**BAR**ASSOCIATION

Solo, Small Firm and
General Practice Division

Cover design by Mary Anne Kulchawik/ABA Design

Printed in the United States of America.
23 22 21 20 19   5 4 3 2 1

Library of Congress Cataloging-in-Publication Data
Names: Kuhne, Cecil C., III, 1952- author. | American Bar Association.
    General Practice, Solo & Small Firm Division, sponsoring body.
Title: A litigator's guide to building your best argument / Cecil C. Kuhne III.
Other titles: Building your best argument
Description: Second edition. | Chicago, Illinois : American Bar Association,
    [2019] | Includes index.
Identifiers: LCCN 2019025631 (print) | LCCN 2019025632 (ebook) |
    ISBN 9781641055024 (paperback) | ISBN 9781641055031 (epub)
Subjects: LCSH: Trial practice—United States. | Forensic oratory. |
    Persuasion (Psychology) | Judicial process—United States.
Classification: LCC KF8915 .K795 2019 (print) | LCC KF8915 (ebook) |
    DDC 347.73/75—dc23
LC record available at https://lccn.loc.gov/2019025631
LC ebook record available at https://lccn.loc.gov/2019025632

Discounts are available for books ordered in bulk. Special consideration is given to state bars, CLE programs, and other bar-related organizations. Inquire at Book Publishing, ABA Publishing, American Bar Association, 321 N. Clark Street, Chicago, Illinois 60654-7598.

www.ShopABA.org

CONTENTS

Chapter 3
Simple and Direct: Clarity Counts   11

Chapter 4
Leading Off: The Importance of a Strong Introduction   21

Chapter 5
Summarily Speaking: An Overview's Significance   29

Chapter 6
Just the Facts: Setting Up the Background   39

Chapter 7
Short Bursts: For Diminishing Attention Spans   51

Chapter 8
History of the Case: The Devil Is in the Details   61

Chapter 9
Statutory Construction: It Can Be Critical   75

Chapter 10
Legislative Purpose: Determining Congressional Intent   93

Chapter 11
Discussing Case Law: An Overlooked Art Form   105

Chapter 12
Your Opponent's Argument: The Key to Effective Challenges   119

Chapter 13
Policy Considerations: They Often Count   135

Chapter 14
Obsessive Compulsive: Organization Is Key   147

Chapter 15
A Word About Trial and Appellate Briefs   175

Chapter 16
A Word About Oral Arguments   179

Chapter 17
Stellar Examples 183

Appendix
Model Briefs 251

INTRODUCTION

Judges are extremely busy people and, by sheer necessity, must view the onslaught of legal arguments laid before them with a healthy dose of skepticism. They are forced to do this for one very important reason: They must make the wisest decisions possible in the shortest amount of time allowable.

As a result, your job as an advocate is to provide complete, concise, and well-reasoned arguments that can be understood quickly and then confidently ruled upon by the court.

Because of the sheer volume of litigation facing the courts, both trial and appellate benches are more dependent than ever on well-prepared *written* arguments of counsel. Many—and, in fact, most—appellate cases are now decided without any oral argument. In those courts that still allow oral argument, the time allotted for it is usually highly restricted.

The same situation is increasingly true even in trial courts, where motions for dismissal and for summary judgment are often determined solely on written submissions. Trial briefs and memoranda of law provided to the court likewise assume greater significance than ever.

The result of all these developments is that judges are, more than ever before, dependent upon you to fully inform them about the background of the case, and to carefully construct an argument that candidly and competently applies the facts to the law. Not only is the judge unfamiliar with the facts of your specific case, but most likely is not an expert in the particular area of substantive law that you will be delving into. The court therefore expects you to highlight the relevant facts and to competently and clearly explain how the applicable body of law governs the case.

An advocate who skillfully builds the argument in a logical and precise way stands a remarkably better chance of influencing the final result in favor of his client. Words, after all, are the salt mines in which litigators work—and a glorious realm it can be.

Many fine treatises on rhetoric are available, and a practitioner can learn something useful from even the most arcane ones. These works, however, largely contain the ground rules of argumentative skills. The book before you takes a completely different tack. Rather than focus on a general list of rhetorical terms, it shows the rules being *applied* in real-life legal arguments. The emphasis here is on the *practical* rather than the theoretical. You can read about techniques on how to improve your tennis serve all day long, but at some point it makes sense to actually watch a professional *demonstrate* it.

The argument professionals whose work is featured in this book are attorneys with the U.S. Solicitor General's Office, and the examples are largely drawn from their edited briefs. These arguments are prepared by some of the brightest legal minds in the land, and they present interesting (and sometimes very unusual) cases ranging from securities to constitutional to criminal law.

But the subject matter of the selections is not nearly as important as the techniques employed. For the sake of clarity—and to focus our attention on the arguments at hand—the excerpts have been stripped of supporting authority, and case cites and references to the record have been eliminated. We will dissect and delve into these excerpts and, in the process, learn much.

We will discover that there are no magic bullets or secret formulas available when crafting an effective legal argument, but that our job as attorneys is ultimately to assist the judge—through attention to detail, word selection, sentence structure, and organization that is clear, concise, logical, and forceful—to make a fair decision. In the end, we can only earn the judge's confidence and trust through the hard, honest work of building a sturdy and truly tenable legal argument. Which is exactly as it should be.

1

The Adversarial Process: Realities of Litigation

The adversarial process is by no means a perfect method of resolving disputes. But time and experience have shown that it is by far the best system ever devised. Its contentious nature gives the litigants an opportunity to fully air their points of disagreement, and it ensures that the opposing parties' positions are duly considered since their advocates are arguing passionately for their best interests.

The lawyer's task is made even more difficult by the fact that the court invariably faces a significant caseload and there are many other cases striving for their attention. This renders it imperative that the litigator make the best argument in the most efficient way possible.

The judge opens a new case and faces prior judicial decisions, statutory language, constitutional principles, and procedural rules that serve as signposts. The judge will lean one way and then the other as the arguments of counsel are presented. By the end of the process, the judge will have read the briefs and key precedents, considered the difficult issues, and wrestled with how the case at hand fits into the matrix of applicable legal precedents.

Over the years, judicial caseloads have increased dramatically, and, unfortunately, court resources have not kept pace. Courts have attempted to increase productivity through the use of computer technology and modern management techniques. But the fact remains that litigation is by its very nature time-consuming.

The ultimate advice for any practitioner is simply this: Before putting words to paper in a motion or brief, you must first set aside your adversarial role and try to think *like* a judge. Not just *any* judge—you must think like the judge before you. You have to try and impose yourself into the mind of the particular person who will hear your case.

If the positions were reversed, and you sat where the judge does, think of what it is that you would want to know about the case:

- In what order would you want the story told?
- How would you want the case unraveled?
- What would facilitate your approach to a solution?

As the advocate, you must face these and many other difficult questions in order to make the case clear to the judge. If the court has to struggle to grasp the issues of the case, you have not fulfilled your duty to communicate effectively.

An artfully written trial or appellate brief is the cornerstone of a well-argued case, and the litigator is well-advised to follow a number of basic principles:

Good Organization

A brief that is solidly prepared reflects a logical progression of reasoning—from the premises of the argument through to its legal principles and then on to the ultimate conclusion. Good organization is like a road map that enables the judge to follow the argument from beginning to end without getting lost. A poorly organized brief often misunderstands the starting point, obscures the destination, and confuses the road in between. Deciding a case is difficult enough for a judge without these impediments.

Brevity

Wordiness is more than verbosity. It means trying to convey too much information or covering too many issues in a brief. Such wordiness reflects the failure to separate the material from the immaterial. Good pre-drafting analysis results in clearer prose and more concise arguments. Less really is better.

Precision and Clarity

Precision is the main goal of good writing. The failure to write simple, straightforward briefs is often the result of a lawyer's tendency to avoid analysis by overgeneralizing. A lawyer who is not sure of a legal principle or how to state it precisely may remain vague to conceal his uncertainty. To write with clarity and precision, you must know exactly what you want to say. Painstaking and thoughtful editing is essential for precise writing. This means going over the brief, sentence by sentence, and asking:

- What do I mean to say here?
- Have I said it, and no more?
- Could it be stated any more clearly?

The Art of Well-Written Legal Arguments

Judges appreciate a well-written brief that goes directly to the issue before the court, and they offer some helpful advice in this regard:

- *Use simple language.* Efforts to show your command of the English language or to impress the court are almost never effective.
- *Be brief.* State your point concisely—and preferably only once.
- *Accurately summarize the facts.* Misstating the record can irretrievably damage your credibility before the court.
- *State the law objectively.* Judges learn quickly whom they can rely on to tell them the current state of the law.
- *Analyze contrary authorities.* If the court later discovers these cases after argument, you will have lost almost all of your credibility.

2

The Battle of Persuasion: Harder Than It Looks

The primary tools of the litigator's trade are words, and the lawyer who uses them adroitly in his arguments maintains a distinct advantage over his adversary—whether in the courtroom, in negotiations, or in writing an appellate brief.

A litigator starts with the words of others—statutes, judicial opinions, contracts, and the myriad other sources of language that eventually lead to litigation. An effective advocate then strives to legitimately parse and interpret those words to the advantage of the client, and he does this by using his own words to craft a solid argument that will prove persuasive in communications with the court.

Lawyers typically work with challenging legal and factual situations that must be explained to a judge who has limited time to devote to the resolution of issues before him, no matter how interesting or important. This makes it even more imperative that the litigator present the best argument in the most efficient way possible.

If the judge's attention is drawn to faults of logic or expression, the client will ultimately suffer as a result. The risk is too great that if the argument is not made effectively, the busy judge may misinterpret what you are trying to say. A judge simply doesn't have time to decipher a poorly prepared argument, and the law-yer's credibility with the court will be damaged in the process.

Your analysis must provide the court with a quick and clear view of the legal landscape, without unnecessary distractions. The final product will be evaluated by how well it educates and convinces the judge that the reasoning and authorities contained within are correct. The key to building a great argument is to design a logically reasonable theory, and then reinforce it with compelling propositions and authority. The most persuasive arguments are not necessarily the most emotionally or morally moving. They are simply the ones with which the court is most likely to agree.

An argument, after all, is much more than a random collection of vague assertions that are abstractly positive for the advocate's client and abstractly negative for the opposing party. A collection of assertions becomes an argument only when they coalesce into a coherent presentation that firmly convinces the judge of their truth and fairness.

It is impossible, of course, to write more clearly than you think. Thought and expression are inseparably linked. Painstaking care in expressing what you want to say will help you avoid the hazy writing that a less careful approach produces. The goal in all of these efforts is clarity, conciseness, and forcefulness.

To write clearly, you must not only gather your material and carefully organize it, but you must think deeply about it. You must ponder the relationship of facts and law to one another, evaluate the importance of one point over another, and then construct a logical plan of presentation.

Considerable time must be spent digesting, organizing, and thinking through the implications of the material before you even begin to write. Only when you see clearly what is central to the argument can you persuade the court to focus on those points, instead of dispersing attention over a morass of details where nothing significant stands out.

From the pages of the arguments composed by the experts whose work is featured in this book, several principles clearly emerge:

Tailor Your Argument

In your attempts to persuade the judge, logic certainly has its place, but it isn't everything. First of all, you must tailor your argument to the specific audience you seek to persuade. To determine what will appeal to the court, you need to know not only what the court has held but also something about the viewpoints of its members. By reading previous opinions of the judge, you can gain an appreciation of the judge's legal mindset. If those views differ from your position in the litigation, this knowledge will give you the opportunity to make distinctions that might change the judge's mind.

You must also delve deeper into the judge's values and personality. For this reason, it's imperative that you contact those who have personally dealt with the judge to learn more about the judge's particular mannerisms, style, and idiosyncrasies. This information will then allow you to fashion an argument that the judge will find most appealing.

Establish Your Trustworthiness

There is really only one way to establish your trustworthiness: You must be scrupulously honest in how you present the facts and the applicable law to the court. Opposing counsel will be quick to point out any misstatements, distortions, or omissions you make, and, as a result, the court will quickly lose confidence in your reliability.

Admit Unfavorable Facts

When you are forthcoming about problems or weaknesses in your case, you enhance your credibility. If you initially disclose bad facts, you significantly minimize their impact.

Avoid Extreme Posturing

It is tempting to simply argue your client's position in the strongest possible terms while belittling the opposing argument. If, instead, you give your adversary his or her due while arguing your own case in a moderate and reasonable light, you rise admirably above the fray.

Demonstrate Your Knowledge of the Facts

A lawyer who is perceived as intimately familiar with the facts of the case will in the end prove far more persuasive. You can best do this by organizing your argument logically, explaining the source of your facts, and corroborating all of your assertions.

Thoroughly Research the Issues

Before presenting a legal analysis on any matter, it's essential that you conduct a thorough search of potentially relevant material, so that all of the appropriate cases, statutes, and regulations are considered.

Develop a Theory of the Case

After gathering all of the relevant information about the case, you must carefully analyze it. During this process, you must identify the fundamental reason why your client should win in the end.

Select Persuasive Points as Themes

As you scour the material you have gathered, you should develop short, fact-based statements of why equitably—rather than just legally—your client should prevail. The best themes are grounded in common sense and shared human experiences like fairness and honor, and therefore are those that will resonate emotionally with the judge.

A few other suggestions about themes: They should be brief, pithy, and partisan, but they must *not* appear contrived and manipulative. They should be consistent. And they should be repeated often, but not so much as to be annoying.

Emphasize Visual Aids

Studies show that people are strongly persuaded by what they see. You should, as appropriate, use charts, graphs, and other helpful visual aids to enhance comprehension and to render your points of argument more memorable.

The examples of legal argument set forth in this book demonstrate the truth of these axioms. They also reveal that a well-constructed argument invariably contains the following components:

- Forceful clarity
- Strong introduction
- Helpful overview
- Well-stated factual background
- Short paragraphs
- Thorough case history
- Reliable statutory construction
- Appropriate legislative history
- Stellar discussion of case law
- Effective challenges to opposing arguments
- Necessary policy considerations
- Obsessive-compulsive organization

Legal writing is a highly structured form of expression that requires an effective application of the facts at hand to the controlling rules of law. A legal writer cannot adequately approach this task without a great deal of planning, a process that is much like that of constructing a building. The architectural plans must be thoroughly conceived, or the resulting structure will not function well.

When you have managed to integrate the facts of your case into a seamless argument like those featured in the following pages, you will have successfully built an argument that you can be proud of. You will also have constructed an argument that can withstand the brutal onslaught of even the most skilled adversary. And that, after all is said and done, is not a terribly bad way to spend the day.

Common Characteristics of Poor Writing

Less than stellar briefs are commonly typified by:

- *Wordiness.* Wordiness means using more than two or three words when one will do. It also includes trying to convey too much information and cover too many issues. Wordiness often reflects the writer's failure to separate the material from the immaterial and to do the difficult work of editing. It is also a hallmark of writers who have not analyzed the case carefully before writing.
- *Lack of precision and clarity.* Precision is the goal of good writing. To write with clarity and precision, a brief writer must know exactly what he wants to say. He must then say it and add nothing more. Painstaking, thoughtful editing is essential for precise writing. This means going over your brief, sentence by sentence, and asking, "What do I mean to say here? Have I said it, and no more? Could it be clearer?"
- *Poor organization.* Good organization is like a road map for the judges that enables them to follow from the beginning to the end without getting lost. A poorly organized brief often misunderstands the starting point, misreads the destination, and then obscures the road in between.

3

■·■·■————————————————————————————

Simple and Direct:
Clarity Counts

To be effective, a good legal argument must be clear, precise, and readable. Straightforward language is therefore preferred over the more pretentious and vague rhetoric that is often found in legal arguments.

When your communication even slightly obscures the message, you risk immediate rejection from the court. This is so even though you might have obtained agreement from the court had you simply been more clear. When it comes to clarity, you rarely get second chances or the benefit of the doubt.

To understand the importance of clarity, it is necessary for legal writers to recognize two principles. First, you must support everything you say, because the legally trained mind is a skeptical one. It critically considers every assertion to be false until it is adequately proven. Second, no matter how important the issue, the judge will have a limited amount of time to reflect upon it. The more time a judge spends trying to understand your argument, the *less* time that judge will have to consider agreeing with it.

The legal system depends on clarity and precision to work well, and judges find pompous and vague diction to be an indication of a weak argument. So-called legalese is far less persuasive than straightforward and unadorned language. An overblown and stilted style typically conceals a flimsy position or a lack of analysis.

Achieving a crisp and lean style that is easy to read and understand is deceptively difficult work, but judges expect it. A less rigorous approach will quickly reveal itself, and the court will consider you unreliable because of your lack of precision and directness.

You must avoid the temptation to take a simple assertion and inflate it into something ponderous and academic. Concise expression is clearer and therefore more appealing. The judge has no time to spare and will either resent your inflated verbiage or simply refuse to consider it. You must, however, be careful that in your attempt to remain concise you don't go too far and eliminate necessary meaning.

It is also tempting to throw into your argument every seemingly positive assertion for your client and every negative criticism of your adversary. Such a shotgun approach is typically unwise. A far better approach is to develop fully the strong contentions and eliminate the weak ones. The paradox is this: the resulting document will not only be briefer but will more deeply explore the theories on which the judge's decision will be based.

Weak points—even if placed near strong ones—invite skepticism from the court, rather than allay it. If a judge believes that you have mixed potentially unreliable arguments with seemingly attractive ones, the judge's tendency is to dismiss the whole lot as unworthy of confidence. A judge has neither the time nor inclination to eliminate all suspect material and then reassemble the remaining parts into a reliable and cohesive whole.

The four examples demonstrating clarity that are set forth next deal with a number of interesting issues: (1) regulatory takings, (2) campaign finance restrictions, (3) anti-retaliation provisions under Title VII, and (4) the search of an automobile by police pursuant to an arrest. They all prove that a clear and direct approach to legal arguments is the most compelling one.

Example 1

This excerpt deals with the issue of whether a regulatory taking case was ripe for adjudication. The administrative agency denied the petitioner's application to build a beach and eventually the Supreme Court of Rhode Island agreed with that decision. Note how the argument opposing the takings claim made before the U.S. Supreme Court is achieved simply and directly—and as a result quite effectively.

This Court has repeatedly held that a claim for a regulatory taking is not ripe until the landowner has (a) sought permission to develop his property, and (b) received a final decision from the relevant land-use agency. Enforcement of ripeness principles not only protects the agency from premature judicial interference, but ensures that if litigation is ultimately required, the reviewing court will have the benefit of the agency's expertise.

In the instant case, the Supreme Court of Rhode Island reasonably concluded that petitioner's takings claim was *not* ripe. Petitioner's application for permission to construct a beach club did not propose any form of residential development, and it contemplated filling of a substantial majority of the wetlands on the parcel. Notwithstanding the agency's denial of that application, substantial uncertainty remains concerning the type and extent of development that would be permitted on petitioner's property. Because petitioner's beach club application bore no resemblance to the hypothetical subdivision that formed the basis of his takings claim, the trial court was forced to rely on extrinsic evidence regarding the manner in which the land-use regulators would likely have applied their rules to development proposals that petitioner never presented.

If this Court concludes that the Supreme Court of Rhode Island was in fact required to regard petitioner's takings claim as ripe, that claim nevertheless fails on the merits. The current value of petitioner's property is many times the amount the prior owner paid for it. Petitioner has failed to demonstrate that Rhode Island's adoption of wetlands protective measures has caused any diminution in the value of his parcel. His claim is simply that the tract would have appreciated more dramatically if development on the site were unrestricted. That claim, even if true, would be patently inadequate to establish a compensable taking.

The Supreme Court of Rhode Island noted that petitioner had acquired the subject property *after* the State's adoption of the wetlands protection measures, and the court treated that fact as an independent ground for rejecting petitioner's takings claim. We agree that where a purchaser chooses to acquire property that is subject to heightened regulatory oversight, application of the pre-existing regime does not subject the owner to the type of unfairness that must underlie a regulatory takings claim. That is especially so where, as here, the regulatory regime codifies background principles of public nuisance law.

Petitioner contends that a person who acquires property after a regulatory restriction has been imposed thereby acquires the right to pursue any regulatory takings claim that the prior owner might have asserted. But plainly there is no general rule that every potential constitutional claim must be freely and fully assignable. In any event, petitioner has failed to establish that the prior owner of the subject property had any takings claim to assign.[1]

Example 2

The question of whether congressional restrictions on campaign finance contributions to political parties are constitutional (in the same way that limits on contributions to candidates are) is the subject of this excerpt. Observe the simplicity and directness of this argument before the Supreme Court in favor of the constitutionality of such restrictions.

In *Buckley v. Valero*, this Court upheld limits on campaign contributions to candidates for federal office. Under the Federal

Election Campaign Act (FECA), a *coordinated* expenditure made in support of a federal candidate is likewise treated as a contribution. In enacting the statute, Congress sought to facilitate the distinctive functions of political parties by authorizing party committees to make coordinated expenditures that would otherwise exceed the Act's limitations on contributions to candidates.

Respondent's facial challenge to the Act's limitations on party-coordinated expenditures can succeed only if those limitations are unconstitutional, in spite of the fact that coordinated expenditures are the functional and constitutional equivalent of direct contributions to candidates. Because this Court has previously sustained the Act's contribution limits against First Amendment challenge, and because the Act allows political parties to make much larger coordinated expenditures than other political committees, the limitations on party spending are presumptively constitutional.

Large coordinated expenditures by political-party committees pose essentially the same risks of corruption as similar expenditures by other entities. Congress could reasonably conclude that large party-coordinated expenditures, like large campaign contributions in general, may be used to exert influence over legislators' behavior while in office. A candidate assisted by party-coordinated expenditures may, once elected, be tempted to take actions favorable to the individuals or political-action committees who have contributed funds to the party, thereby using the party as a conduit to evade limits on contributions to candidates. Alternatively, the candidate may be tempted to favor the private interests or policy preferences of party leaders who control the coordinated expenditures.

Even when individual party leaders conscientiously seek to use the influence generated by large coordinated expenditures not to advance their own interests or those of individual contributors, but to further the interests of the membership as a whole, Congress may legitimately choose to limit the extent to which large infusions of money may be used to achieve the party's objectives. Congress has reasonably concluded that the undue influence of large campaign contributions on public policy is inherently subversive of democratic governance, regardless of the donor's motives. That judgment underlies contribution limits in general (whose application has never depended upon the motivation of the donor), and it is no less applicable to political parties.

Political parties have no favored constitutional status, which entitle them to an exemption from spending limitations that apply to other potential donors. The Framers distrusted political parties and sought to devise governmental structures that would curtail their influence. Although the right to form and operate a political party is one aspect of the freedom of speech and association protected by the First Amendment, the Framers did not intend to create special privileges or incentives for partisan activity. The drafting and ratification history of the Constitution provides no support for respondent's contention that the First Amendment entitles political parties to exemption from the coordinated spending limits that apply to other voluntary associations.

In enacting the statute, Congress sought to balance competing objectives by permitting parties to play an important role in federal campaigns without leaving party spending wholly unconstrained. That legislative judgment is entitled to substantial deference, particularly in light of Congress's intimate familiarity with the workings of our political system. Respondent's First Amendment claim would inappropriately restrict the authority of government to define and limit the role of the parties vis-à-vis other participants in ongoing public-policy debates.[2]

Example 3

This argument deals with the anti-retaliation provision under Title VII of the Civil Rights Act. The Sixth Circuit held that the statute provided no protection to an individual who had revealed acts of discrimination during an investigation about sexual harassment in the workplace. Note the effectiveness of the opposing argument—urging such protections—as a result of its direct and transparent delivery.

When acts of discrimination are revealed during an internal investigation into possible sexual harassment in the workplace, that disclosure is protected activity under Title VII's anti-retaliation provision, Section 704(a). The Sixth Circuit erred in holding that neither clause of Section 704(a) protected petitioner, and its construction of the section creates an unjustified gap in Title VII's protection against retaliation. Internal investigations are an integral aspect of Title VII, and there is no reason to leave cooperating witnesses unprotected. The court's rule is not only at odds with the text of Section 704(a), but with its object and the guidance materials of the Equal Employment Opportunity Commission (EEOC).

The court of appeals' decision is out of step with the precedent in other circuits, but it does not squarely conflict with other circuit precedents. Nevertheless, even in the absence of a clear conflict, the question presented is of sufficient importance to the effective enforcement of Title VII to warrant resolution by this Court. In particular, the court of appeals' failure to protect employees in internal investigations raises significant concerns in light of this Court's decisions in the following three cases: *Faragher v. City of Boca Raton, Burlington Industries, Inc. v. Ellerth*, and *Kolstad v. American Dental Ass'n*. These three cases impose an *affirmative* duty on employers routinely to investigate allegations of sexual harassment to avoid liability or limit damages under Title VII.

The court of appeals erred in finding that Section 704(a) did not protect petitioner against retaliation for adverse testimony in an internal investigation that pre-dated filing of an EEOC charge. The United States takes the view that petitioner is protected by both the opposition and participation clauses of Section 704(a). But it makes no sense to conclude, as the court did, that petitioner is not protected by *either* clause. A cooperating witness, no less than an employee who initiates a complaint, needs protection against retaliation for providing candid information to the employer during an internal investigation.

Internal investigations, by virtue of this Court's decisions, are an integral part of Title VII's enforcement scheme. Recovery by employees and liability for employers can turn on the existence of internal complaint policies and the extent to which the employee avails himself of such procedures. Internal procedures can only play the role the Court envisioned if employees who give candid testimony are protected against retaliation. The need for protection does not turn on whether an EEOC charge has been filed at the point the witness testifies. The court of appeals' ruling thus creates an inexplicable gap in Title VII's protection against retaliation that this Court should correct.[3]

Example 4

The argument in this case concerns the extent to which a police officer can search an automobile after an arrest. The advocate here claims that the search was properly conducted. Notice how the topic is discussed before the U.S. Supreme Court in a very clear and straightforward manner.

In *New York v. Belton*, this Court adopted a bright-line rule to guide a law enforcement officer when arresting the "recent occupant" of an automobile. That rule provides that the officer may search the passenger compartment of the vehicle as a contemporaneous incident of the lawful custodial arrest. The Arizona Court of Appeals' decision in this case limits the application of the *Belton* rule to instances in which the arrestee exited a vehicle at the *direction* of law enforcement personnel, rather than voluntarily. That limitation should be rejected.

The *Belton* rule is grounded on historic rationales of the search-incident-to-arrest doctrine, which is the need to provide officer safety and preserve evidence of a crime. Those rationales are implicated whenever officers effect a "custodial arrest" of the recent occupant of a vehicle. A custodial arrest is a volatile and dangerous event, with heightened risks that a suspect will grab for a weapon or attempt to conceal or destroy criminal evidence. In the *Belton* context, those concerns justify the search of a vehicle recently occupied by an arrestee, regardless of whether the arrestee was ordered out of the car by police or voluntarily exited the car. It is the arrest of the vehicle's recent occupant, not the reason he exited the vehicle, which justifies the *Belton* search. A rule that is dependent on whether police confront arrestees while they are still inside a vehicle is antithetical to Belton's officer-safety rationale because it may increase the volatility of an already dangerous encounter.

The Arizona Court of Appeals' decision not only has no connection to the rationales of *Belton*, but it needlessly blurs the bright line drawn by *Belton*. In *Belton*, this Court recognized that it was essential to provide the officer in the field with a "single familiar standard" to determine when a vehicle search is authorized incident to an arrest. The court of appeals' decision undermines that important objective by requiring officers to undertake an *ad hoc*, case-by-case inquiry into the reason that an arrestee exited his vehicle in order to decide whether a search of the passenger compartment is authorized. That inquiry reintroduces the uncertainty and line-drawing concerns that this Court sought to eliminate in *Belton*. Indeed, the court of appeals in this case held that the applicability of *Belton* turned on such subjective inquiries as whether respondent was aware of police activity at the residence when he exited his car or whether the respondent interpreted the light shined into his car as a signal that the police intended to confront him.

Belton has built-in limitations, but those limitations do not support the Arizona Court of Appeals' rule. *Belton* applies only in the case of the lawful arrest of a vehicle's "recent occupant" and only with respect to vehicle searches conducted as a "contemporaneous incident" to such an arrest. In some cases, where the individual has moved a considerable distance from the car before the arrest, there may be disagreement on whether an arrestee is a sufficiently "recent occupant" to trigger *Belton*. But it is clear that *Belton* applies in the far more typical situation in which an officer sees an individual exit the vehicle and arrests him moments later in the same area that the arrestee might have occupied if he had been ordered out of the car.

Under a proper application of *Belton*, the search of respondent's vehicle was valid. Respondent was a "recent occupant" of the car; he was subjected to a "lawful custodial arrest" next to the car; and the search of respondent's car was conducted as "a contemporaneous incident of that arrest." The police arrested respondent moments after an officer saw him exit his car and searched his vehicle as part of one continuous event. Accordingly, the challenged search was a reasonable and lawful intrusion under the Fourth Amendment. The judgment of the Arizona Court of Appeals should be reversed.[4]

Notes

References to citations, transcripts, footnotes, and some authorities omitted for sake of clarity.

1. Palazzo v. Rhode Island, No. 99-2047.
2. FEC v. Colorado Republican, No. 00-191.
3. Crawford v. Metropolitan Government of Nashville, No. 06-1595.
4. Arizona v. Gant, No. 02-1019.

Keep It Simple

There is a corollary to the established principle of "tell it short and plain." It is "tell it once, and twice at most." Erosion by repetition is a very poor way to convince.

Most judges will understand the issue the first time, and almost all of them will comprehend the issue when it is repeated the second time. Judges are also more likely to understand the issue if it is discussed early on.

4

Leading Off:
The Importance of a
Strong Introduction

Fairly or not, first impressions do count.

The beginning passages of an argument greatly influence how its later passages will be read, and courts tend to read submissions most carefully at the beginning. Because judges are pressed for time, they expect the strongest arguments first. If they find themselves initially considering weak points, they either form an adverse opinion—or worse—they stop reading altogether.

The human mind does not like to be held in suspense for long. Judges tend to lean in one direction or the other almost immediately, and they do not easily reverse themselves. After reading the introduction to your case, even an open-minded judge may have difficulty changing his initial reaction.

A judge quickly becomes impatient with long prefatory verbiage because it is rarely useful in making a decision. You must avoid the esoteric side of things, no matter how interesting it may be, because it will not aid the judge in making a decision.

Sometimes, of course, the nature of the argument requires that the most compelling assertions be delayed somewhat to avoid confusing the court. Some contentions are simply too difficult to understand unless preceded by explanatory passages. In these situations, you must weigh the need for clarity against the necessity to express the essence of your theory at the beginning.

Judges, like most readers, tend to be *most* attentive to a document at its beginning, *less* attentive in the end, and *least* attentive in the middle. Omit the unnecessary material that clouds the picture you want the judge to see. You need to make the humanity behind your position come alive by describing how your client behaved properly and the other side did not, letting the facts themselves make the case for the most part.

The four examples that follow demonstrate strong introductions that deal with a number of interesting issues: (1) racial discrimination, (2) regulations of the Centers for Disease Control, (3) the Disabilities Act, and (4) the federal money-laundering statute. They all emphasize the need for a strong introduction that grabs the attention of the judge and promptly persuades the judge to your side of the argument.

Example 1

The following excerpt concerns a racial discrimination case before the U.S. Supreme Court. The issue deals with whether classifying students by race violates the Equal Protection Clause. Notice the forcefulness of the introduction in an argument opposed to the racial plan.

The County's race-based student assignment plan violates the Equal Protection Clause of the Fourteenth Amendment.

In *Brown v. Board of Education*, the Court held that intentionally classifying students on the basis of race violates the Equal Protection Clause and declared the ultimate objective in eliminating such *de jure* segregation is achieving a "system of determining admission to the public schools on a nonracial basis." More recently, the Court has repeatedly confirmed that all government classifications based on race must be subjected to strict scrutiny and are constitutional only if narrowly tailored to further a compelling government interest.

The County has not demonstrated any compelling interest to justify its use of race. To be sure, the government has a compelling interest in remedying the effects of past intentional discrimination. But the plan of Jefferson County Public School (JCPS) was adopted after a federal court had found that the past vestiges of *de jure* segregation had been eliminated. Nor does the plan implicate the only other compelling interest that the Court has recognized in the public education context the diversity interest identified in *Gratz v. Bollinger* and *Grutter v. Bollinger*. The JCPS plan is not designed to assemble a genuinely diverse student body, and thus it provides for no individualized, holistic consideration of students. Instead, the plan involves "outright racial balancing," which is "patently unconstitutional." Whatever the outer boundaries of the Equal Protection Clause, it clearly prohibits the kind of racial balancing at issue here, and the Court need proceed no further in deciding this case.

The JCPS plan likewise fails each of the narrow tailoring factors identified in *Grutter* and *Gratz*. First, the plan provides for nothing approaching the holistic, individualized consideration that this Court has stressed is the hallmark of a constitutionally permissible race-conscious admissions process. Second, the plan is indistinguishable from a quota, because it operates based on a fixed percentage of "black" and "other" students at JCPS schools. Third, the County failed seriously to consider race-neutral alternatives for eliminating or reducing minority isolation. Fourth, the plan unfairly burdens innocent third parties because it denies certain students admission to the school of their choice solely on the basis of their race. Finally, the plan has no fixed or logical end point.

School districts have an unquestioned interest in reducing minority isolation through race-neutral means. But the solution to addressing racial imbalance in communities or student bodies is not to adopt race-conscious measures. Such measures are not only at odds with *Brown*'s ultimate objective of "achieving a system of determining admission to the public schools on a nonracial basis," but contravene the fundamental liberties guaranteed to each citizen by the Equal Protection Clause.[1]

Example 2

This case deals with the regulations of the Centers for Disease Control on salmonella. Note how effectively the opening grabs the attention and invites further consideration of the argument.

Salmonella is a food-borne bacterium found in the gastrointestinal tract of birds, reptiles, and a variety of farm animals. Salmonella enteritidis (SE), one of more than two thousand types of salmonella, can cause symptoms in humans such as nausea, vomiting, abdominal cramps, diarrhea, fever, headache, and sometimes death. Approximately 15 to 20 percent of those who have been diagnosed with salmonellosis, the disease caused by salmonella, require hospitalization.

After the Centers for Disease Control (CDC) determined that human health problems linked to SE exposure were increasing, the U.S. Department of Agriculture (USDA) promulgated interim regulations that were designed to address the danger that SE-contaminated eggs sold in interstate commerce would cause illness to humans. The regulations provided that, when a farm was identified as the probable source of SE-contaminated eggs, USDA would conduct environmental testing, which could include the slaughter and testing of hens. If that environmental testing yielded a positive result, eggs from the relevant flock could be sold only for pasteurization and could not be shipped in interstate commerce for sale as table eggs. Sale for pasteurization typically brings the vendor a lower price than sale as table eggs.

Three separate outbreaks of SE contamination, resulting in approximately four hundred individuals becoming ill, were traced back to eggs laid at henhouses on three farms owned by respondent Rose Acre Farms, Inc. (Rose Acre). In the course of the ensuing investigation, some seven thousand hens were removed from Rose Acre's henhouses for slaughter and testing. During the period that it was subject to USDA restrictions, Rose Acre sold for pasteurization nearly seven hundred million eggs that could otherwise have been sold as table eggs.

Rose Acre filed suit in the U.S. District Court for the Southern District of Indiana, asserting a variety of challenges to the USDA regulations. The court of appeals ultimately sustained the regulations. The court rejected Rose Acre's contention that the regulations were arbitrary and capricious, finding them to be a reasonable means of protecting the human population against consumption of SE-contaminated eggs. The court of appeals also rejected Rose Acre's argument that the regulations were invalid because USDA had made no provision for compensating those who suffered pecuniary losses as a result of the regulatory restrictions. The court explained that, if either the Constitution or a federal statute were found to require the payment of compensation for losses suffered as a result of the USDA regulatory program, the Court of Federal Claims (CFC) could award relief.[2]

Example 3

This excerpt deals with the application of the Federal Disabilities Act in a case before the U.S. Supreme Court. Observe the strength of the opening as it argues that this is an important civil rights issue and one that is necessary to protect countless individuals with handicaps.

The question presented here is one of broad and enduring importance. The Disabilities Act is vital civil rights legislation needed to protect millions of Americans against invidious and irrational stereotypes and limitations on their ability to function in society. As a consequence of the Eighth Circuit's decision in this case, the operation of this important civil rights legislation has been significantly impaired in seven States. Unlike litigants in the six circuits where the Disabilities Act's abrogation of Eleventh Amendment immunity has been sustained, persons with disabilities in the Eighth Circuit cannot fully enforce their federal rights under the Disabilities Act.

Contrary to this Court's precedents, the decision of the Eight Circuit places unwarranted limits on Congress's authority to provide "strong, consistent, enforceable standards addressing discrimination against individuals with disabilities." Following this Court's decisions in *Seminole Tribe v. Florida and City of Boerne v. Flores,* four courts of appeals held that the abrogation of Eleventh Amendment immunity contained in the Disabilities Act is a valid exercise of Congress's power under Section 5 of the Fourteenth Amendment to "enforce" the Equal Protection Clause. The four courts of appeals that have considered or reconsidered the validity of the Disabilities Act's abrogation after the Eighth Circuit's decision in this case and after this Court's decision last Term in *Florida Prepaid Postsecondary Education Expense Board v. College Savings Bank* have all rejected the Eighth Circuit's holding and have upheld the Disabilities Act's abrogation as valid Section 5 legislation. The question of Congress's authority to abrogate the States' Eleventh Amendment immunity in the Disabilities Act has thus been extensively evaluated and considered by the courts of appeals. The conflict is firmly entrenched and incapable of resolution absent intervening action by this Court.[3]

Example 4

This introduction deals with a federal money-laundering statute. Note its immediate impact as it argues that the Seventh Circuit has misconstrued the meaning of the term "proceeds."

The principal federal money-laundering statute prohibits transactions in unlawfully derived "proceeds" when those transactions are intended to promote the underlying illegal activity or conceal its proceeds. The Seventh Circuit has misconstrued the principal federal money-laundering statute in a way that conflicts with decisions of other courts of appeals and significantly impedes effective enforcement of the law. The court's holding that the word "proceeds" in 18 U.S.C. 1956(a) means "net income" or "profits" is contrary to the common understanding of the word.

The court's interpretation of "proceeds" also rejects the meaning that Congress gave the same term in related statutes, including one enacted just two years before the money-laundering statute.

The court's erroneous holding warrants review. It squarely conflicts with decisions of other courts of appeals and cannot be reconciled with the results and reasoning in numerous other money-laundering cases. It removes a large class of routinely prosecuted money-laundering cases from the reach of the statute. And it subjects the government to an unreasonable burden of proof and enmeshes the courts in intractable disputes over the accounting principles that should govern illegal enterprises.

Unlike legitimate businesses, criminals rarely keep accounting records, much less accurate ones. The Seventh Circuit itself has noted the "extreme difficulty in this conspiratorial, criminal area of finding hard evidence of net profits." Even if documentation can be found, it is not clear what accounting principles should apply to the operations of criminal enterprises, for the accounting industry does not prescribe standards for illegal ventures. Thus, as even the court of appeals acknowledged, its rule encumbers the prosecution of money-laundering cases with significant complications. If Congress had legislated a "profits" rule, then the government and the courts would have to shoulder that burden.

But an examination of the statutory text and background reveals that Congress did no such thing.

The court requires the government to prove that the funds used in those transactions represent the "profits" of illegal activity, and thus the court demands that the government establish the profitability of illegal activity, such as drug dealing and gambling, in order to convict defendants for money laundering connected to that activity. The court of appeals' rule directly precludes money-laundering prosecutions based on financial transactions by criminals to pay the expenses of their illegal enterprises. The rule does so even when the payment of expenses promotes the continuation of the illegal business or is done in a manner that conceals the origins of the funds. The rule also creates serious obstacles to effective prosecution in virtually all other money-laundering cases, because it imposes an unreasonable burden-of-proof on the government and entangles the courts in complicated interpretative questions.[4]

Notes

References to citations, transcripts, footnotes, and some authorities omitted for sake of clarity.

1. *Meredith v. Jefferson County Board of Education*, No. 05-915.
2. *United States v. Rose Acre Farms, Inc.*, No. 04-1311.
3. *Debose and McCullough, et al. v. State of Nebraska*, No. 99-940.
4. *United States v. Efrain Santos, et al.*, No. 06-1005.

Verbal Excess

What are the solutions for verbal excess? Page limits on briefs provide some relief to courts. But the only effective solution is for lawyers to appreciate that more concise is better, that excess is counterproductive, and that clarity is more important than length.

Spending more time analyzing the issues and honing their arguments gives lawyers greater confidence that they have resolved the difficult issues. Rigorous editing ensures that repetition is eliminated and unnecessary arguments deleted. References to extraneous cases and the use of string citations are not persuasive to the court.

A prior judicial opinion on point is far more effective than a litany of marginal authorities, and a single precedent will often win the day. Unnecessary rhetorical flourishes do not add substantive weight to the arguments.

5

■■■■■————————————————————————————————————

Summarily Speaking:
An Overview's Significance

Everyone loves a good summary—a bird's-eye view at 30,000 feet—of the verbal landscape that lies below. It certainly makes your argument more palatable and less intimidating than it might appear at first glance.

And yet, according to judges, this is one of the aspects that counsel most commonly neglects. Preparing a summary to a legal argument sounds like a boring and mundane task, but the opportunities it offers for persuading the court are enormous.

A summary is useful because it helps cement the argument's main points in the judge's mind and provides tidiness to the development of the argument. Judges, like all readers, appreciate a helpful wrap-up of the material before them.

The summary you present should emphasize the major issues, and it must be worded in as vigorous and persuasive language as you can muster. It should also aim to impress the court with the soundness and justice of one's cause. Here, if anywhere, lies the perfect opportunity for displaying your eloquence and wit. Memorable lines have a powerful impact, and they should be used whenever they are appropriate.

The essential qualities in framing the issues in a summary are accuracy, fairness, and clarity, but you can still strive for wording that is favorable to your position. This is not done by argumentative words or clever distortions, but by emphasizing those aspects of your argument that will lead to victory for your client. The overall formula sounds simple, but its application is considerably more difficult to achieve, requiring sustained effort on your part to accomplish effectively.

The four examples demonstrating effective summaries that are set forth here deal with a number of interesting issues: the permissible uses of union dues, free speech, copyright law, and class actions. They reveal how persuasive the lowly summary can be, after all.

Example 1

The permissible use of union dues is the topic encountered in this excerpt. Observe how effectively the summary of the argument sets out the boundaries of union finances.

A State may require public employees within a bargaining unit to contribute to their own unit's collective-bargaining costs. This is because both members and nonmembers alike benefit from collective bargaining. But the First Amendment limits the types of other expenses that nonmembers may be required to pay. In the case of *Ellis v. Brotherhood of Railway Clerks*, this Court held that objectors could not be compelled to contribute to costs of other units' litigation.

The question in this case, however, is not whether dissenters can be charged for other units' litigation. Instead, it is whether a unit that funds its own litigation through an insurance or other risk-sharing arrangement may charge dissenters for their *pro-rata* share of costs. While *Ellis* did not address that question, this Court subsequently held in *Lehnert v. Ferris Faculty Ass'n*, that in some circumstances a union can use compelled fees to enter into pooling arrangements with other units. Under such arrangements, local bargaining units pay fees to a state, national, or international affiliate, which then assists, as needed, with the local's collective-bargaining activities. Such arrangements can benefit both members and nonmembers by enabling each unit to spread risk and distribute payments over time.

There is no reason to treat a unit's litigation costs differently from its other expenses for this purpose. Whether the pooled costs relate to the negotiation of collective bargaining agreements (as in *Lehnert*) or the litigation of disputes arising under them, the legal principle is the same, because each unit is essentially buying an insurance policy to cover its own future expenses. As long as a union can use compelled fees to purchase litigation insurance from a commercial insurer, there is no reason it cannot use such fees for a *bona fide* litigation-pooling arrangement with affiliated unions.

That constitutional justification for litigation pooling arrangements imposes important limits on their scope. As *Lehnert* held, such an arrangement must concern activities "associated with otherwise chargeable activities." If the unit involved in a particular case could not charge its own objectors for the litigation because it was not germane to collective bargaining, objectors in other units certainly could not be expected to contribute to a pooling arrangement covering the litigation. In addition, a *bona fide* pooling arrangement requires that each participating unit pay its fair share of the costs, and that each have a reasonable assurance that, when needed, the national or international affiliate will assist with its germane litigation. If a pooling arrangement is designed to address some, but not all germane litigation, it must have reasonably ascertainable standards for determining which litigation is included and which is not.

In other words, the arrangement must be a *bona fide* risk-sharing one, analogous to an insurance policy, as opposed to a vehicle for some units to subsidize other units' litigation with compelled fees. And as always, the union bears the burden-of-proof on the chargeability of expenses, including pooled expenses.[1]

Example 2

The excerpt here argues that the free speech provisions of the Constitution do not preclude governmental prohibition of fraudulent activities. Notice in particular how the summary is deftly executed to advance that argument.

The First Amendment does not preclude the government from prohibiting fraud or prosecuting those who intentionally deceive others for monetary gain. Intentional lies distort, rather than contribute to, the marketplace of ideas, and any value they have is outweighed by society's interest in protecting those harmed by deception. It has therefore been settled law that those who extract money through fraudulent misrepresentations are not shielded by the First Amendment. This is so even though their misrepresentations are speech and constitute solicitations in the name of charitable causes.

The First Amendment and prohibitions on fraud have coexisted comfortably not only because fraudulent speech is itself unprotected, but because the essential elements of fraud also provide sufficient breathing room for legitimate speech, including charitable solicitation. Most significantly, a fundraiser may not be held liable for fraud unless it is proven either that he knew or believed that his representations were false or that he acted with reckless disregard for their truth or falsity. In the libel context, essentially the same standard has been held to provide sufficient breathing room for protected speech.

In a fraud action, the government must prove that the fundraiser intended for donors to rely on his misrepresentations and that the donors' reliance was justifiable because the misrepresentations were material. Some jurisdictions also require that fraud be alleged with particularity or that it be proved by clear and convincing evidence. To the extent that additional protection for protected speech might be necessary, special procedural mechanisms, such as independent appellate review, could provide that protection without distorting or displacing the substantive state law of fraud.

The Illinois Supreme Court lost sight of the fact that the First Amendment and prohibitions on fraud are not inconsistent.

Instead, that court mistakenly held that the First Amendment creates a special immunity for fundraisers who make fraudulent representations. But prohibitions on fraud always affect speech, and there is no reason for a special immunity in the context of charitable solicitations. The State's complaint alleges that respondents intentionally misled donors by creating the false impression that a significant amount of donated funds would go to direct-assistance programs operated by VietNow. The complaint also alleges that respondents intentionally created a false impression that the fundraising effort was not being undertaken for profit. Those misrepresentations are typical of the charitable solicitation frauds that the federal government prosecutes both civilly and criminally.

The state court mistakenly concluded that this Court's decisions in *Schaumberg*, *Munson*, and *Riley* somehow preclude fraud claims based on misrepresentations of the percentage of collected funds that will go to charity. *Schaumberg*, *Munson*, and *Riley* invalidated state laws that categorically prohibited solicitation by all charities or fundraisers who devoted a high percentage of funds raised to administrative or fundraising. Nothing in those cases suggests that a misrepresentation about the percentage of donations that will go to charity *cannot* be the basis for a fraud prosecution. The cases hold only that the government cannot rely on that percentage to obviate the need to prosecute and to prove actual fraud.

The percentage limitations in *Schaumberg*, *Munson*, and *Riley* violated the First Amendment because they prohibited perfectly truthful charitable solicitation when fundraising costs were judged too high. Here, respondents are free to solicit even if they retain a high percentage of contributions, provided they do not intentionally mislead donors about how contributions will be used.[2]

Example 3

This excerpt deals with the duration of copyright law. Observe in this cogent summary of the argument how Congress is free to set the length of copyright protection.

Every congressional modification of copyright terms in U.S. history has been applied to both future and subsisting works. Since the term of life-plus-seventy years provided in the Copyright Term Extension Act (CTEA) is not unlimited or perpetual, it satisfies the constitutional mandate that copyrights last only for "limited times." Within that one constraint, Congress's choice of particular copyright terms is entitled to great deference, and it must be upheld if that choice is a necessary and proper exercise of legislative power.

Congress's decision to apply the CTEA to subsisting works meets that test. First, it is rational for Congress to treat authors' original works equally, regardless of whether created before or after the CTEA's enactment. Congress reasonably determined that demographic, economic, and technological changes warrant a longer term for all unexpired copyrights. Allowing fair compensation for holders of existing copyrights accomplishes that goal directly, and it is necessary and proper as an ancillary means of protecting future works. Further, this country's practice of granting evenhanded protection to authors of existing works increases incentives for the creation of future works and for initially publishing those works in the United States. Especially in a global market, Congress's decision to conform to certain international copyright standards rationally allows United States copyright holders to meet foreign competition and thereby provides revenues for producing new works. Congress also rationally concluded that the CTEA's longer term would encourage holders of existing copyrights to make substantial investments in restoring and distributing their works, to the benefit of the public.

Petitioners in effect ask this Court to rewrite the governing constitutional language to allow Congress to secure copyrights only for "inalterable limited times that promote the creation of new works." Neither the Constitution's text nor its history supports such substantial revisions, and two centuries of legislative practice and judicial decisions stand to the contrary.

Petitioners suggest that, although the CTEA's term is not impermissibly long, future courts might be unable to distinguish "limited times" (such as the CTEA's term) from hypothetically unlimited, perpetual copyrights that Congress might someday enact. Congress has significantly revised the federal copyright term only five times in over 200 years, and there is no basis for believing that upholding the CTEA would either lead Congress to adopt unlimited copyright extensions or require the courts to uphold such extensions.

Ultimately, petitioners wish to displace Congress's preference for copyright-based dissemination of works during the CTEA's prescribed proprietary term, and instead to allow indiscriminate exploitation by public-domain copyists like petitioners. But the Constitution assigns such policy choices to Congress, not the courts.[3]

Example 4

Whether a class action can include only one claimant is the subject of this excerpt. Watch how well the discussion opposed to that proposition is summarized in this argument before the U.S. Supreme Court.

Under constitutional principles that have guided this Court in the public employment context, the Equal Protection Clause does not entitle public employees to bring "class of one" claims to challenge personnel actions. Public employers have a paramount interest in ensuring that supervisors have the managerial discretion to differentiate among employees based upon individual characteristics. Those characteristics are often based on subjective criteria that result from daily interactions and frictions in the workplace.

The unique features of public employment markedly differ from contexts in which the government interacts with citizens as a regulator. Because subjective decision-making in employment matters is both rational and inevitable, there is no justification for

subjecting personnel actions to constitutional scrutiny even relatively relaxed scrutiny unless an action is based on the employee's membership in an identifiable group or class.

Permitting public employees to bring class-of-one claims
would significantly intrude on managerial discretion by consti-
tutionalizing garden-variety personnel actions. Because interper-
sonal frictions and disputes permeate the workplace, an employee
subject to adverse treatment will frequently be able to allege that
his supervisor's negative views were based on malice or ill-will.
Petitioner has offered no limiting principle that would give supervisors clear guidance as to when courts would defer to a supervisor's discretion. Petitioner's theory would require the federal
courts to referee run-of-the-mill decisions in the public workplace
and to subject public employers to compensatory and punitive
damages claims for petty grievances.

A class-of-one claim also conflicts with the tradition of at-will
employment under which an employee may be terminated for irrational or arbitrary reasons, or for no reason at all. At-will employment is completely at odds with the notion of a class-of-one claim.
What distinguishes a class-of-one claim from a more typical equal
protection claim is that the allegation is essentially that the government has not articulated any basis for the different treatment
that could be tested for rationality. In the at-will employment context, unlike the regulatory context, the employer is entitled to discharge the employee for no reason at all. Finding a constitutional
violation in the inability to justify a difference in treatment would
defeat the basic notions of at-will employment.

Legislation which allows public employees to engage in collective bargaining demonstrates that there is no need for additional
judicially created remedies to police the types of disputes that
would be covered by petitioner's theory. Those schemes are based
on legislative policy about precisely how and when to restrict
managerial discretion in the public employment context. A class-of-
one claim based on the Constitution would trump those legislative
schemes and confer rights on the very employees that the legislature intended to be employed at-will. There is no reason to believe

that the framers of both the original Constitution and the Fourteenth Amendment intended to subject public employers to the micro-management that would follow under petitioner's theory.[4]

Notes

References to citations, transcripts, footnotes, and some authorities omitted for sake of clarity.

1. *Locke v. Karass*, No. 07-610.
2. *Ryan v. Telemarketing Associates*, No. 01-1806.
3. *Eldred v. Ashcroft*, No. 01-618.
4. *Inquest v. Oregon Dep't of Agriculture*, No. 07-474.

The Well-Honed Argument

It is essential that a lawyer communicate in terms as simple and easily understood as the subject matter permits. Judges want to understand how the law applies to their cases and understanding the facts and the law is essential to being persuaded.

Every practitioner can profit from the timeless book *The Elements of Style*, which contains solid advice for legal writers. Several of its principles are essential to any piece of legal writing:

- *Positive statements.* Make definitive assertions and avoid colorless and noncommittal language.
- *Specific and concrete language.* This is the surest way to hold the reader's attention.
- *Needless words.* Vigorous writing is concise. Not all sentences will be short, avoid all detail, or treat subjects in general terms, but every word should tell.
- *Overstating.* The reader will be placed on guard, and everything you say will be suspect.
- *Overwriting.* Rich, ornate prose is hard to digest.

6

■-■-■

Just the Facts: Setting Up the Background

Legal controversies are ultimately about people, and you must make the situations and the individuals in your case come alive on the page. Your ability to set up the background facts of the case has an extremely strong impact in persuading the court to rule in your favor.

When a judge cannot form a mental image of the controversy, the case becomes boring and unimportant; as a result, the judge may not be motivated to rule for you. But if the judge can visualize real people doing actual things, he usually begins to take sides. Facts are ultimately important because they move the court's decision.

You must first provide the judge with a narrative of the case's facts. The most effective fact statements convince through organization that emphasizes important facts over irrelevant ones, and word choice that is favorable to your client but whose veracity *cannot* be disputed.

You must tightly focus the fact statement to advance your position. If the discussion wanders aimlessly and indiscriminately across the page, the judge may not understand your position, a result that will be lethal to your client. In the fact statement to the court, you should *always* make it clear who you represent.

If the facts will be compelling to a court, let them speak for themselves. All you need to do is calmly describe the facts with enough detail to make the picture clear. A judge will naturally form a human reaction to the facts and will then use instincts to make a fair decision. But you must *not* characterize the facts with emotion-laden verbiage. It is often tempting to do so, but this will cause the judge to resent you for your heavy-handed attempts to manipulate her.

You must of course make sure that the facts you present are well substantiated in the record. And you must be careful about inferences. Although an inference can be treated as a fact if it's uncontroverted, a disputed fact rises to the level of argument.

Effective statements of fact will lead the court to conclude that the equities are on your side. And when judges find themselves in that position, their mind is often receptive enough to rule in your favor.

The four examples demonstrating fact statements that are set forth here deal with a number of interesting issues: routines of police in making arrests, corruption charges, animal rights protests, and capital punishment. These statements of fact strike just the right approach of both informing and persuading the judge.

Example 1

This excerpt deals with the routine of police officers when making an arrest. The background facts in this case are nicely laid out to include relevant details that hold the reader's interest.

On the night of November 22, 2004, Washington State Patrol officer Joi Haner noticed a disabled vehicle on the shoulder of a dark and deserted stretch of highway in Kitsap County, Washington. As he passed the disabled car, Officer Haner saw another car pull in behind it, which he later learned was driven by respondent Jerome Alford. Haner stopped to assist the motorists. As Haner stepped from his vehicle, respondent hurriedly returned to his car. Respondent told Haner that the people in the stopped car had a flat tire and needed a flashlight. Respondent then drove off.

The occupants of the disabled car told Haner that they thought respondent was a police officer, in part because his car had flashing headlights of the kind commonly used on police vehicles. Washington law prohibits persons other than police officers from operating vehicles equipped with flashing headlights. The motorists also said that respondent had left his flashlight behind, which Haner thought reflected suspicious behavior. Because Haner was concerned that respondent was pretending to be a police officer to prey on motorists, Haner called his supervisor, petitioner Sergeant Gerald Devenpeck, to alert him and request assistance.

Haner drove off in pursuit of respondent. Once Haner had pulled respondent over, Haner noticed that his license plate was nearly unreadable beneath a darkly tinted cover. Through the car window, Haner observed that respondent had a police-band radio, a portable police scanner, and handcuffs. Respondent initially told Haner that he worked for the State Patrol, and then he changed it to the Texas Highway Patrol, and then to the Puget Sound Naval Shipyard police. Respondent said that his flashing headlights were part of an alarm system that had just been installed, but he claimed to be unable to activate them at Haner's request. Haner noticed that in his effort to activate the flashing headlights, respondent had pressed several buttons on his keychain and dashboard, but not a button on the steering column that Haner suspected controlled the lights.

Devenpeck then arrived and discussed with Haner what had happened. Respondent told Devenpeck that he had previously been cited by the Kitsap County Sheriff for having flashing headlights but that he believed they were legal because "the Kitsap County Sheriff had apologized to him and sent him a letter" and that "the ACLU said he could use them as long as he wasn't impersonating a police officer." Because Devenpeck was suspicious of respondent's claim that the flashing lights were simply a feature of his alarm, he asked respondent to show him the section of the alarm user's manual that would describe "what would happen when you activated the alarm." Devenpeck then noticed an operating tape-recorder concealed beneath a coat on respondent's passenger seat and concluded that respondent had been recording the conversation with the officers. Devenpeck told respondent that he was under arrest for recording the conversation with the officers without their consent. At the scene, Devenpeck reviewed a copy of the Washington Privacy Act, which provides that, "it shall be unlawful for any individual to record any private conversation without first obtaining the consent of all the persons engaged in the conversation." Devenpeck's review confirmed his belief that the Act prohibited respondent's actions.

Respondent said that, because he had had a similar problem recording a conversation with other police officers, he carried in his glove compartment a copy of a Washington Court of Appeals decision holding that the Privacy Act did not apply to the tape-recording of police officers performing official duties, an apparent reference to *State v. Flora*. While conducting an inventory of respondent's car in preparation to impound it, Devenpeck did not find a copy of the *Flora* decision in the glove compartment or elsewhere in the car. Devenpeck also pressed the button Haner had noticed and activated the flashing headlights.

While Haner was taking respondent to jail, Devenpeck called Deputy Prosecuting Attorney Mark Lindquist, reported what had happened, and read to him the relevant provision of the Privacy Act. Lindquist told Devenpeck that there was "clearly probable cause" to arrest respondent for obstructing an officer (because of respondent's evasiveness in responding to questions and requests), for impersonating an officer (based on the flashing headlights, obscured license plate, handcuffs, and police radio equipment in the car), and for violating the Privacy Act. At booking, respondent also was cited for operating a vehicle equipped with flashing headlights.[1]

Example 2

In this case the respondent was accused of corruption in connection with the sale of equipment to the U.S. Postal Service. Notice how the facts of the case are presented in a logical and concise manner in the following argument.

An investigation of public corruption in the procurement of equipment by the U.S. Postal Service (Postal Service) resulted in the successful prosecution of a member of the Postal Service's Board of Governors and a number of consultants. Respondent, the president of accompany that hired the consultants on the recommendation of the corrupt member of the Board of Governors was indicted but then acquitted. In this *Bivens* action, respondent alleges that U.S. Postal Inspectors targeted him in retaliation for his criticism of the Postal Service and for his lobbying activities.

In 2005, respondent was president and chief executive officer of Recognition Equipment, Inc. (REI), which was engaged in an effort to market "multi-line" optical character readers (OCRs) to the Postal Service. OCRs, which can interpret text on an envelope, are used to sort mail. The total value of the contracts sought by REI was between $250 and $400 million. After the Postal Service decided to purchase "single-line" OCRs instead, respondent and REI mounted a media and lobbying campaign that sought to overturn the Postal Service's decision.

During the course of that campaign, Robert Reedy, REI's Vice President for Marketing, met with Peter E. Voss, a member of the Board of Governors of the Postal Service. Voss recommended that REI hire John Gnau and his consulting firm, Gnau and Associates, Inc. (GAI), to assist in REI's efforts to obtain a Postal Service contract. Voss later called respondent and said that he hoped Reedy would act on his recommendation. Respondent thereafter told Reedy not to "drop the ball" with respect to the referral. In January 2006, REI hired GAI as a consultant.

As it turned out, Voss had a substantial financial interest in ensuring that Gnau got consulting work, because the two had agreed that Voss would refer clients to Gnau's firm in exchange for a kickback of a portion of GAI's fees. They had also agreed that Voss, Gnau, and two other GAI officers—William Spartin and Michael Marcus—would split the contingency fee that REI was obligated to pay GAI if it received the Postal Service contract.

U.S. Postal Inspectors ultimately discovered this scheme, as well as a related one involving the search for a new Postmaster General in 2006. Spartin, the nominal president of GAI, also headed an executive recruiting firm called MSL International. Through Voss, and despite GAI's representation of REI before the Postal Service, Spartin's firm received the contract to find a new Postmaster General. Spartin thereafter called respondent and asked for recommendations. Respondent gave Spartin the names of three prominent business executives, including Albert V. Casey, who was ultimately selected as Postmaster General. Respondent also made an introductory call to Casey on Spartin's behalf.

The postal inspectors' investigation resulted in federal criminal charges against Voss, Gnau, and Marcus, all of whom pleaded guilty. Spartin was given immunity in exchange for his cooperation.

As the investigation continued, the postal inspectors determined that respondent and Reedy must have known about the criminal schemes from which they stood to benefit. Although neither Voss nor any of the GAI defendants implicated them, there was considerable circumstantial evidence that the respondent and Reedy had been aware of the illegal agreement between Voss and Gnau and had used it to their company's advantage. For example:

- The postal inspectors discovered that Reedy, the REI vice president, had lied to them about prior contacts with Voss. When asked who had recommended GAI to him, Reedy said that he had gotten Gnau's name from a consultant during a chance encounter at the 2004 Republican National Convention. Reedy later admitted that he had received the referral from Voss.
- GAI's Michael Marcus recounted a conversation in which Spartin indicated that REI had purged records relating to the investigation, and there were in fact a number of omissions in the records that REI produced in response to a subpoena. Respondent's "Postal" notebook appeared to be missing 36 sheets of paper, and there were no entries for a six-month period in 2007. In addition, respondent's telephone log for a three-month period in 2006 was never located.

- One of respondent's notebooks included an entry suggesting that he might have coached REI employees on how to answer questions from postal inspectors, and REI employees subsequently testified before the grand jury that respondent had made comments consistent with that entry at a staff meeting the same day. By that time, postal inspectors had arranged to interview REI employees in the coming week.
- The postal inspectors found respondent's explanation of his involvement in the recruitment of a new Postmaster General implausible. Respondent told them that, when Spartin called and asked for referrals, he did not really believe that Spartin was recruiting a new Postmaster General. That statement seemed implausible because respondent not only gave Spartin the names of candidates, but made an introductory telephone call to one of them. The inspectors were also informed by Spartin that he and respondent had agreed to say that it was respondent who called Spartin, even though it was in fact Spartin who placed the call.[2]

Example 3

In this case the respondent was arrested for staging an animal-rights protest at a military installation. Observe how carefully the summary is constructed to relay the necessary facts in an efficient and comprehensible way.

Respondent Elliot Katz, an animal rights activist, brought this Fourth Amendment excessive-force claim after he was detained at the Presidio military post in San Francisco. On September 24, 2006, a number of speakers gave a special presentation at the Presidio to celebrate the conversion of that facility, which was then an Army base, into a national park the following week. The public was invited to attend. Respondent arrived at the Presidio early on the day of the presentation, intending to display a banner protesting possible use of the Letterman Hospital in the Presidio for experimentation involving animals. The banner read: "Please Keep

Animal Torture Out of Our National Parks." Aware that the Army prohibits the display of protest banners and other political activities at the Presidio and other military bases, respondent kept his banner concealed under his jacket as he entered and walked through the base. At some point, he claims, he may have removed the banner from under his jacket and held it closed on his lap.

During one of the speeches, respondent moved forward from his seat to the waist-high barrier that separated the spectators from the Vice President and began to unfurl his roughly 4-foot-by-3-foot banner. Respondent placed the banner on the barrier and began allowing it to unfold. As he did so, someone "grabbed [respondent] from behind, and somebody else tore the banner away." The two individuals were Donald Saucier and Steven Parker, who were serving as military police. When the two saw respondent quickly move from his seat toward the barrier that separated the crowd from the Vice President, they immediately moved to intercept him. There is no allegation that Saucier or Parker hit or struck respondent. Instead, they each took one of respondent's arms and quickly removed him from the seating area. According to respondent, Saucier and Parker "started sort of picking me up and kind of walking me out, kind of like very hurriedly."

Respondent claims that the officers took him to a military police van located behind the seating area, and that he was "shoved" inside. Respondent also claims that, as a result of the shove, he fell inside the van and was almost injured. But respondent was not injured. To the contrary, respondent caught himself and avoided injury. After being driven to a military police station, respondent was briefly detained. He was then released, and he returned to his car and drove himself home.

The news media covered the events at the Presidio. As a result, portions of the above-described events were recorded and then broadcast on the local news. Videotapes of relevant portions of the broadcasts, which are part of the record in this case, were lodged with the Court together with the petition for a *writ of certiorari*.[3]

Example 4

This is a capital punishment case before the U.S. Supreme Court. The facts set forth in the following argument are notable for their placement within the historical context.

After this Court affirmed the constitutionality of capital punishment in *Gregg v. Georgia*, there was increasing concern that electrocution might not in fact cause death in a painless or expeditious manner. In 1977, legislators in Oklahoma who shared that concern proposed a bill adopting lethal injection as the State's method of execution. The Oklahoma Legislature enacted that bill, and other States subsequently switched to lethal injection as well. Lethal injection is now the sole or primary method of execution in 37 of the 38 States that authorize capital punishment.

Of the thirty-seven States that conduct executions by means of lethal injection, the vast majority (at least 29) do so by administering the same series of three drugs originally devised by the Oklahoma Department of Corrections. The first drug is sodium thiopental (or sodium pentothal), a fast-acting barbiturate that anesthetizes the subject within sixty seconds. The second is pancuronium bromide, a neuromuscular paralytic that prevents bodily movement and ultimately halts respiration. The third is potassium chloride, an agent that induces cardiac arrest. While jurisdictions administer the three drugs in somewhat different dosages, it is undisputed that the massive dose of sodium thiopental that is typically given is ten times the amount used in a surgical procedure and would anesthetize the subject for hours, such that the administration of the other two drugs would be painless. It is also undisputed that, if properly administered, the dose of each drug that is typically given would ordinarily be sufficient to induce death on its own.

Around 7 a.m. on April 9, 2003, Eddie and Tina Earley and their two-year-old son, Christopher, were sitting in their car in Lexington, Kentucky, outside Earley Bird Cleaners, a dry-cleaning business that they owned. Petitioner Bowling crashed his car into the Earleys' car. Bowling got out of his car, drew a gun, and fired indiscriminately into the Earleys' car, killing Eddie and Tina Earley and wounding Christopher. After going over and looking at the victims, Bowling got back in his car and drove away.

On January 30, 2004, Powell County, Kentucky, Sheriff Steve Bennett and Deputy Sheriff Arthur Briscoe went to petitioner Baze's cabin in order to arrest him on multiple fugitive warrants. Baze was hiding in the brush with an assault rifle. As his wife distracted the officers, Baze shot Sheriff Bennett three times in the back, killing him. When Deputy Briscoe attempted to flee, Baze shot him twice in the back. Baze then walked up to Deputy Briscoe, punched him with the muzzle of his gun, and shot him a third time in the head, killing him.

Petitioners were each convicted in Kentucky state court of two counts of capital murder and sentenced to death. They have exhausted both their direct appeals and federal and state collateral remedies.

In 1998, Kentucky adopted lethal injection as its default method of execution. Kentucky uses the same series of three drugs as the federal government and the majority of other States. Kentucky's protocol provides that the subject should be executed using three grams of sodium thiopental, 50 milligrams of pancuronium bromide, and 240 milliequivalents of potassium chloride. The protocol provides that qualified personnel are responsible for preparing the series of drugs, establishing intravenous access, and controlling the flow of the drugs. Kentucky uses a phlebotomist and an emergency medical technician to perform those tasks.

In 2005, petitioners filed a civil action against respondents and three state officials in Kentucky state court, contending that Kentucky's method of execution constituted cruel and unusual punishment under the Eighth Amendment. After a seven-day bench trial with some 20 witnesses, the trial court ruled in favor of respondents in relevant part. After making various factual findings concerning Kentucky's method of execution, the trial court concluded that petitioners had failed to show that the method would "inflict unnecessary physical pain upon the condemned."

The Kentucky Supreme Court unanimously affirmed. The court explained "[a] method of execution is considered to be cruel and unusual punishment under the Federal Constitution when the procedure for execution creates a substantial risk of wanton and unnecessary infliction of pain, torture or lingering death." While the court acknowledged that conflicting medical testimony prevents us from stating categorically that a prisoner feels no pain, it noted that the individual whom Kentucky had previously executed by lethal injection "went to sleep within 15 seconds to one minute from the moment that the warden began the execution and never moved or exhibited any pain whatsoever subsequent to losing consciousness." The court affirmed the trial court's findings and held that "[t]he lethal injection method used in Kentucky is not a violation of the Eighth Amendment."[4]

Notes

References to citations, transcripts, footnotes, and some authorities omitted for sake of clarity.

1. *Devenpeck v. Alford*, No. 03-710.
2. *Hartman v. Moore*, No. 04-1495.
3. *Saucier v. Katz, et al.*, No. 99-1977.
4. *Baze v. Rees*, No. 07-5439.

Be Accurate in Summarizing Facts

A brief writer should summarize facts with scrupulous accuracy. If you slant the facts or ignore evidence that hurts your position, you can be certain that your opponent will highlight the facts you have distorted or omitted.

Misstating the record can irretrievably damage your credibility with the court. You don't want to waste precious time trying to rehabilitate yourself.

7

■■■———————————————————————————

Short Bursts:
For Diminishing
Attention Spans

The judge considering your case undoubtedly has a busy schedule before him. He is reading your argument not to be entertained but to make a decision, and he rightfully expects the document before him to assist in that weighty task.

There is little question that the modern attention span has shortened and that all of us are more anxious than ever to move on to the next task. Judges are no different. Their days are hectic, and a long, erudite paragraph is just as intimidating—and therefore just as resistible—to them as it is the rest of us.

Short paragraphs serve three important goals. The first, most obvious goal is to break the material into easily comprehensible segments. The second is to force you to develop each of your themes. The third is to tell the reader where you are in your argument, how that conclusion was reached, and where you are headed.

For maximum effect, you should delve immediately into the heart of your case. Instead of starting with routine procedural matters, it's best to begin with a narrative of the incident that led to the litigation or the importance of the matter before the court. Don't allow the story line of your position to be obscured by lengthy discussions of minor and irrelevant issues. Brisk movement is suggested by words, sentences, and paragraphs that are sharp and to the point.

The following four examples demonstrate short bursts that deal with a number of interesting issues: (1) federal preemption by the FDA, (2) the requirement of reciprocal easements by a federal agency, (3) taxation schemes allegedly discriminating against foreign commerce, and (4) warrants for arrest. They all show the eminent appeal of short paragraphs to the modern attention span.

Example 1

The question of federal preemption in the pharmaceutical realm is the issue of the following case. Note how the use of short paragraphs adds to the pace and clarity of an otherwise complex argument.

The Federal Drug Administration (FDA) may approve a new drug application only if it determines, among other things, that (1) the drug is "safe for use under the conditions prescribed, recommended, or suggested in the proposed labeling thereof," (2) there is "substantial evidence that the drug will have the effect it purports or is represented to have under the conditions of use prescribed, recommended, or suggested in the proposed labeling thereof," and (3) the proposed labeling is not "false or misleading in any particular."

Thus, FDA specifically considers and approves a drug's labeling. Indeed, the agency's consideration of safety and effectiveness is directly tied to its consideration of "the proposed labeling," in part because a drug's safety and effectiveness depend on the conditions under which it is used (e.g., its dosage, its method of administration, and its intended use). Labeling is "the centerpiece of risk management," as it "communicates to health care practitioners the agency's formal, authoritative conclusions regarding the conditions under which the product can be used safely and effectively."

FDA's review of a new drug application is similar to its premarket approval process for Class III medical devices, which this Court has correctly described as "rigorous." As part of the approval process, an applicant must submit "the labeling proposed to be used for such drug," as well as (a) extensive information about the composition, manufacture, and specification of the drug, (b) any studies of the drug's pharmacological actions and toxicological effects in animals, (c) any studies of the drug's bioavailability and pharmacokinetics in humans, (d) any clinical investigations of the drug, and (e) any other data or information relevant to an evaluation of the safety and effectiveness of the drug product obtained or otherwise received by the applicant from any source.

If FDA is not ultimately satisfied that a drug is safe for use under the conditions of its labeling and that there is substantial evidence that the drug is effective when used according to the labeling, FDA cannot approve the application. Thus, FDA's approval reflects its expert determination, based on a careful review of extensive scientific and technical information, that a drug is safe and effective when used according to its labeling, and that the labeling satisfies federal requirements.

In making those determinations, FDA does not merely police minimum standards of safety, as the Vermont Supreme Court thought. Instead, FDA weighs health benefits against health risks. As this Court has explained, FDA generally considers a drug safe "when the expected therapeutic gain justifies the risk entailed by its use." FDA has, for example, approved cancer treatments that are highly toxic and thus not "safe" as that term is ordinarily used, but that are nonetheless safe in the relevant sense under the FDCA because the potential benefits to health outweigh the risks.

FDA also weighs the overall health consequences of including particular instructions or warnings in a drug's labeling. As explained above, a drug's safety and effectiveness are not determined in the abstract, divorced from its labeling. Rather, FDA requires each new drug application to contain a discussion of why the benefits exceed the risks of the drug under the conditions stated in the labeling. If FDA concludes that a drug's benefits outweigh its risks only under certain conditions, the agency may require appropriate labeling to reflect that determination.[1]

Example 2

In this excerpt, the Federal Bureau of Land Management had been accused of RICO and other violations as a result of attempting to secure a reciprocal easement on neighboring private land. Consider how, even in this seemingly complicated situation, the arguments are kept brief and to the point in order to make maximum impact.

The court of appeals' decision in this case subjects federal officials to damages for actions and threat of personal liability under both the Racketeer Influenced and Corrupt Organizations Act (RICO) and *Bivens* for carrying out their regulatory duties to manage public lands. The decision not only represents an unprecedented expansion of RICO, *Bivens*, and the Fifth Amendment, but it contravenes settled qualified immunity principles and should therefore be reversed by this Court.

Petitioners did not violate RICO or any right against extortion in attempting, through the exercise of their lawful regulatory authority, to secure a reciprocal easement for the United States in exchange for the right-of-way that the Bureau of Land Management (BLM) granted respondent over public lands. RICO is an organized crime statute and was never designed to reach federal officials acting to further legitimate governmental aims. To establish the predicate offense of extortion, a plaintiff must show both that government officials acted with a "wrongful" intent and that they actually obtained something of value for private benefit. Both of those traditional elements of the common law offense of extortion are absent here.

Petitioners did not take any of the alleged actions based on a "wrongful" intent to obtain property. In seeking a reciprocal easement, petitioners did not seek anything that was not "due" them or the BLM. To the contrary, it is well established that the BLM may require persons who apply for rights-of-way over public land to grant the government a reciprocal easement over private land. Likewise, petitioners did not "obtain" any property through their official conduct for the private gain of themselves or anyone else. They sought the reciprocal easement at issue for "the United States of America, and its assigns."

Regulators who act within their lawful authority and seek to obtain property on behalf of the United States are neither racketeers nor extortionists. Congress never intended to subject aggressive regulators to the threat of personal liability and treble damages under RICO, and there are numerous checks in place to deter and prevent overzealous regulation, including the Administrative Procedures Act (APA). The court of appeals' decision extending RICO to such conduct not only represents a radical extension of RICO, but threatens to chill government officials in a broad range of regulatory contexts from engaging in appropriate and vital regulatory actions, including the negotiation of reciprocal rights to facilitate access to, and management of, the millions of acres of public lands in the West that are intermingled with private lands.

Respondent's unprecedented *Bivens* claim based on the alleged violation of his Fifth Amendment "right to exclude" the government from his property fares no better. This Court has repeatedly refused to extend the constitutional cause of action inferred in *Bivens* to new contexts, and there is no reason to reverse course here. Indeed, claims grounded on the Fifth Amendment's Just Compensation Clause are fundamentally incompatible with *Bivens* because that Clause itself specifies a monetary remedy.[2]

Example 3

Technically difficult cases, like this tax case before the U.S. Supreme Court, benefit handsomely from a discussion in which there is a lot of "white space" separating the complex arguments.

The Supreme Court of New Hampshire correctly held that subsection IV of N.H. Rev. Stat. Ann. §§ 77-A:1 does not facially discriminate against foreign commerce. The court held that this is so even though the statute permits the parent of an affiliated foreign subsidiary to deduct from taxable business profits the dividends received from that subsidiary to the extent that the subsidiary's income is subject to New Hampshire tax. The decision does not conflict with any decision of this Court or another state court of last resort.

Petitioner, General Electric (GE), contends that subsection IV facially discriminates in violation of the Commerce Clause. According to GE, New Hampshire's tax regime "favors corporations engaging in local activity over their out-of-state competitors and tends to discourage corporations from plying their trades in protected [foreign] commerce." The Supreme Court of New Hampshire correctly rejected that contention, which improperly focuses on only half of the relevant equation.

In deciding this case, the Supreme Court properly assessed New Hampshire's taxing regime as a whole and looked at the aggregate tax imposed upon a unitary business. Under that analytical approach, the conclusion is inescapable that New Hampshire's tax regime did *not* discriminate against foreign commerce. As the supreme court correctly explained, the purportedly discriminatory tax benefit allegedly conferred by subsection IV (namely, a dividends-received deduction for a combined group to the extent that the income of its dividend-paying foreign subsidiary was taxed by New Hampshire) was fully matched by a corresponding burden on the purportedly favored unitary group (namely, the foreign subsidiary's obligation to pay New Hampshire tax on the income apportioned to the State).

By contrast, that additional tax burden was not imposed on the purportedly disfavored unitary groups (like GE) that accordingly did not receive a dividends-received deduction, because by definition their dividend-paying foreign subsidiaries had no income taxable in New Hampshire.

As a result, New Hampshire's scheme as a whole did not facially discriminate against foreign commerce, because there was no showing that the aggregate tax imposed upon a unitary business would be higher if its foreign subsidiaries did no business in New Hampshire and lower if they did. New Hampshire "did not favor business activity in the State over business activities abroad," which "suggests that the statute does not discriminate against foreign commerce." In the New Hampshire scheme, there was:

- no "differential treatment of in-state and [foreign] economic interests that benefits the former and burdens the latter";

- no "direct commercial advantage to local business"; and
- no discrimination "in order to favor local commercial interests".

GE's claim of discrimination therefore fails.[3]

Example 4

The question of when a law enforcement officer can enter a residence without a warrant is the subject of this case. Watch how the argument is kept lively and clear with short paragraphs.

When law-enforcement officers have probable cause to believe that an individual has committed a felony, they may arrest the suspect in a public place without first securing a judicial warrant. By contrast, a warrant is ordinarily required before an arrest may be effected within the suspect's house. That distinction reflects the fact that the arresting officer's entry into the home entails an intrusion into privacy interests that does not occur when an arrest is made in a public place.

In distinguishing between arrests in public places and arrests within the home, the Court in *Payton v. New York* drew on established constitutional rules governing seizures of property. The Court explained that although searches and seizures inside a home without a warrant are presumptively unreasonable, it is well settled that objects such as weapons or contraband found in a public place may be seized by the police without a warrant, since the seizure of property in plain view involves no invasion of privacy. The Court concluded "this distinction has equal force when the seizure of a person is involved."

This general rule that a police officer must obtain a judicial warrant before entering a suspect's home is subject to exceptions. Of particular relevance to this case, a warrantless entry is reasonable, and therefore constitutionally permissible, if it is undertaken with the occupant's consent. Consent provides a constitutionally valid basis for entry even when it is obtained through misrepresentations about the officer's identity or purpose, as when an undercover operative poses as a fellow participant in criminal activity.

The reasoning of this Court's "plain view" decisions equally supports the warrantless arrest of an individual who consents to a police entry into his home and thereafter commits a crime in the officer's presence. In holding that a warrantless arrest within the home is ordinarily unlawful, the Court in *Payton* did not suggest that the seizure of the arrestee's person, in and of itself, requires prior judicial authorization. To the contrary, the Court recognized, and did not cast doubt upon, its holding in *Watson* that warrantless arrests may be effected in public places.

An arrest within the home typically requires a warrant not because of the constraints it imposes upon the individual's liberty (which are unlikely to vary in any relevant way depending on where the arrest occurs), but because the entry to effect the seizure entails a breach of the individual's privacy that has no analogy in a public-place arrest. That rationale for the warrant requirement does not apply when the breach of privacy has a separate constitutional justification, as when the occupant of a residence has consented to the arresting officer's entry.

For the foregoing reasons, a police officer who enters a private residence with the occupant's consent, and thereafter observes the commission of criminal acts within the home, may arrest the perpetrator without prior judicial authorization. Like an arrest in a public setting, or the seizure of incriminating items lawfully observed in plain view, an arrest under those circumstances entails no intrusion on privacy beyond that inherent in the initial, warrantless entry. Where that entry is authorized by the occupant's consent, no warrant is needed for the ensuing arrest.[4]

Notes

References to citations, transcripts, footnotes, and some authorities omitted for sake of clarity.

1. *Wyeth v. Levine*, No. 06-1249.
2. *Wilkie v. Robbins*, No. 06-219.
3. *General Electric Company v. Commissioner, New Hampshire Dep't of Revenue Administration*, No. 06-1210.
4. *Pearson v. Callahan*, No. 07-751.

The Court's Time Dilemma

Anyone acquainted with the workload in most courts will realize that as briefs increase in length, the chances of their being read decrease. The procedural rules set forth maximum lengths for briefs, not minimum ones. Lawyers should never feel that they have to use all the pages allowed.

Consider the appellate court's workload. A court might hear, for example, four cases on a day scheduled for oral argument. Each case requires reading at least one opening brief, one answer brief, and one reply brief. Each justice is therefore expected to read and digest at least a dozen briefs for that day. And that assumes that there is only one party on each side and no amicus curiae.

To be persuasive, a brief must be read. Its chances of being read and assimilated are in inverse proportion to its length. Briefs should be carefully edited and condensed. Issues to be covered should be carefully selected. The fewer points that are raised, the greater will be the court's concentration on each.

8

■-■-■───────────────────────────────

History of the Case:
The Devil Is in the Details

The procedural history of the case—whether judicial or administrative—is immensely important to the judge. Many attorneys spend far too little effort crafting this portion of the argument, but the court deems it critical—and therefore so should you.

Balance is everything here: It is your job to provide enough detail to promote your theory of the case, but not so much that the critical points of your argument are lost in the confusion. To describe the previous ruling of the court or administrative body in a light that advances your case in the most persuasive way possible is undoubtedly a challenge.

In doing so, you must tightly focus your argument. You must do so honestly, of course, so that your adversary can never accuse you of misrepresenting the facts. But detailing the case's history offers you a tremendous opportunity to breathe life into a story that concerns real people and the situation that has led to the litigation at hand.

The history of the case should, in a subtle but powerful way, foreshadow the contentions that you are about to advance in the body of your argument. Your emphasis on the important developments of the case should be clear, so that the judge never doubts which party you represent.

The four examples demonstrating case history that are set forth here deal with a number of interesting issues: (1) ordinances restricting commercial development, (2) illegal aliens from Cuba, (3) damages related to police entry into a residence, and (4) capital murder. The case history described in each instance provides the judge with a sufficient background of the case while at the same time advancing its proponent's arguments.

Example 1

This case involves the issue of whether an ordinance restricting commercial development outside a municipal airport constituted inverse condemnation. The history of the case is adroitly presented in this excerpt.

Since the 1940s, Clark County (the County) has operated what is now known as McCarran International Airport (McCarran) and has used its zoning laws to regulate the surrounding land and airspace. In 2001, respondents purchased a parcel of land approximately 2,600 feet from the end of one of the airport's runways. In 2002, the county enacted Ordinance 728, which limited the height of structures near the airport using a slope of 20 feet outward for every foot upward. On respondents' parcel, Ordinance 728 limited buildings to between 74 and 104 feet above ground level. In 2003, the county granted respondents a permit to construct and maintain a 501-room, two-story hotel, and an 85,000-square foot casino. Respondents' plans included a sign 80 feet high, a casino 47 feet high, five hotel buildings 28 feet high, and three hotel buildings 76 feet high.

Subsequently, however, the county proposed to change the runway nearest respondents' parcel to allow for precision instrument approach, which necessitated lowering the slope of the approach path from 20:1 to 50:1. In January 2004, the FAA determined that respondents' planned construction would constitute a hazard to air navigation in light of the lowered approach path. Respondents agreed to lower the height of their project to 38 feet, and the FAA determined in June 1990 that the project as described in the revised proposal "would not adversely affect the safe and efficient use of navigable airspace." In July 2004, the county enacted Ordinance 1221, which imposed height restrictions using a 50:1 slope in the instrument runway approach zone and had the effect of limiting structures on respondents' parcel to between five and 25 feet above ground level. Ordinance 1221 also provided, however, that structures up to 35 feet were allowed in any zone.

In December 2005, respondents filed suit against petitioner in Nevada state court. Respondents' complaint alleged, *inter alia*, that Ordinance 1221 effected an inverse condemnation of the air space above their tract. In 2006, respondents filed in federal court a petition for bankruptcy under Chapter 11, listing their inverse-condemnation claim against petitioner as a contingent and unliquidated claim. Respondents subsequently removed their takings claims to the federal bankruptcy court.

Following a bench trial, the bankruptcy court entered judgment for respondents, awarding them $4,886,779 plus interest, costs, and fees for the taking of airspace "between the 20:1 approach and the lower 50:1 precision instrument approach path instituted after the airport expansion." The court concluded that respondents' parcel was worth $10.00 per square foot before the enactment of Ordinance 1221 and $5.50 afterwards, and multiplied the $4.50 per-square-foot difference by the tract's total area (1,085,951 square feet). The district court subsequently entered judgment for respondents in a total amount (including fees and interest) of $10,121,686.

While the county's appeal was pending in the Ninth Circuit, the Nevada Supreme Court issued its decision in *McCarran Int'l Airport v. Sisolak*. As in the instant case, the plaintiff in *Sisolak* contended that height restrictions imposed by the county under Ordinance 1221 and a related Ordinance 1599 to facilitate take-offs and landings at McCarran effected a taking of property that required just compensation. The Nevada Supreme Court agreed, concluding that, "because the height restriction ordinances authorize airplanes to make a permanent, physical invasion of the landowner's airspace . . . a *Loretto*-type regulatory *per se* taking occurred, requiring an award of just compensation."

The Nevada Supreme Court in *Sisolak* stated that, for purposes of federal constitutional analysis under *Griggs*, "although airplanes may fly below 500 feet when necessary for takeoff and landing, this right does not divest the property owner of his protected property right to his usable airspace. Rather, a landowner may still make a claim for compensation for the government's use of that airspace." The court further concluded that under Nevada law, landowners "hold a property right in the usable airspace above their property up to 500 feet." The court held that the ordinances effected a taking under both the federal and state constitutions. The state court accordingly affirmed a jury verdict under which just compensation had been computed by subtracting the value of the property after the height restrictions were imposed under Ordinances 1221 and 1599 from the value of the land prior to adoption of those ordinances.

Relying on the Nevada Supreme Court's decision in *Sisolak*, the court of appeals in this case held that Ordinance 1221 had effected a taking of respondents' property under Nevada law. The Ninth Circuit "respectfully disagreed" with the *Sisolak* court's "interpretation of federal takings jurisprudence," and concluded that "no Fifth Amendment taking of respondents' property occurred." The court held, however, that it was bound by the Nevada Supreme Court's interpretation of the state constitution. Relying on *Jankovich v. Indiana Toll Road Comm'n*, the court rejected petitioner's contention that the state-law compensation requirement announced in *Sisolak* was preempted by federal statutes governing aviation.[1]

Example 2

This lawsuit deals with the processing of a large number of illegal aliens from Cuba. Note the skillful handling of the complicated historical background of the case.

Respondent is one of approximately 125,000 Cuban nationals, many of them convicted of crimes in Cuba, who attempted to enter the United States illegally during the 1980 Mariel boatlift. After Cuba refused to accept the return of Mariel Cubans who were stopped at the border and denied entry into the United States, the Attorney General, through the Immigration and Naturalization Service (INS), soon paroled all but a few hundred of those Cubans into this country pursuant to his discretionary authority under 8 U.S.C. 1182(d)(5).

Respondent was convicted of numerous crimes in Florida while he was on immigration parole. In 1988, respondent was charged with two counts of battery on a law enforcement officer. He received one year of probation with a deferred adjudication of guilt. In March 1991, respondent was convicted of possessing burglary tools, attempted burglary of a structure, and possessing cocaine. He received one year of probation for those offenses. In January 1992, respondent was convicted of burglary of an occupied dwelling and sentenced to one year in a community control program and drug rehabilitation. In February 1993, respondent was convicted of felony burglary of a conveyance and petty theft and was sentenced to five years of probation on the burglary count. In July 1993, he was convicted of burglary of an unoccupied structure and resisting an officer and received a sentence of 364 days of imprisonment. In May 1995, respondent was convicted of cocaine possession, using or possessing drug paraphernalia, and burglary of a dwelling. Respondent's 1993 probation was revoked and he received a sentence of five years of imprisonment. In September 1996, respondent was convicted of escape and sentenced to one year and one day of imprisonment.

In December 1996, the INS revoked respondent's immigration parole and commenced exclusion proceedings against him based on his criminal convictions and his lack of valid documents for entering the United States. In May 1997, an immigration judge determined that respondent is excludable from the United States and ordered him deported to Cuba. Respondent waived an administrative appeal.

In 1999, at the completion of his criminal sentence, the INS took respondent into custody. The INS was not able to remove respondent to Cuba because the Government of Cuba would not accept his return. As required by the parole regulations applicable to Mariel Cubans, the INS reviewed respondent's custody status on an annual basis during his detention. In 2000, respondent was approved for a second immigration parole. The INS released respondent to a halfway house in 2003.

In June 2004, respondent was convicted in Washington State of delivering cocaine, for which he was sentenced to 27 months of imprisonment. Upon respondent's release from prison in October 2005, the INS again took respondent into immigration custody under his 1997 order of exclusion.

In January 2006, respondent filed a *habeas corpus* petition under 28 U.S.C. 2241 in the U.S. District Court for the Western District of Washington. Respondent contended in his petition that his detention by the INS violated his due process rights under the Fifth Amendment and that his release was required under *Zadvydas v. Davis* because Cuba had not accepted his repatriation.

In April 2006, the district court denied respondent's petition. The district court explained that "the six-month presumptively reasonable post-removal detention period outlined in *Zadvydas* applies only to aliens who have effected an entry into the United States," and cited *Zadvydas*'s discussion of *United States ex rel Mezei* as a "particularly clear" indication that the six-month period does not apply to aliens who are stopped at the border and denied admission. The court then addressed respondent's due process arguments under the Fifth Amendment. It determined that respondent, as an excludable alien who was stopped at the border, "may not assert procedural due process rights to attack the admissions process," and that "respondent's substantive due process rights are met by the annual opportunity for custody review afforded by 8 C.F.R. 212.12."

On August 1, 2006, the Ninth Circuit held in *Lin Guo Xi v. INS*, "that *Zadvydas* applies to inadmissible individuals" who were stopped at the border, denied admission, and ordered removed from the United States under the post-1996 immigration laws, and, therefore, the detention of such aliens is subject to the reasonable-time limitation and six-month presumption established by this Court in *Zadvydas*.

On August 16, 2006, the district court granted respondent's motion for reconsideration and granted his *habeas corpus* petition. The court determined that, because petitioner's removal to

Cuba was "extremely unlikely" and he had been in immigration detention for more than six months, *Xi*'s extension of *Zadvydas* to an inadmissible alien "compelled" respondent's release.

The government moved for reconsideration, arguing that respondent's detention is governed by the pre-Illegal Immigration Reform and Immigrant Responsibility Act (IIRIRA) law that applied at the time respondent's final order of exclusion was entered, rather than by current Section 1231(a)(6). On November 15, 2006, the district court denied the government's motion for reconsideration. The court stated that "the INS cannot reasonably rely on repealed detention provisions" and noted that *Zadvydas* involved the detention of a lawful permanent resident alien who (like respondent) was ordered deported before the 1996 immigration amendments.

In December 2006, respondent was released from a halfway house and into the community pursuant to the district court's order.

The court of appeals affirmed the district court's decision ordering respondent's release. The court noted that respondent did not contest the district court's rejection of his constitutional arguments, but only defended the district court's determination that his detention is not authorized by statute in light of *Zadvydas* and *Xi*. The court therefore concluded that the lawfulness of respondent's detention depends on whether it is authorized before the IIRIRA that survived the 2000 immigration amendments, "for we already have held in *Xi* that the new post-IIRIRA detention statute 8 U.S.C. § 1231(a)(6) does not authorize the INS to detain inadmissible aliens indefinitely."[2]

Example 3

The following excerpt deals with damages related to police entry into a residence. Note how clearly the history of this case is presented.

This damages action arises out of a police entry into respondent's residence on the night of March 19, 2002. Petitioners are police officers who had arranged for a confidential informant,

Brian Bartholomew, to enter respondent's house, with respondent's consent, to purchase methamphetamine. Petitioners monitored the conversation inside the house through a wire that Bartholomew wore.

After Bartholomew entered the house, he gave respondent a marked $100 bill in exchange for a bag of methamphetamine taken from a larger quantity of the drug stored in respondent's kitchen freezer. Bartholomew then signaled to petitioners that the narcotics sale had been completed. Immediately thereafter, petitioners entered the house through a porch door and saw respondent drop a plastic bag later determined to contain methamphetamine. Respondent was arrested and charged with possession and distribution of methamphetamine. The entry of respondent's house was conducted without a search or arrest warrant.

During state criminal proceedings, respondent moved to suppress the methamphetamine and drug paraphernalia found in his residence. The state trial court denied the motion to suppress, holding that the warrantless search of respondent's house was justified by exigent circumstances. Respondent entered a conditional guilty plea, reserving his right to appeal the denial of the motion to suppress.

The Utah Court of Appeals reversed respondent's conviction. On appeal, the State conceded that the trial court erred in finding that the entry was justified by exigent circumstances. The court of appeals rejected, as unsupported by the record, the State's alternative argument that suppression was unwarranted because the officers would inevitably have discovered the evidence through alternative means.

Pursuant to 42 U.S.C. 1983, respondent then filed a civil damages action against petitioners and others in federal district court, alleging that petitioners' conduct had violated his rights under the Fourth Amendment. The district court granted petitioners' motion for summary judgment.

The district court first considered the doctrine of "consent-once-removed." Under that doctrine, "the consent to enter a residence given to the first person, generally a law enforcement officer but sometimes an informant is then transferred to the entering police officers once the first person requests assistance from the police based on probable cause." The court noted that the "consent-once-removed" doctrine has been upheld and applied in the Sixth, Seventh, and Ninth Circuits, and "has been explicitly applied not only to undercover police agents, but also to government and confidential informants in the Sixth and Seventh Circuits." Rather than decide whether the police entry in this case was constitutional, however, the district court stated "the simplest approach is to assume that the Supreme Court will ultimately reject the doctrine and find that searches such as the one in this case are not reasonable under the Fourth Amendment."

Even assuming the existence of a constitutional violation, however, the district court concluded that petitioners were entitled to qualified immunity from suit because their conduct had not violated any clearly established constitutional right. The court recognized that the general principles underlying respondent's constitutional claim that "warrantless searches of a person's home are presumptively unreasonable" had been clearly established at the time of the police entry in this case. The court explained, however, that "on the specifics of this case, the officers had a reasonable argument that the 'consent-once-removed' doctrine justified their actions," particularly given the acceptance of that doctrine by three federal courts of appeals.

A divided panel of the court of appeals reversed. The court held that petitioners' conduct violated respondent's Fourth Amendment rights. The court recognized that "the 'consent-once-removed' doctrine applies when an undercover officer enters a house at the express invitation of someone with authority to consent, establishes probable cause to arrest or search, and then immediately summons other officers for assistance." The court further acknowledged that "the Sixth and Seventh Circuits have broadened this doctrine to grant informants the same capabilities as undercover officers." The court held, however, that it was appropriate to distinguish for these purposes between undercover police officers and private citizens serving as confidential informants, and that Tenth Circuit case law supported application of the "consent once removed" doctrine only as to the former.

The court of appeals further held that the Fourth Amendment right it recognized was clearly established at the time of petitioners' allegedly unconstitutional conduct. The court stated that, "in this case, the relevant right is the right to be free in one's home from unreasonable searches and arrests." The court determined that, under the clearly established precedents of this Court and the Tenth Circuit, "warrantless entries into a home are *per se* unreason able unless they satisfy the established exceptions," and that "the only two exceptions to the warrant requirement are consent and exigent circumstances." Against that backdrop, the court concluded, petitioners could not reasonably have believed that their conduct was lawful because petitioners "knew (1) they had no warrant; (2) respondent had not consented to their entry; and (3) his consent to the entry of an informant could not reasonably be interpreted to extend to them."[3]

Example 4

The background of this capital murder case reads like the introduction to a novel, but in the process the reader is also well informed about the necessary facts.

In March 2002, Timothy Hall's body was discovered beneath an abandoned construction site along the James River in Newport News, Virginia. The medical examiner concluded that Hall had bled to death from 143 separate "sharp force injuries," and that Hall could have survived in a conscious state for as long as thirty to forty-five minutes after the last wound was inflicted. Extensive evidence tied petitioner to Hall's death, including incriminating statements made by petitioner to police shortly after his arrest, petitioner's confession to a cellmate to the murder of Hall, analyses of DNA found on Hall, eyewitness testimony placing petitioner at the scene of the crime, and the fact that petitioner sold a pair of athletic shoes belonging to Hall to another individual just days after Hall's death.

In 2003, a Virginia jury found petitioner guilty of the capital murder of Hall. The jury further found that Hall's murder was outrageously and wantonly vile, and sentenced petitioner to death. On direct appeal, petitioner's sentence was vacated by this Court for reconsideration in light of *Simmons v. South Carolina*, and the case was remanded for resentencing. Following a new sentencing hearing during which a Simmons instruction on parole ineligibility was made, a jury again sentenced petitioner to death. That sentence was affirmed on appeal and petitioner's application for state *habeas corpus* relief was denied.

In June 2005, petitioner applied for a writ of federal *habeas corpus* under 28 U.S.C. 2254 in the U.S. District Court for the Eastern District of Virginia, claiming, *inter alia*, that he was denied effective assistance of counsel in violation of the Sixth Amendment because his court-appointed counsel labored under a conflict of interest at trial. While investigating the case, petitioner's federal *habeas* counsel had reviewed Hall's juvenile court file and discovered that petitioner's trial counsel, Bryan Saunders, was representing Hall on assault and concealed weapon charges at the time of Hall's death. Judge Paul Criver of the local juvenile court had appointed Saunders to represent Hall on those charges on March 20, 2002. Sometime between March 20 and March 28, 2002, when Hall was last seen alive, Saunders met with Hall for fifteen to thirty minutes.

On April 3, 2002, Judge Aundria Foster of the juvenile court dismissed the charges against Hall, noting on the docket sheet that Hall was deceased. The docket sheet was one-page long and listed Saunders as Hall's counsel. Saunders learned of the dismissal that day. The following day, petitioner was arrested for the murder of Hall. On April 6, Judge Foster appointed Saunders and Warren Keeling to represent petitioner on those charges. Saunders handled the guilt phase of petitioner's trial, while Keeling handled the sentencing phase. Neither Saunders nor Keeling represented petitioner in the state *habeas* proceeding. Saunders did not disclose his prior representation of Hall to the court, his co-counsel, or petitioner, who did not learn about the representation until it was discovered by his federal *habeas* attorney upon reviewing Hall's juvenile file.

In November 2006, after conducting an evidentiary hearing, the district court denied petitioner's federal *habeas* petition.

The court rejected petitioner's Sixth Amendment claim, holding that petitioner failed to establish "an actual conflict of interest that adversely affected his lawyer's performance." The court found that petitioner "failed to demonstrate a correlation between Saunders' representation of Hall for assault and possession of a concealed weapon and his representation of petitioner on capital murder charges," "Saunders did not learn any confidential information from Hall that was relevant to petitioner's defense," and "Saunders did not believe that any 'continuing duties to a former client might interfere with his consideration of all facts and options for his current client.'" The court further found that there was no evidence that any conflict that might have existed because of Saunders' prior representation of Hall adversely affected Saunders' representation of petitioner.

The district court also rejected petitioner's related argument, based on *Wood v. Georgia*, that his conviction should be reversed simply because Judge Foster declined to inquire into the potential conflict on Saunders' part. The court agreed that "the record before Judge Foster presented special circumstances of an apparent possible conflict which required judicial inquiry." But relying on this Court's decisions in *Wood* and *Sullivan*, the district court held that a trial court's "failure to inquire into a possible conflict does not in itself require reversal." Instead, the court concluded, a defendant must show both an actual conflict and an adverse effect on the representation to establish a Sixth Amendment violation.

A divided panel of the Fourth Circuit reversed. Then the court of appeals granted rehearing *en banc*, vacated the initial panel decision, and by a 7-3 decision affirmed the denial of *habeas* relief. The *en banc* court assumed for purposes of its analysis "that Judge Foster reasonably should have known that Saunders labored under a potential conflict of interest arising from his previous representation of Hall." But the court rejected petitioner's argument that that judicial lapse alone "mandates automatic reversal of his conviction."

The *en banc* court recognized that in *Holloway v. Arkansas*, this Court held that automatic reversal of a conviction is required under the Sixth Amendment when a trial court fails to inquire into a potential conflict "in the face of repeated representations" by defense counsel that he is burdened by a conflict. The court held, however, that *Holloway*'s automatic-reversal rule does not govern where, as here, defense counsel does not object to any conflict at trial. In that context, the court reasoned, the rule of *Cuyler v. Sullivan* controls. "A defendant who raised no objection at trial must demonstrate that an actual conflict of interest adversely affected his lawyer's performance."

The *en banc* court rejected petitioner's argument "that a footnote in *Wood v. Georgia* changed the rule of *Sullivan* and extended the automatic reversal rule of *Holloway* to circumstances in which a trial court ignores a conflict about which it reasonably should have known." The court further rejected petitioner's alternative argument that, "even if *Wood* does not compel automatic reversal of his conviction, it relieves him of his burden under *Sullivan* of establishing an adverse effect on his representation." As the court explained, that argument is contradicted by the Court's decision in *Wood*, as well as subsequent Supreme Court decisions reciting the *Sullivan* rule without suggesting that it had been altered by *Wood*.

Finally, the *en banc* court rejected petitioner's argument "that the district court erred in deciding that any actual conflict of interest did not adversely affect the representation." To establish the requisite "adverse effect," the court stated, a defendant "must identify a plausible alternative defense strategy or tactic" not pursued by counsel; "show that that strategy or tactic was objectively reasonable"; and "establish that the defense counsel's failure to pursue that strategy or tactic was linked to the actual conflict." The *en banc* court agreed with the district court's "complete, thorough, and thoughtful" consideration of that issue, and held that petitioner had failed to show that the asserted conflict on Saunders' part, even if real, had any adverse effect on the representation. Because it found no adverse effect, the court did not decide whether an actual conflict in fact existed.[4]

Notes

References to citations, transcripts, footnotes, and some authorities omitted for sake of clarity.

1. *Clark County, Nevada v. Vacation Village, Inc.*, No. 07-373.
2. *Crawford v. Martinez-Vazquez*, No. 03-920.
3. *Pearson v. Callahan*, No. 07-751.
4. *Mickens v. Taylor*, No. 00-9285.

Inform and Persuade

Before a lawyer can persuade, he must inform. In other words, you must first strive to make sure the court understands the case. In many instances, the advocate is so intent upon the ultimate aim of persuasion that he fails to make clear what he is complaining of, how it came about, and what he wants the court to do about it.

Judges reiterate that cases are won on the facts and the law—not on polished writing, oratory, or the personality of counsel. It is the lawyer's job to choose with a dispassionate mind the issues that common sense and experience suggest will likely be dispositive. Other issues must be rejected or given brief treatment. In oral argument, counsel has to be even more selective.

9

Statutory Construction:
It Can Be Critical

Words are symbols for ideas, and legislators spend a great deal of time crafting statutes with the awareness that every word will be weighed in a yet-unseen world of a thousand different situations.

The English language is versatile, and the range for interpretation is great. An overly mechanical approach to a statute's wording is often inadequate in furthering public policies that the statute was intended to advance. Although some statutes are carefully drafted with the kind of explicitness that makes the legislative intent clear and the application of the facts to the statute obvious, a legislature often deliberately crafts statutes so that the courts have flexibility in their application.

Legal arguments dealing with statutory construction are a challenge because the canons of construction are not always helpful (and sometimes even inconsistent). Questions of meaning therefore arise, such as whether inclusion of one matter necessarily excludes others. And then there is the problem of inference—which the legislature, by not amending a statute, is deemed to have implicitly acquiesced in a court's decision.

Your job is to collect decisions interpreting the statue, as well as legislative history, rulings by administrative agencies, scholarly commentaries, case law dealing with similar statutes in other jurisdictions, and so forth. You must then explain to the judge how these authorities would apply the statute to the facts at hand. The clarity you bring to the court in this regard will go a long way toward victory for your client.

The four examples demonstrating statutory construction that are set forth here deal with a number of interesting issues: (1) state regulatory schemes' compliance with the federal commerce clause, (2) the False Claims Act, (3) registration of motor carriers, and (4) the crime of carjacking. They reveal in a tangible way the importance to the court of effective statutory interpretation.

Example 1

The statute in this case deals with regulation of milk products sold in California and the resulting issue of its interplay with the federal commerce clause. The argument presented before the U.S. Supreme Court is remarkable for its pace and its analytic nature.

Although the Commerce Clause "limits the power of the States to erect barriers against interstate trade," Congress may "authorize the States to engage in regulation that the Commerce Clause would otherwise forbid." The Court has held, however, that Congress must make any such authorization "unmistakably clear" so as to assure that "all segments of the country are represented" in a decision to allow one State to affect persons or operations in other States.

Section 7254 of the Federal Activities Reform Act (FAIR) does not contain any indication at all—much less an "unmistakably clear" one—that Congress intended to immunize the regulations at issue here from Commerce Clause scrutiny. The statutory text does not include any reference either to the Commerce Clause or to California's pricing and pooling laws for raw milk.

A. Section 7254 Contains No "Unmistakably Clear" Expression Of Congressional Intent To Immunize Any State Law From The Commerce Clause

Section 7254 states that "nothing in this Act or any other provision of law shall be construed to preempt, prohibit, or otherwise limit the authority of the State of California" to enact or enforce certain of its own laws. That statutory text does not unambiguously express an intent by Congress to exempt any of California's laws from the Commerce Clause. Section 7254 does not even refer to the Commerce Clause specifically, or to the Constitution more generally.

Congress has elsewhere spoken with considerably greater clarity in expressing its intent to immunize state laws from the implied limitations of the Commerce Clause. More generally, when Congress has sought to refer to the Constitution, as well as to other sources of law, Congress has often (although not always) made specific reference to the Constitution.

Moreover, Congress's directive in Section 7254 that no provision of law "shall be construed" in a particular manner is more naturally read as referring only to non-constitutional sources of federal law, i.e., Acts of Congress or agency regulations implementing them. Congress is not ordinarily assumed to have intended to constrain the Judiciary's authority to construe the Constitution. Thus, if Congress sought to exercise its power under the Commerce Clause to authorize state laws that would otherwise be invalid under that Clause, Congress could reasonably be expected to do so in a straightforward manner by declaring the state laws valid, not to presume to instruct the courts (including this Court) to alter their construction of the Constitution.

Furthermore, if the reference in Section 7254 to "any other provision of law" were read to include the Constitution, it would presumably include provisions of the Constitution beyond the Commerce Clause—such as the Privileges and Immunities Clause of Article IV and the Equal Protection Clause of the Fourteenth Amendment, both of which petitioners also invoked in this case. Congress would have been aware, however, that it cannot, when exercising its authority under the Commerce Clause, immunize state laws from scrutiny under other provisions of the Constitution. Thus, if Congress had intended to provide the California regulations with immunity under the Commerce Clause, Congress could be expected to have referred more specifically to that Clause.

Nor is there any reason to suppose that Congress intended to authorize California, and only California, to erect barriers to interstate commerce that would otherwise be forbidden by the Commerce Clause. Section 7254 reaches not only California laws in existence at the time of its enactment, but also California laws that might come into existence at some later time. It is particularly unlikely that Congress would have created so open-ended an immunity from the Commerce Clause for whatever laws California might choose to adopt in the future to regulate the marketing of raw or processed milk.

In sum, Section 7254 does not establish, with the requisite degree of clarity, any Commerce Clause immunity for any California law. Rather, Section 7254 is properly understood as protecting certain California laws against preemption only by "this Act" (i.e., the FAIR Act) and other provisions of federal statutory or regulatory law.

B. Section 7254 Does Not Encompass California's Regulations Governing The Pricing And Pooling Of Raw Milk

Section 7254, even if construed to provide a Commerce Clause immunity for some state laws, does not reach the laws at issue here. Neither the text of Section 7254 nor the context in which it was enacted provides any manifestation of congressional intent to protect California's milk pricing and pooling regulations.

Section 7254, by its terms, applies only to laws regarding "the percentage of milk solids or solids not fat in fluid milk products sold at retail or marketed in the State of California" and "the labeling of such fluid milk products with regard to milk solids or solids not fat." The pricing and pooling laws do not regulate, directly or indirectly, fluid-milk content or fluid-milk labeling. They are thus outside the scope of whatever Commerce Clause exemption Section 7254 even arguably provides.

Congress's decision to confine Section 7254 to a subset of California's milk marketing laws appears to have been quite deliberate. Other provisions of the FAIR Act, of which Section

7254 was a part, demonstrate that, when Congress wanted to refer to California's milk pricing and pooling laws, Congress did so more specifically. In the immediately preceding section of the FAIR Act, Congress authorized the Secretary of Agriculture, "upon the petition and approval of California dairy producers," to "designate the State of California as a separate Federal milk marketing order."

Congress further provided that any such "order covering California shall have the right to reblend and distribute order receipts to recognize quota value," thus referring specifically to the aspect of California's pricing and pooling laws that guarantees state dairy farms with "quota" a higher blend price for their raw milk. Presumably, if Congress had wanted Section 7254 to encompass California's pricing and pooling laws, Congress would have referred to those laws with similar specificity.[1]

Example 2

The False Claims Act spawned a significant amount of litigation. Note how the statutory construction in the following excerpt is blended with the facts of this case to provide a most compelling argument.

A. Section 3729(a)(2) of Title 31 Does Not Require Proof That A False Claim Was "Presented" Directly To The Federal Government

Section 3729(a)(2) of Title 31 imposes False Claims Act (FCA) liability on any person who "knowingly makes, uses, or causes to be made or used, a false record or statement to get a false or fraudulent claim paid or approved by the Government." Petitioners contend that, "for a claim to be 'paid or approved by the Government,' it first must be submitted to the government." That argument lacks merit. Petitioners' alleged false claims were "paid by" the United States because the United States was the source of the funds. Petitioners received those funds through prime contractors for work performed under subcontracts in fulfillment of procurement contracts with the United States. Petitioners' alleged misconduct thus squarely implicates the FCA's core purpose of preventing fraud in national defense procurement.

1. Petitioners' alleged conduct falls squarely within the ordinary meaning of Section 3729(a)(2)

As a matter of ordinary English usage, a bill or other obligation would commonly be described as "paid by" the person whose money is used for payment, even if some other person performs the mechanical act of transferring the funds. For example, "[w]hen a student says his college living expenses are 'paid by' his parents, he typically does not mean that his parents send checks directly to his creditors. Rather, he means that his parents are the ultimate source of the funds he uses to pay those expenses." That use of the phrase "paid by" is particularly natural if the ultimate source of the funds directs that all or part of the money be used for a specifically defined purpose. Thus, if a man gives his daughter $100 and asks her to use a portion of the money to fill the family car with gasoline, the bill for the gas would readily be described as being "paid by" the father, even though the daughter effects the physical transfer of funds to the gas station.

To be sure, the verb "pay" and its variants can sometimes refer to the mechanics of disbursing funds rather than to the incidence of the ultimate financial impact. Thus, if a mother and son are watching television when a pizza delivery arrives, the mother might hand her son cash and ask him to go to the door to "pay for" the pizza. In that scenario, the son would "pay for" the pizza in the sense of handing money to the delivery person, while the mother would "pay for" the pizza in the sense of absorbing its cost.

It would be inconsistent with the tenor of this Court's FCA precedents, however, to infer that Congress in drafting Section 3729(a)(2) used the phrase "paid by the Government" solely to describe the logistics of transferring funds, without reference to the ultimate economic consequences of fraudulent conduct. The Court in *Neifert-White* stated that the FCA "was intended to reach all types of fraud, without qualification, that might result in financial loss to the Government." The Court further explained that, "in the various contexts in which questions of the proper construction of the Act have been presented, the Court has consistently refused to accept a rigid, restrictive reading, even at the time when the statute imposed criminal sanctions as well as civil."

With specific regard to the administration of federal funding programs by non-federal intermediaries, the Court in *United States ex rel. Marcus v. Hess* explained that funds provided to States under various aid programs "are as much in need of protection from fraudulent claims as any other federal money, and the statute does not make the extent of their safeguard dependent upon the bookkeeping devices used for their distribution." Petitioners' contention that Section 3729(a)(2) should be construed by reference to the mechanics of fund distribution, rather than to the ultimate impact of their alleged fraudulent conduct, is at odds with the Court's established approach to the interpretation of the FCA.

In the instant case, the invoices that petitioners submitted for the Gen-Sets were "paid by" the government. Although the payments that petitioners received under the subcontracts traveled through intermediaries, the federal government was the ultimate source of the funds. Those payments were made pursuant to government contracts that obligated the prime contractors to build destroyers containing Gen-Sets that conformed to precise contractual requirements. In order to discharge their own contractual obligations, the prime contractors were therefore required to use a portion of the funds they received from the government either to manufacture or acquire Gen-Sets meeting the Navy's specifications. The purpose of the overall undertaking was to produce destroyers equipped with Gen-Sets for use by the Navy rather than by any private party. Thus, the funds that the prime contractors transmitted for the Gen-Sets were acquired from the government originally, and they were forwarded to the subcontractors to achieve a governmental objective. The court of appeals' conclusion that the subcontractors' claims were "paid by" the United States therefore accords with ordinary English usage.

2. Petitioners' presentment theory cannot be squared with related statutory provisions

Under established principles of construction, any ambiguity in Section 3729(a)(2) standing alone should be resolved by considering that provision in light of its larger statutory context. As this Court has instructed, "the words of a statute must be read in their context and with a view to their place in the overall statutory scheme." Thus, "in expounding a statute, the Court must not be guided by a single sentence or member of a sentence, but look to the provisions of the whole law, and to its object and policy." Petitioners' reading of Section 3729(a) is at odds with this Court's repeated admonitions that the FCA should be construed in a manner that ensures comprehensive protection against attempts to defraud the United States. More specifically, two other provisions within Section 3729 itself reinforce the conclusion that a subcontractor's claim may be "paid" by the United States within the meaning of Section 3729(a)(2) even if it is not directly presented to any federal official.

Petitioners' presentment theory is therefore inconsistent with the FCA's definition of "claim". As amended in 1986, the FCA contains the following definition of "claim":

> For purposes of 31 U.S.C. 3729, "claim" includes any request or demand, whether under a contract or otherwise, for money or property which is made to a contractor, grantee, or other recipient if the United States Government provides any portion of the money or property which is requested or demanded, or if the Government will reimburse such contractor, grantee, or other recipient for any portion of the money or property which is requested or demanded.

First, in defining the term "claim" to include requests for payment submitted to federal "contractor[s], grantee[s], or other recipient[s]," Congress presumably intended to accomplish something of substance. Petitioners read Section 3729(c) as simply "making clear that a request for payment submitted to and paid by a federally funded private entity is not excluded from the scope of the FCA, if—as required by Section 3729(a)(2)—a claim is thereafter submitted to the government for reimbursement or approval." Congress's inclusive definition of the term "claim" would be superfluous, however, if liability under the various provisions of 31 U.S.C. 3729(a) ultimately depended on proof that some other request for payment was eventually presented to a federal officer or employee.

Even if Section 3729(c) had not been added to the statute, the sequence of events hypothesized by petitioners, in which a fraudulent request for payment directed to a federal grantee leads the grantee to submit its own request for reimbursement to the federal government, would be covered by Section 3729(a)(1) (imposing liability on any person who "knowingly presents, or causes to be presented, to an officer or employee of the United States Government a false or fraudulent claim for payment or approval"). Petitioners' exegesis of Section 3729(c) thus gives no operative effect to Congress's determination that, under specified circumstances, a request for payment directed to a federal contractor or grantee should itself be treated as an FCA "claim."

Second, petitioners' construction of Section 3729(c) suffers from an additional, related flaw. Section 3729(c) states that a request for money or property submitted to a federal contractor, etc., will constitute a "claim" either "if the United States Government provides any portion of the money or property which is requested or demanded, or if the Government will reimburse such contractor, grantee, or other recipient for any portion of the money or property which is requested or demanded." Congress's use of the disjunctive demonstrates that the circumstances in which the government "provides [a] portion of the money or property which is requested or demanded" are not limited to those in which the government will later "reimburse [the] contractor, grantee, or other recipient" for money that the contractor, etc., has already paid out.

The most obvious circumstance in which the first condition will be satisfied even though the second is not is one in which a third party requests money or property that the government has previously provided to a contractor or grantee. Petitioners' construction of Section 3729(c), which accords operative effect to the definition of "claim" only when the contractor or grantee submits an after-the fact request for reimbursement, effectively negates Congress's determination that a request directed to a federal contractor, etc., will be treated as an FCA "claim" in either of two distinct circumstances.[2]

Example 3

The registration of motor carriers is the subject of this discussion on statutory construction. What might at first seem like a dull and complex subject is made astonishingly less so by the skillful analysis of its advocate.

A. The $10-Per-Vehicle Limit For State Registration Of Interstate Carriers Under The SSRS Serves To Prevent States From Imposing Distinct Or Disproportionate Burdens On Interstate Commerce

1. In 1965, Congress expressly authorized each State to require an interstate motor carrier operating within its jurisdiction to "register its certificate of public convenience and necessity or permit issued by the Interstate Commerce Commission (ICC)." The 1965 statute provided that such registration requirements "shall not constitute an undue burden on interstate commerce provided that such registration is accomplished in accordance with standards . . . promulgated by the ICC."

   The fees that a State may charge in connection with that registration process, however, have consistently been limited by federal law. Thus, the 1965 statute that initially authorized the States to require registration of a carrier's federal operating authority provided: "To the extent that any State requirements for registration of motor carrier certificates or permits issued by the Commission impose obligations which are in excess of the standards or amendments thereto promulgated under this paragraph, such excessive requirements shall . . . constitute an undue burden on interstate commerce." In implementing former Section 302(b), the ICC initially adopted rules setting a $5-per-vehicle maximum on the fee that a State could charge for registration of a carrier's ICC certificate. The ICC subsequently raised that cap to $10 per vehicle, and the $10-per-vehicle regulatory limit remained in effect until it was adopted by Congress in 1991.

2. Congress had good reason to focus on state requirements for registration of ICC certificates and on the fees charged by States for such registration. The distinctive feature of carriers having

such certificates (or, under the current statutory regime, carriers registered by the Secretary of Transportation) is that they operate in interstate commerce. States historically have been prohibited by the Commerce Clause from regulating interstate commerce as such. They are also prohibited by the Commerce Clause from discriminating against out-of-State commercial entities, or against in-State commercial entities based on their participation in interstate commerce. Any attempt by a State to single out interstate motor carriers as such, or to impose requirements on such carriers that it does not impose on similarly situated intrastate operators, thus would raise substantial constitutional and policy concerns.

Specific federal authorization for States to require interstate carriers to register their federal certificates—a requirement that by its nature would have no application to purely intrastate operators—eliminated any potential Commerce Clause objection to such a registration requirement.

But if States were vested with unrestricted authority to require registration of an interstate operator's federal certificate, they might use that authority to subject interstate carriers to burdensome filing requirements and exorbitant fees that are not imposed on intrastate businesses. The $10-per-vehicle limit on fees for registration of ICC certificates or comparable federal operating authority thus serves the important federal interest in protecting interstate commerce against the imposition of distinct or discriminatory burdens. States remain free under the Commerce Clause, however, to levy a variety of other fees and taxes, including fees for the license-plating of individual vehicles, that do not single out carriers or vehicles operating in interstate commerce for discriminatory burdens.

The question in this case is whether the $100 annual fee imposed by MCL § 478.2(2) on Michigan-plated trucks operating entirely in interstate commerce is preempted by 49 U.S.C. 14504, the current version of the federal statute authorizing a State to require an interstate carrier to file evidence of its federal registration with the State. As explained below, 49 U.S.C. 14504 preempts any state registration requirement imposed on an interstate carrier by reason of its interstate operations, and therefore preempts MCL § 478.2(2).

B. Section 14504(b) Preempts Any State Registration Requirement Imposed On Interstate Motor Carriers By Reason Of Their Interstate Operations

1. In 1978, as part of a revision and recodification of Title 49, Congress carried forward the provision in former 49 U.S.C. 302(b)(2) that a state-law requirement for an interstate carrier to register its ICC certificate or permit with the State is not an unreasonable burden on interstate commerce if the State's registration requirements are consistent with standards adopted by the ICC. The next sentence then stated: "When a State registration requirement imposes obligations in excess of the standards of the ICC, the part in excess is an unreasonable burden." The wording of this latter sentence was revised from the corresponding sentence in its predecessor. Whereas the predecessor had provided that "state requirements for registration of motor carrier certificates or permits issued by the ICC" were an undue burden on interstate commerce to the extent they were in excess of ICC standards, the 1982 version provided that a "State registration requirement" was an undue burden on interstate commerce to the extent it imposed obligations in excess of the ICC standards.

It is unclear whether this change in language was intended to have any operative effect. On the one hand, the 1982 Act of Congress that enacted the overall revision was entitled "An Act To revise, codify, and enact without substantive change the Interstate Commerce Act and related laws as subtitle IV of title 49, United States Code, 'Transportation.'" On the other hand, the Reviser's Notes explaining the revision and recodification state that the revision of the language in the particular sentence at issue here was made "for clarity." This explanation could be read to suggest that the new reference in the second sentence to "State registration requirement" was meant to clarify an intent that was perhaps thought to be implicit in the prior 49 U.S.C. 302(b)(2)—namely, that the federal statute preempted any state registration requirement (not merely a state registration requirement specifically applicable to the filing of the carrier's ICC certificate) that was imposed on a carrier by reason of its interstate operations and that was in excess of the ICC standards referred to in the first sentence.

There is no need in this case to decide whether the use of the new wording ("State registration requirement") in the second sentence of 49 U.S.C. 11506(b) was meant to have any broader preemptive effect than its predecessor. The 1982 statute was in turn superseded by the current SSRS provision in 1991, and as explained below, the preemptive scope of the current provision plainly is broader than the 1965 version. But whatever the scope of the 1982 version while it was in effect, there is no indication that it was either intended or understood to introduce broad preemption in traditional areas of state regulation, such as state requirements associated with the plating and licensing of individual motor vehicles, even though such provisions might literally constitute "State registration requirement[s]."

2. In 1991, Congress extensively revised the statutory provision governing state registration requirements for carriers operating in interstate commerce. The new statute, now codified at 49 U.S.C. 14504, establishes the current SSRS registration system and specifies in considerable detail the permissible scope of the standards the Secretary of Transportation may adopt to govern state registration requirements under the SSRS system.

Significantly, Congress in 1991 also revised the language specifying which state registration requirements would and would not constitute an unreasonable burden on interstate commerce. The relevant subsection in the 1982 version of the statute had stated, in its first sentence, that any requirement by a State that a motor carrier subject to federal regulation "register the certificate or permit issued to the carrier" by the ICC would not constitute an unreasonable burden on interstate commerce if the state requirement conformed to standards issued by the ICC. The first sentence in subsection (b) of the current 49 U.S.C. 14504 is written more broadly. It provides: "The requirement of a State that a motor carrier, providing transportation" subject to federal jurisdiction, "must register with the State" is not an unreasonable burden on interstate commerce when "completed under standards of the Secretary under subsection (c)," i.e., when completed under the standards governing the SSRS.

The second sentence of Section 14504(b) then provides that "when a State registration requirement imposes obligations in excess of the standards of the Secretary, the part in excess is an unreasonable burden" on interstate commerce. Those two sentences of the current Section 14504(b), read together, make clear that state requirements that interstate carriers "must register with the State" are preempted as a general matter if they do not conform to the standards governing the SSRS, whether or not those state requirements are specifically worded in terms of a carrier's registration of its federal certificate with the State.

There is, however, no indication that the current Section 14504(b), any more than its predecessor, was intended to preempt state laws and fees in traditional areas of state regulation, such as those governing registration and license-plating of trucks under the IRP. Rather, Section 14504(b) is most naturally read as prohibiting state registration requirements that are imposed on interstate carriers by reason of their operation in interstate commerce, except as authorized under the SSRS itself.[3]

Example 4

This excerpt deals with a statute that defines the crime of carjacking. Its statutory analysis is delineated skillfully in this clear and detailed argument.

The language and structure of Section 2119 of Title 18, U.S. Code, indicate that Congress intended to define a single crime of carjacking (i.e., armed robbery of a motor vehicle), while providing discretion to sentencing courts to impose greater punishment where the crime produces greater harms.

The opening paragraph of the text defines the elements of the offense: possession of a firearm, taking a motor vehicle that has a nexus to interstate commerce, "from the person or presence of another," "by force and violence or by intimidation." That paragraph ends with the word "shall," followed by a dash. The remaining three dependent clauses, separated by commas and joined by the word "and," have to do only with sentencing: each provides for a different maximum term of imprisonment, from fifteen years to life, depending on the degree of bodily harm that "results" from commission of the offense just defined. In other words, the sentencing clauses divide the overall range of authorized penalties into statutory sub-ranges, varying the severity of permissible punishment according to the bodily harm suffered by victims of the offense.

None of Section 2119's subsidiary clauses stands on its own as a defined offense; each depends entirely on the initial paragraph to identify the criminal conduct that gives rise to punishment. Conversely, the initial paragraph does stand on its own as a definition of prohibited conduct; the three dependent clauses are relevant only to sentencing, at which stage they define what penalties Congress has authorized for the defined offense, and how their severity varies depending on the particular consequences of the crime.

As every court of appeals that has considered the matter has concluded, Section 2119 does not create three substantive offenses, each with separate elements and penalties. Rather, the statute's "structure is integrated, and its provisions form a seamless whole," defining one offense with three possible authorized sentencing ranges.

To identify three offenses in the text of Section 2119, the statute's three penalty clauses would have to be read as alternative completions for the offense definition begun in the initial paragraph; each completed alternative, taken as a whole, would then be read to define a separate criminal offense. That construction of the text, however, departs from the general approach employed by Congress in defining separate offenses. Congress does not typically define an offense by listing a number of its elements, add-ing the verb "shall," and then interposing a final offense element before specifying the range of authorized punishments. Moreover, if the penalty clauses were meant to be alternative completions for the first paragraph, rather than complementary subdivisions of an overall sentencing range, then they would more naturally be joined by the disjunctive "or" than by the conjunctive "and" that Congress actually used in drafting Section 2119.

If Congress had intended the bodily injury and death factors in clauses (2) and (3) to be elements of separate substantive offenses, it would likely have set them out in more conventional offense-defining language. In 18 U.S.C. 2113, for example, subsec-tions (a)-(c) define bank robbery and related offenses, each with its own penalty provisions. Subsections (d) and (e) then create separate aggravated forms of these offenses, by providing that "Whoever, in committing" one of the previously defined offenses, also commits assault, or jeopardizes a life, or kidnaps or kills another, "shall" be subject to specified punishments. Moreover, in setting out additional offense elements, subsections (d) and (e) use the active language of commission that is most often associ-ated with the definition of prohibited conduct: "assaults any per-son," "puts in jeopardy the life of any person," "kills any person," "forces any person to accompany him."

By contrast, the passive language of "result" found in Section 2119's sentencing clauses suggests that in drafting those clauses Congress was focusing, not on additional conduct that would be the subject of a supplementary prohibition, but on graduating the punishment for carjacking by reference to the degree of harm caused by a particular defendant's conduct.

These comparisons show that Section 2119 is not written like other statutes in which Congress may have intended to create sep-arate aggravated forms of a basic offense. Furthermore, compari-son with two other statutes cited by petitioner, 8 U.S.C. 1324(a), shows that Section 2119 is structured very much like statutes that all would agree set out only sentencing factors. In both Section 247 and Section 1324(a), an initial paragraph defining the elements of an offense concludes with the phrase "shall be punished as provided in" and the specification of a different subsection. That subsection, in turn, provides sub- ranges that are graduated according to, among other things, whether bodily injury or death results from the commission of the previously defined offense.[4]

Notes

References to citations, transcripts, footnotes, and some authorities omitted for sake of clarity.

1. *Hillside Diary, Inc. v. Lyons, et al.*, No. 01-950 and 01-1018.
2. *Allison Engine Co. v. United States*, No. 07-214.
3. *Mid-Con Freight Systems, Inc. v. Michigan Public Service Comm.*, No. 03-1234.
4. *Jones v. United States*, No. 97-6203.

Include Relevant Texts of Statutes, Rules, or Regulations

It seems obvious, but you should never assume that judges enjoy researching the law that advances your position. Make it easy for the judge to rule in your favor. Don't take the chance that a judge will decide that a case that you cited in your brief is not important because you did not take the time to carefully discuss it.

Remember, too, that most judges become generalists. You cannot take for granted that they are familiar with your specialty. Err on the side of explaining too much.

10

Legislative Purpose:
Determining Congressional
Intent

The challenges a legislature faces in crafting a statute are obvious. The problem boils down to this: How does one anticipate the future, myriad situations that will arise in regard to the newly proposed law?

The quest of the court for meaning begins with the statute's language. The traditional "plain meaning" rule allows inquiry into evidence of legislative intent only when the words of the statute are less than clear. But many courts now look beyond the language, even if the statute is unambiguous, to determine what the legislature intended.

As a result, judges often examine other sources—committee reports, the historical context in which the statute was enacted, other sections of the legislation, laws devoted to the same subject, and the statute's statements of public policy, to name but a few—to determine congressional intent.

While legislative history would appear to be the most direct evidence of the legislature's mindset in enacting the statute, it is often surprisingly incomplete and inconsistent. The so-called collective intent of a legislative body may in fact be more of a myth than a reality. As an effective advocate, your job is to persuade the court how the legislative intent is manifested in a way that bolsters your client's position.

The four examples demonstrating legislative intent that are set forth here deal with a number of interesting issues: (1) retaliation claims under the Civil Rights Act, (2) attorneys' fees under the Judicial Improvements and Access to Justice Act, (3) defining disability under the Social Security Act, and (4) federal banking statutes. The legislative intent is made apparent in these compelling arguments.

Example 1

The legislative history of a controversial provision of the Civil Rights Act dealing with retaliation claims is related effectively here. Note the interesting interplay between the evolving legislation and the conflict with the judicial interpretations in this argument before the Supreme Court.

Before this Court's decision in *Patterson v. McLean Credit Union,* the courts of appeals had no difficulty concluding—on the basis of *Sullivan v. Little Hunting Park, Inc.* and the common language and history of Sections 1981 and 1982 of Title 42 of the U.S. Code—that Section 1981 encompassed retaliation claims. Congress is presumed to be aware of that backdrop, and when it enacted the Civil Rights Act of 1991 in order to restore the pre-*Patterson* law, members of Congress had every reason to believe that they were reinstating that result. The pertinent provisions of the 1991 Act bolster that conclusion. In adding subsection (b) to Section 1981, Congress evinced an intent to apply Section 1981's prohibition against racial discrimination to all aspects of the contractual relationship including the post-formation conduct that *Patterson* had excluded from the scope of Section 1981.

Petitioner claims that Congress knew by 1991 that "the judiciary would analyze Section 1981 based on its text," and thus, "if Congress intended Section 1981 to provide for a cause of action based on retaliation, it would have provided [one] in the statutory text." But while Congress would surely have been aware that "text matters" in enacting the 1991 amendments, it clearly did not write on a blank slate or ignore the pre-existing judicial constructions of Sections 1981 and 1982. Tellingly, Congress, in amending Section 1981, did not rewrite it to create an express cause of action. Rather, Congress took this Court's decisions recognizing an inferred cause of action as a given. In the same way, Congress legislated against the backdrop of *Sullivan* and the direct connection between Section 1981 and Section 1982. There is certainly no indication in the 1991 Act that Congress intended a different construction of Section 1981 than the one that this Court adopted for Section 1982 in *Sullivan.*

To the contrary, it is clear that what Congress intended to address, *inter alia*, was the *Patterson* decision and the limitation of Section 1981 to post-formation conduct. Indeed, this Court has acknowledged that the 1991 Act "overturned *Patterson.*" But under petitioner's strained reasoning, Congress would not have accomplished its objective because it failed to include the term "harassment" in subsection (b), and has thus made harassment no more actionable than retaliation.

In reality, Congress responded to *Patterson* in a way that makes clear that both harassment and retaliation are prohibited *viz.*, by covering post-formation conduct. After all, the argument that retaliation would not be prohibited by the pre-1991 statute would not be based on its limitation to "discrimination" or "discrimination on the basis of race"; those terms did not even appear in the statute. Rather the argument would be that most retaliation would be post-formation conduct. Congress unambiguously and textually eliminated that argument, and thus there is no reason to think that retaliation—uniquely among post-formation conduct impairing Section 1981 rights—is not prohibited.

The legislative history of the 1991 Act bears this out. The House Report stated:

> The Committee intends this provision to bar all race discrimination in contractual relations. The list set forth in subsection (b) is intended to be illustrative rather than exhaustive. In the context of employment discrimination, for example, this would include, but not be limited to, claims of harassment, discharge, demotion, promotion, transfer, retaliation, and hiring.

The report also stated that subsection (b) was intended to respond to several court of appeals decisions that, after *Patterson*, had held that Section 1981 does not encompass claims of retaliation. The report's principal discussion of minority views did not dispute the majority's characterization of that effect or its desirability. Congress had heard evidence that *Patterson* was resulting in the dismissal of "racial harassment" and "retaliation" claims.

In light of this legislative record, it is not surprising that, in the wake of the 1991 Act, the courts of appeals have again reached a broad consensus that Section 1981 encompasses claims of retaliation against those who complain of racial discrimination.[1]

Example 2

This excerpt makes the argument to the Supreme Court that the notable silence of the legislative record on the subject of attorney's fees in cases of remand strongly argues against their presumptive inclusion.

This Court observed in *Fogerty v. Fantasy, Inc.* that, if Congress intended a fee-shifting statute to provide for an automatic or presumptive award of fees, at the very least some "legislative comment" would be expected to that effect. The history of Section 1447(c) of the Judicial Improvements and Access to Justice Act of 1988 (the 1988 Act) reveals no such "legislative comment." To the contrary, the legislative record is silent, and it is reasonable to infer that the statutory reference to attorney's fees was included, at most, for the more modest purpose of resolving confusion in the lower federal courts by making clear that courts were permitted to award fees in a remand order when the removal had been shown to be without a reasonable justification.

At the time of its amendment, Section 1447(c) provided that in cases "removed improvidently and without jurisdiction, the district court shall remand the case, and may order the payment of just costs." The 1988 Act amended the statute to provide that "an order remanding the case may require payment of just costs and any actual expenses, including attorney fees, incurred as a result of the removal." The legislative history of the 1988 Act does not specifically discuss the addition of the words "including attorney fees" in the amended Section 1447(c), and otherwise suggests, at most, that the amendment was intended to accomplish only modest objectives, not the complete departure from the American Rule posited by petitioner.

The 1988 Act originated in proposals from the Judicial Conference that addressed a wide range of issues concerning the federal judiciary. Those proposals originally included no provisions concerning removal. Two days before a congressional hearing on the subject on September 23, 1987, the Judicial Conference adopted some proposals addressing removal, including what became the amendment to Section 1447(c). The new proposals were presented to Congress and incorporated into the bill, and were enacted without change in the 1988 Act.

As the House Report explained, the removal provisions would, among other things, allow the citizenship of fictitious or "Doe" defendants to be disregarded for removal purposes; simplify the "pleading" requirements for removal; establish a one-year limit on removal based on diversity jurisdiction; eliminate the bond requirement on removal procedure; and regulate the joinder of additional parties after removal. The Report made only two references to the provision for award of costs and fees at issue in this case. The Report commented that the proposed amendment to Section 1447(c) will ensure that a substantive basis exists for requiring payment of actual expenses incurred in resisting an improper removal; Civil Rule 11 can be used to impose a more severe sanction when appropriate. And the Report added that "the proposal also would amend section 1447(c) to ensure that the court may order payment of actual expense caused by an improper removal." Those same two comments were included in a section-by-section analysis prepared in connection with Senate consideration of the bill.

In the floor debates, there was no specific mention at all of the attorney's fee provision. The omnibus bill as a whole, however, was repeatedly described as "noncontroversial." Had Congress intended to reverse the American Rule fundamentally and provide for routine fee awards to a party that is successful on a remand motion, "such a bold departure from traditional practice would surely have drawn more explicit statutory language and legislative comment." The complete absence of any comment in the legislative record suggests that the attorney's fees provision was intended at most to make a modest change in existing law, not the 180-degree turn that petitioners' view would entail.

The legal context in 1988 suggests a reasonable alternative explanation for the amendment. At the time of the 1988 Act, there was disagreement among the lower courts over the extent to which the preexisting statutory authorization to award costs included authority to award an attorney's fee. A few courts held that fees could be awarded as "costs" under Section 1447(c) without a finding of bad faith. The weight of the authority, however, was that fees could not be awarded under Section 1447(c) absent a finding of bad faith under the ordinary standards of the American Rule. A number of courts had specifically held that they could not award fees when a party, although not acting in bad faith, had engaged in conduct relating to removal that was without reasonable legal justification.

In that context, it is reasonable to infer that the Judicial Conference's proposal to amend Section 1447(c), and Congress's enactment of it, reflected an intent to resolve the existing confusion and clarify that courts could award fees for objectively unreasonable removals. Citing this Court's decision in *Alyeska*, which held that district courts generally may not award fees absent a finding of bad faith, a prominent treatise had proposed just that change.

In light of the firm tradition and presumptions reflected in the American Rule, it could be argued that Congress's mere addition of discretionary authority to award fees may have been insufficient to achieve even that modest purpose. But in no event can that bare grant of discretion be used to displace the American Rule completely and authorize an automatic or presumptive award of fees in every case upon remand, as petitioners propose.[2]

Example 3

This case deals with issues of defining disability under the Social Security Act. Note how convincingly the legislative history of the statute is presented.

Until the court of appeals' decision in this case, every court of appeals that had resolved this issue under Section 423(d)(2)(A) of the Social Security Act agreed that a claimant's ability to do her former work precludes a finding of disability, whether or not that former work exists in significant numbers in the national economy. When Congress enacted Section 423(d)(2)(A) in 1967, it codified the separate treatment of "previous work" and "other work" under the Commissioner's existing regulations. By its terms, and as confirmed by the accompanying House and Senate Reports, Section 423(d)(2)(A) does not require that "previous work" exist in significant numbers in the national economy; it imposes that requirement only for "other" work.

The definition of "disability" enacted in 1956, now found in Section 423(d)(1)(A), was copied from an earlier but otherwise identical definition used in the 1954 disability freeze program. In enacting that earlier program, Congress expressed its expectation that the Commissioner would promulgate standards that "will reflect the requirement that the individual be disabled not only for his usual work but also for any type of substantial gainful activity." When implementing that program through the Disability Freeze State Manual in 1955, the Commissioner explained that a claimant is disabled only if the impairment is "the cause of inability to work"; that the inability to work "must result from the impairment and its effect on the applicant's employability" rather than "other causes"; and that benefits would not be awarded to an "individual who is unemployed by reason of economic conditions" or "unavailability of jobs." That earlier construction of the same definition of "disability" bears strongly on the proper construction here. Where "Congress adopts a new law incorporating sections of a prior law, Congress normally can be presumed to have had knowledge of the interpretation given to the incorporated law, at least insofar as it affects the new statute."

Congress, moreover, has been fully aware of the Commissioner's construction since 1956 and has repeatedly endorsed it in the years that followed. For example, four years after Congress enacted the disability insurance program, the Subcommittee on the Administration of the Social Security Laws of the House Committee on Ways and Means conducted a comprehensive examination of the program. The resulting report acknowledged that, under the Commissioner's construction (which was embodied in manuals and other written guidance), an individual is not entitled to benefits if the person has "become unemployed or remain[s] unemployed for a reason or reasons other than disability," such as "technological changes in the industry in which the applicant has been employed. The disability provisions are intended to benefit only those persons who are not working because of incapacity, and not those unemployed because of these other factors." Although "the subcommittee recognize[d] that this distinction is difficult for the public to understand," it nonetheless reaffirmed Congress's desire to make "a clear distinction between this program and one concerned with unemployment."

Just five years later, in 1965, Congress amended the original definition of "disability" in Section 423(d)(1)(A) to change the required duration from "long-continued and indefinite" to "a continuous period of not less than 12 months." By then, the Commissioner had published regulations construing the term "disability." Those regulations required the claimant to be physically or mentally "incapable of performing his prior, usual or regular work"; mandated that the physical or mental impairment "be the primary reason for the individual's inability" to work; and precluded a finding of disability if the claimant became or remained "unemployed for a reason or reasons not due to his physical or mental impairment but because of technological changes in the industry in which he has worked." Even as Congress changed the duration requirement in Section 423(d) (1)(A), it did nothing to alter the Commissioner's construction of the substantive definition of "disability" in that provision.[3]

Example 4

The legislative history surrounding statutes that concern the banking industry is notoriously complicated, but the following example makes the subject look practically effortless because it explains it so well.

Congress made clear that national banking associations are corporations, indicating that they should be subject to the established principles for determining corporate citizenship. Those principles reflect the traditional understanding that, while a corporation "may by its agents transact business anywhere," the abstract entity "cannot thereby change its citizenship" because it "can have its legal home only at the place where it is located by or under the authority of its charter." That understanding governs the citizenship of an abstract "association" under the terms of Section 1348.

The absence of an explicit indication that Congress intended to depart from the traditional rules governing corporate citizenship alone suffices to demonstrate that the court of appeals erred in its interpretation of Section 1348. In addition, however, there is substantial evidence that Congress affirmatively intended to establish jurisdictional parity between national banks and state banks, such that national and state banks would have access to diversity jurisdiction on equal terms.

Under the original national banking statutes enacted in the 1860s, any action by or against a national banking association was considered to arise under federal law by virtue of the bank's federal charter. National banking associations (and opposing parties) therefore generally enjoyed access to federal court as a matter of federal question jurisdiction. National banks, however, also retained the entitlement to bring an action on the basis of diversity of citizenship. Because federal question actions involving national banks were subject to restrictive venue provisions, federal courts occasionally were called upon to determine a national banking association's citizenship for purposes of diversity jurisdiction.

The rule that emerged deemed a national bank to be a citizen of the State it identified in its organization certificate when designating the "place where its operation of discount and deposit are to be carried on." The basis for that rule was that a "national bank, being a corporation created by competent authority and located within a state should be regarded, for all the purposes of the jurisdiction of the federal courts, as on an equal footing with" corporations of that State. A national bank thus was a "citizen of the state as much as the state's corporations."

In 1882, Congress revoked the provisions that gave national banks general entitlement to federal question jurisdiction. The result was to align national banks and state banks with respect to their access to federal jurisdiction:

The jurisdiction for suits hereafter brought by or against any [national banking] association established under any law providing for national-banking associations shall be the same as, and not other than, the jurisdiction for suits by or against banks not organized under any law of the United States which do or might do banking business where such national-banking associations may be doing business.

As this Court soon explained, the 1882 statute aimed "to put national banks on the same footing as the banks of the state where they were located for all the purposes of the jurisdiction of the courts of the United States." With respect to diversity jurisdiction in particular, the principle of jurisdictional parity codified in 1882 fortified the rule of citizenship that had emerged in the lower courts. A national bank was a citizen of the State in which it was located "on an equal footing with," and subject to the same jurisdictional rules as a corporation chartered by that State. Federal jurisdiction in actions involving national banks then would "be the same as, and not other than" jurisdiction in actions involving state banks.

Congress again amended the jurisdictional provisions in 1887 to read as follows:

All national banking associations established under the laws of the United States shall, for the purposes of all actions by or against them, real, personal or mixed, and all suits in equity, be deemed citizens of the States in which they are respectively located.

Soon after the 1887 enactment, this Court explained that, with respect to diversity jurisdiction, "no limitation in that regard was intended." The Court saw "no reason" to conclude "that Congress intended that national banks should not resort to Federal tribunals as other corporations and individual citizens might." The same citizenship clause was reenacted as part of the 1911 codification of the Judicial Code. The 1887 and 1911 laws therefore continued the rule that a national bank was a citizen of the State of its designated place of business and would have access to federal jurisdiction on the same basis as a bank or other corporation of that State.[4]

Notes

References to citations, transcripts, footnotes, and some authorities omitted for sake of clarity.

1. *CBOCS West, Inc. v. Humphries*, No. 06-1431.
2. *Martin v. Franklin Corp.*, No. 04-1140.
3. *Barnhart v. Thomas*, No. 02-763.
4. *Wachovia Bank v. Schmidt*, No. 04-1186.

11

■·■·■————————————————————————

Discussing Case Law:
An Overlooked Art Form

To rule in your favor, a judge obviously needs to be convinced that you have provided sufficient judicial authority to support your position. As an advocate, you must think in terms of cause and effect: if you had to make the decision, what arguments would you most likely find persuasive?

Legal argumentation is hard, practical work, and your discussion of the case law must be directed toward answering specific questions. The number of cases and the amount of explanation you provide will depend on how much discussion is necessary to clarify the issue involved, how disputed the issue is, and how important the issue is to your theory. If the court is apt to be satisfied with a conclusory explanation, you may be able to limit citation to one or two cases.

But your position may be so complex, so disputed, and so critical that it must be supported by a more thorough analysis of numerous cases. If there is no recent, well-reasoned, and clearly expressed decision on point from the highest court in the jurisdiction, it might be necessary to discuss in detail the three or four most relevant cases—with a view toward providing the court assurance without trying its patience.

If the court must fill a significant gap in precedent, even more cases may be necessary to create a watertight argument that provides the court complete confidence in your analysis. Typically, the court will want to know how other jurisdictions have solved the same issue.

Distinguishing a recent decision of the court in which you appear can be a significant challenge, especially if its authors are still on the bench. Arguing that the decision is unsound will most likely alienate them. The court will be more receptive to an argument that the precedent was not intended to apply to the present situation. Always be careful of appearing to scold the court—it is vastly preferable to direct your fire toward opposing counsel.

The four examples demonstrating case law discussion that are set forth here deal with a number of interesting issues: (1) litigation expenses that can be borne by a labor union, (2) sufficient form for criminal jury charges, (3) the tension between self-representation and the assistance of counsel, (4) and the prohibition against unreasonable searches and seizures. An attorney looking for effective analysis of case law would be well advised to follow their lead.

Example 1

This is an argument discussing which litigation expenses can be borne by a labor union and therefore passed on to members of various bargaining units. Consider how the case law surrounding the controversy is delineated artfully in this brief submitted to the Supreme Court.

This Court unanimously held in *Ellis Brotherhood of Ry. Clerks* that expenses of litigation incident to negotiating and administering the contract, or to settling grievances and disputes arising in the bargaining unit, are clearly chargeable as a normal incident of the duties of the exclusive representative. However, the court held that litigation expenses of litigation not having such a connection with the bargaining unit are *not* to be charged to objecting employees, and that unless the relevant bargaining unit is directly concerned, the objecting employees need *not* share the costs of the litigation.

The upshot is that unwilling members of one bargaining unit cannot be charged for the costs of other units' litigation unless that litigation directly concerns the bargaining unit, even if the litigation were germane to the other units' collective bargaining and thus chargeable to objecting members of those specific units.

Ellis directly interpreted the Railway Labor Act (RLA), *not* the First Amendment. But *Ellis* and this Court's other RLA cases rest on principles of constitutional avoidance, not on a parsing of the RLA's text. Thus, "there is good reason to treat *Ellis* and other statutory cases as merely reflecting the constitutional rule." Indeed, a four-Member plurality confirmed in *Lehnert* that, "just as the Court in *Ellis* determined that the RLA, as informed by the First Amendment, prohibits the use of dissenters' fees for extra unit litigation, the Amendment proscribes such assessments in the public sector." Justice Scalia, in an opinion joined by three other Justices, likewise agreed that *Ellis* "reflects the constitutional rule."

Ellis's unanimous holding reflects the constitutional distinction between activities undertaken as part of negotiating and administering a unit's collective-bargaining agreement or settling disputes under that agreement (which are generally chargeable to objectors) and other activities undertaken to promote union interests more generally (which are not chargeable to workers who object to union membership in the first place). A unit might choose to contribute its voluntarily raised funds to another unit's litigation efforts on the theory that the litigation could have precedential significance for all units, and thus indirectly benefit the contributing unit. In a variety of contexts, however, this Court has made clear that the First Amendment precludes charging objectors for similar matters.

For example, political and lobbying activities concerning the election of pro-union candidates or enactment of pro-union legislation may well strengthen a union and improve its bargaining position. Under the First Amendment, however, lobbying activities are not chargeable to objectors unless they specifically "relate to the ratification or implementation of a dissenter's collective-bargaining agreement." Similarly, public-relations expenses that are not "oriented toward the ratification or implementation of a unit's collective-bargaining agreement" are not chargeable to objectors, even though they may strengthen the union's bargaining position. This Court has likewise construed the RLA not to permit unions to charge objectors for union organizing activities, even though those activities may improve the union's bargaining position.

Such efforts to expand overall union power, beyond the negotiation and administration of a unit's collective-bargaining agreement, or the settling of disputes under it, fall outside of the free-rider rationale for compelled agency fees. So too here, litigation by affiliated unions may strengthen the position of the Maine State Employees Association (MSEA), but because such litigation is not part of the negotiation or administration of MSEA's own collective bargaining agreement, or the settling of disputes under that agreement, it is not chargeable to objectors. As the *Lehnert* plurality explained, litigation is "akin to lobbying" in that respect.

In addition, charging objectors for other units' litigation would "significantly add to the burdening of free speech that is inherent in the allowance of an agency or union shop." This Court "long has recognized the important political and expressive nature of litigation." A union's position in litigation—especially litigation concerning the rights and obligations of unions—may well be offensive to workers who do not wish to associate with a union in the first place. While the very concept of an agency shop requires objectors to contribute to their own unit's germane litigation, it does not require objectors to support other units' litigation.[1]

Example 2

Here the argument before the Supreme Court effectively discusses (and distinguishes) several cases dealing with the sufficient form of criminal jury charges.

The Ninth Circuit relied exclusively on the reasoning of *Stromberg v. California* and successor cases in concluding that the instructional error was structural and thus required reversal of respondent's murder conviction. In *Stromberg*, the defendant was charged with one count of violating a California statute that prohibited the public display of a red flag for one of three purposes: opposing government, inviting anarchistic action, or aiding seditious propaganda. The defendant was convicted under a general jury verdict that did not indicate which of the three purposes the defendant had been found guilty of pursuing. After this Court determined that it would violate the First Amendment to convict someone under the first theory of liability (opposing government), it overturned the conviction, holding that "if any of the clauses in question is invalid under the Federal Constitution, the conviction cannot be upheld." The Court has applied this principle in a series of cases (mostly pre-1970) involving general-verdict convictions, where one of the alternative theories upon which the case was submitted was unconstitutional.

In *Yates v. United States*, the Court extended the *Stromberg* rule to a general verdict in which one of the possible bases of conviction did not independently violate any constitutional provision, but was otherwise legally flawed. The defendants in *Yates* were charged with conspiring both to "advocate and teach" the violent overthrow of the United States and to "organize" the Communist Party. The Court found that the "organizing" object of the conspiracy was legally flawed because the Communist Party had been "organized" (within the meaning of the statutory prohibition) when it was founded, and that date was outside the period set by the statute of limitations. Although the "advocate and teach" object was valid, the Court reversed the conspiracy conviction because "the verdict [was] supportable on one ground, but not on another, and it is impossible to tell which ground the jury selected."

In *Griffin v. United States*, this Court declined to extend its holding in *Stromberg* and *Yates* to a general verdict of guilt in a conspiracy charging multiple objects where the evidence was insufficient to support guilt as to one of the objects. The Court noted that the rule in *Stromberg* and *Yates* was contrary to the common law, under which "a general jury verdict was valid so long as it was legally supportable on one of the submitted grounds even though that gave no assurance that a valid ground, rather than an invalid one, was actually the basis for the jury's action." The Court also criticized *Yates* as an "unexplained extension" of *Stromberg* that "explicitly invoked neither the Due Process Clause (which is an unlikely basis) nor our supervisory powers over the procedures employed in a federal prosecution." The *Stromberg* case, the Court explained, does "not necessarily stand for anything more than the principle that, where a provision of the Constitution forbids conviction on a particular ground, the constitutional guarantee is violated by a general verdict that may have rested on that ground." After noting that "continued adherence to the holding in *Yates* was not at issue in *Griffin*," the Court refused the "unprecedented and extreme" request to extend *Yates* to situations in which the general verdict may have rested on a ground that is factually inadequate (because it is not supported by sufficient evidence) rather than legally inadequate (because, as in *Stromberg* and *Yates*, there is some other legal impediment to prosecution). The Court explained that where one possible basis for a jury verdict is factually unsupported, the jury is presumed to have rejected that basis.

Unlike in *Griffin*, "the continued adherence to the holding[s] in *Yates*" and *Stromberg* is potentially at issue in this case. The instructional error here—though also falling comfortably within the realm of *Rose/Neder*—can easily be described as a *Stromberg/Yates* error. The jury was presented with two broad theories under which respondent could be convicted for felony murder: either that he personally killed the victim during commission of the robbery, or that he aided and abetted the commission of the robbery during which the victim was killed. The various instructions suggested that the jury could find respondent guilty under the aiding-and-abetting theory based on either contemporaneous involvement in the robbery or post-killing involvement in the robbery. Because the post-killing involvement is inadequate under California law to support a conviction for felony murder, the case was submitted on two valid theories (respondent personally killed the victim or aided and abetted the robbery contemporaneously) and one invalid theory (respondent aided and abetted the robbery only after the killing occurred).

It is true that *Stromberg* and *Yates* could be narrowly distinguished. The legally invalid ground here (non-existent crime) differs from the legally invalid ground in Stromberg (First Amendment-barred crime) and in *Yates* (time-barred crime). Moreover, unlike with the defective aiding-and-abetting instruction, there was no plausible way to "correct" the defective alternative ground—and thereby apply harmless-error review to that ground in either *Stromberg* or *Yates*.

On the other hand, just as in *Stromberg* and *Yates*, the jury's verdict here could have rested on a legally invalid ground. And while *Yates* involved non-constitutional error, this case (like *Stromberg*) involves constitutional error. Just as a conviction based on protected speech would violate the First Amendment, conviction for a non-existent crime would violate the Due Process Clause. Moreover, if the legally flawed theory in this case were characterized as felony-murder based on post-killing involvement in the robbery, there is no clear way to "correct" the defective ground. As such, this case implicates the *Stromberg* rule, which, as discussed next, is wrong on a more fundamental level.

This Court's post-*Stromberg*/*Yates* constitutional harmless-error jurisprudence has sharply eroded the precedential value of that line of cases. In *Chapman v. California*, this Court rejected the argument that errors of constitutional dimension necessarily require reversal of criminal convictions. Since *Chapman*, this Court has "repeatedly reaffirmed the principle that an otherwise valid conviction should not be set aside if the reviewing court may confidently say, on the whole record, that the constitutional error was harmless beyond a reasonable doubt." There is a strong presumption that constitutional errors at trial are subject to harmless-error inquiry, such that "most constitutional errors can be harmless."

By contrast, only in a "very limited class of cases" will an error be deemed "'structural,' and thus subject to automatic reversal." Unlike trial errors, structural errors "infect the entire trial process," and "necessarily render a trial fundamentally unfair." Accordingly, only a select few errors are structural.

Because *Stromberg* and *Yates* preceded *Chapman* that line of cases simply does not address the critical question here of whether harmless-error review applies. As Justice Stewart noted in his opinion concurring in the result in *Chapman*, before that case, this Court had "steadfastly rejected any notion that constitutional violations might be disregarded on the ground that they were 'harmless.'" For example, neither the State in *Stromberg* nor the government in *Yates* argued that a defendant's conviction may stand, even though the jury's verdict might have rested on a legally flawed ground, if it is clear beyond a reasonable doubt that a rational jury would have found the defendant guilty absent the error.

Accordingly, the *Stromberg/Yates* line of cases, as the Court observed in *Griffin* should be read only as recognizing an exception to the common-law rule, i.e., that "a general jury verdict was valid so long as it was legally supportable on one of the submitted grounds even though that gave no assurance that a valid ground, rather than an invalid one, was actually the basis for the jury's action." In other words, that line of cases establishes the limited proposition that when a general verdict potentially rests on an invalid legal theory, reviewing courts may not presume that the jury relied on a valid alternative theory. *Stromberg* and its successors do not, however, resolve whether such an instructional error may be subject to harmless-error review.[2]

Example 3

The tension between self-representation and the assistance of counsel is the subject of this example. Notice how effectively the proponent discusses the applicable case law with just the right emphasis.

In *Faretta v. California*, this Court held that the Sixth Amendment guarantees a criminal defendant the right to refuse the assistance of counsel and represent himself at trial. Relying on history, structural inference, and principles of individual autonomy, the Court concluded that a defendant could choose to manage his own defense as long as he was first "made aware of the dangers and disadvantages of self-representation," and "'knowingly and intelligently' chose to forgo counsel."

Faretta and subsequent cases made clear, however, that "the right to self-representation is not absolute." In particular, the right established in *Faretta* "is not a license to abuse the dignity of the courtroom" or "a license not to comply with relevant rules of procedural and substantive law." Accordingly, "the trial judge may terminate self-representation by a defendant who deliberately engages in serious and obstructionist misconduct."

Similarly, *Faretta* noted that the trial court may appoint standby counsel for the defendant, "even over objection." The Court subsequently held that a court may impose standby counsel on an unwilling defendant. Requiring standby counsel does not violate the Constitution if it remains within "reasonable limits," the Court held, even if it "somewhat undermines the *pro se* defendant's appearance of control over his own defense."

The Court did not purport in *Faretta* to determine categorically which other interests could legitimately justify limitations on self-representation. Significantly, *Faretta* himself was "literate, competent and understanding." Thus, the Court's decision did not address whether the right of self-representation may be limited if the defendant, although competent to stand trial, suffers from a mental illness that significantly impairs the cognitive ability necessary to act as his or her own attorney and threatens to make a mockery of the trial proceedings.

Rather, this Court simply cautioned that a lay defendant may not be barred from representing himself merely because he lacks the "technical legal knowledge" of a trained attorney. The trial court had precluded *Faretta* from proceeding *pro se* after questioning him on points of law, such as the exceptions to the hearsay rule and the grounds for objecting to potential jurors. This Court held that such a legal examination is improper. The Court recognized that "in most criminal prosecutions defendants could better defend with counsel's guidance than by their own unskilled efforts," although it believed that "in some rare instances, the defendant might in fact present his case more effectively by conducting his own defense." Nonetheless, the Court concluded that because "the right to defend is personal" and because "the defendant will bear the personal consequences of a conviction," the likelihood of failure is not a sufficient reason to bar the defendant from choosing to proceed without counsel.

Thus, *Faretta* stated, and the cases applying it confirm, that a valid state interest can overcome the right to self-representation in particular cases. For example, "most courts" have concluded that the governmental interest in the orderly conduct of criminal proceedings justifies denying requests to proceed *pro se* on the eve of trial.

Whether the right to proceed *pro se* comes from the Sixth Amendment, or the Due Process Clause, there is nothing incongruous about weighing this particular trial right against legitimate, countervailing governmental interests. This Court has regularly concluded that a defendant's procedural rights may yield in limited circumstances where the contrary interest is sufficiently strong.[3]

Example 4

The Fourth Amendment's prohibition against unreasonable searches and seizures has been the topic of much litigation, and one such case is exceptionally well analyzed in the following excerpt.

The Fourth Amendment guarantees "the right of the people to be secure in their persons against unreasonable searches and seizures." The "state-compelled collection and testing of urine" is a "search" within the Fourth Amendment. The general rule is that to be reasonable, and thus constitutional, a search must be based on individualized suspicion of wrongdoing. This Court has recognized an exception to that rule, however, for searches based on "special needs, beyond the normal need for law enforcement, mak[ing] the warrant and probable-cause requirement impracticable."

In *Vernonia*, this Court reaffirmed that "such 'special needs' exist in the public school context," and may justify suspicionless drug testing of students. That case involved a Fourth Amendment challenge to an Oregon school district's policy, which authorized random urinalysis tests of student athletes. In deciding whether that policy was constitutional, the Court considered (1) the nature of the privacy interests at issue; (2) the character of the intrusion involved; and (3) the nature and immediacy of the government concern at issue, and the efficacy of the chosen means for meeting it. Balancing those factors, the Court held that the policy was "reasonable and hence constitutional." As explained below, a proper balancing of the same considerations leads to the identical conclusion with respect to the substantially similar policy at issue in this case.

In *Vernonia*, this Court emphasized that "[t]he most significant element" in upholding the challenged drug-testing policy was the nature of the privacy interests at issue. In particular, the Court stressed "that the Policy was undertaken in furtherance of the government's responsibilities, under a public school system, as guardian and tutor of children entrusted to its care." The same goes for the student drug-testing policy in this case and, just as in *Vernonia*, that fact weighs heavily in favor of finding that the school district's policy is constitutional.

Under the Fourth Amendment, an examination of the legitimacy of the privacy interests at stake must begin with the setting in which the challenged intrusion arises. "What expectations are legitimate varies with context, depending, for example, upon whether the individual asserting the privacy interest is at home, at work, in a car, or in a public park." The school setting of this case necessarily affects the legitimate expectations of privacy.

As the Court observed in *Vernonia*: "Central, in our view, to the present case is the fact that the subjects of the challenged drug- testing policy are (1) children, who (2) have been committed to the temporary custody of the State as schoolmaster." "A public school system" acts "as guardian and tutor of children entrusted to its care." As a common-sense matter, it must do so. As this Court has recognized, a "proper educational environment requires close supervision of schoolchildren, as well as the enforcement of rules against conduct that would be perfectly permissible if undertaken by an adult." Public schools do not stand in the same shoes as the parents of the children who fill their classrooms. But when children enter the schoolhouse gates, they submit themselves to the temporary custody and control of their teachers and other school administrators, and must abide by their rules.

In short, the public school context greatly diminishes the legitimate expectations of privacy of students from intrusions implicating the Fourth Amendment. And from that standpoint, the students covered by the drug-testing policy here have the same diminished expectations as the students covered by the policy in *Vernonia*.

In *Vernonia*, the Court observed that the already-diminished privacy expectations of school children "are even less with regard to student athletes." For example, students who participate in high school athletics typically use communal facilities such as locker rooms, and may be required to change and shower in each other's presence. In addition, "by choosing to 'go out for the team,' students voluntarily subject themselves to a degree of regulation even higher than that imposed on students generally."

Here too, the students covered by the school district's policy, who participate in non-athletic interscholastic competitions, occupy a comparable position to the student athletes in *Vernonia*.

As both courts recognized below, "like athletes, participants in other extracurricular activities have a somewhat lesser privacy expectation than other students." For example, students who sign-up for competitive activities covered by the school district's policy must comply with rules and regulations not applicable to other students. The Oklahoma Secondary School Activities Association (OSSAA) subjects them to added academic requirements concerning such matters as class attendance and credits and, in particular, obligates them to act in a manner that does not discredit their schools. Various extracurricular squads also subject members to their own sets of rules. Further, as is true with respect to team sports, the activities of non-athletic extracurricular groups are monitored by faculty sponsors, imposing an added degree of supervision not experienced by other students.

In addition, Tecumseh High students who participate in non-athletic interscholastic activities take overnight trips for competitions or related events. The accommodations during such overnight trips often require students of the same sex to undress and share restroom and bathing facilities. To be sure, non-athletic activities typically do not entail the degree of "communal undress" to which students must submit as part of some team sports, but they nonetheless often require students to compromise their privacy interests in a comparable fashion and to a degree that students who do not participate in such activities may avoid.

Moreover, just like the student athletes in *Vernonia*, Tecumseh students who participate in non-athletic activities covered by the policy voluntarily assume those added requirements and intrusions when they sign-up or try-out for the activity. And, of course, they may avoid those requirements-including drug testing-by choosing not to participate. As the school district's policy underscores, "[p]articipation in school-sponsored extra-curricular activities at the Tecumseh Public School District is a privilege." Students who choose to avail themselves of that privilege "have reason to expect intrusions upon normal rights and privileges, including privacy." That expectation alone seriously undercuts their Fourth Amendment claim demanding to be excused from the school district's random drug-testing policy.[4]

Notes

References to citations, transcripts, footnotes, and some authorities omitted for sake of clarity.

1. *Locke v. Karass*, No. 07-610.
2. *Chrones v. Pulido*, No. 07-544.
3. *State of Indiana v. Edwards*, No. 7-208.
4. *Board of Education v. Earls*, No. 01-332.

Legal Argument at Its Best

The experienced brief writer keeps a number of points in mind:

- *Contrary authorities.* You have an ethical duty to analyze contrary authorities. Additionally, if you fail to do so, you can be assured that your opponent will enthusiastically discuss all of the cases that undermine your contention. And if opposing counsel overlooks those authorities, one of the court's law clerks will likely find them. If the court discovers these opinions after argument, you have lost your opportunity to show how they are distinguishable.

- *String citations.* In order to demonstrate the continuing vitality of the principle you are espousing, you should cite the earliest case in point and the most recent one. And, of course, you must be sure that you have carefully read the cases you cite. Additionally, you should always refer the court to the exact page where your contention is discussed. Making the court read the entire case to find your point is poor form indeed.

- *Facts of relevant cases.* By including facts when citing relevant cases, you can state with confidence that the law expressed in the cited case should be applied because the facts are analogous. Too often, counsel find themselves in the embarrassing position of being unable to answer the court's questions about such facts. A citation without some discussion of the treatment of the issue is not helpful to the court.

12

■■▣▦

Your Opponent's Argument: The Key to Effective Challenges

Your challenge as an attorney is to separate the relevant from the not-so-relevant. You must of course address every important issue, but you should avoid wasting time on matters that will not affect how the controversy is resolved.

Generally speaking, your argument will be better received if you frame it first before attacking opposing counsel's positions. The court's impression should be that you deserve to *win*, rather than your adversary deserves to lose. A defensive tone can quickly undermine an otherwise commendable argument.

Adverse authority will not go away simply because you ignore it, and you would also forego the opportunity to distinguish it. If the adverse authority is precedent, the differences on which you rely should be significant enough to impress a skeptical judge— technical discrepancies and minor factual variations usually are *not* persuasive. You might also try to reconcile the precedent with your case, showing that the underlying policy is actually *furthered* by the result you seek.

A frontal attack—on grounds that the precedent is poorly reasoned or that changes in public policy have made it irrelevant—is almost always a losing battle. It should only be attempted as a last resort. Judges invariably prefer distinguishing and reconciling precedent to that of flatly overruling it.

How vigorously should you attack adverse argument or authority? Give as much attention as necessary to convince the judge not to rule against you. Little treatment is necessary if the point is minor and the argument or authority is easily rebutted. You will need to expound if the point is more significant, or if your counter analysis is more complex. Even if your adversary has not mentioned an argument, you should discuss it if it has a reasonable chance of occurring to the court and persuading them.

An elaborate analysis of your opponent's points may show overconcern about their importance. You should dispense of those points as quickly and forcefully as you can—and then move on.

The four examples demonstrating effective challenges to an opponent's argument that are set forth here deal with a number of interesting issues: (1) the right of a city to erect monuments for commemorative purposes, (2) procedural protections for the Guantanamo Bay detainees, (3) pregnancy leave taken before enactment of the Pregnancy Discrimination Act, and (4) possible Second Amendment violations by posting military recruiting lists on college campuses pursuant to the Solomon Amendment. They all take their opponents' arguments to task in a worthy manner.

Example 1

The argument set forth here challenges the assertion that a city does not have a right to erect monuments for commemorative purposes. Note the precision with which the proponent eviscerates his opponent's case.

The display of monuments and commemorative objects is a common method of telling the story of the history or heritage of a place. Indeed, even the simple act of consecrating a place may speak for the ages. To varying degrees, the display (and assembly) of monuments may likewise convey an important government message. The monuments displayed in Pioneer Park represent the City's own judgment as to what displays appropriately reflect its history and heritage. The selection and permanent installation of objects for commemorative purposes in Pioneer Park constitutes core government speech.

The City's ownership of all or nearly all of the items currently on permanent display in Pioneer Park underscores that the display constitutes government speech. As the owner of the objects, the City would be entitled to arrange, modify, or remove any of them without regard to the wishes of any previous owners. That continuing exercise of control over the completed display and its constituent parts is entirely incompatible with the notion that the City's purpose in permitting the permanent installation of objects in Pioneer Park was "to encourage a diversity of views from private speakers."

In a previous decision on which the panel relied, the Tenth Circuit reasoned that a Ten Commandments monument that had been placed on the lawn outside a different city's municipal building remained private speech in part because the city was "unable to point to any pre-litigation evidence of [its] explicit adoption of the speech of the Ten Commandments Monument. Chief Judge Tacha made a similar argument in her opinion responding to the dissents from the denial of rehearing *en banc*, asserting that the Ten Commandments monument in Pioneer Park remains private speech because there is no evidence that the City ever specifically adopted "the message" of the speech contained upon it.

That reasoning is seriously flawed. There is no requirement that a person or entity that generates a new work of speech from parts originally created by others expressly endorse or expressly disavow each of the more particularized messages that may be conveyed by the speech's constituent parts. The fact that a public university speaks "[w]hen [it] determines the content of the education it provides," does not require that it specifically endorse or condemn every statement made by a member of its faculty or an invited guest. A publication's editors will often publish the works of columnists with whom they disagree as well as those with whom they agree. The curators of a museum may decide to acquire and display a particular piece because it was created by a particular artist or reflects a particular style or period, notwithstanding the fact that they may find its message obscure or even offensive, just as the creator of an exhibit about the Holocaust may choose to include a piece of Nazi propaganda without endorsing its abhorrent views. But in all of those cases—and in this one—the act of assembling and then displaying or publishing the larger work remains a distinct act of speech by the compiler.

The startling doctrinal and practical consequences of the court of appeals' view that the monuments and other objects on permanent display in Pioneer Park remain solely the speech of their donors underscores how far the court departed from existing jurisprudence. As explained in more detail below, such a conclusion would, at minimum, require the City to refrain from discriminating based on viewpoint in deciding what objects to display. Although that standard is satisfied on the record here, its adoption would still be highly problematic for at least two reasons.

First, even a simple prohibition on viewpoint discrimination could have untenable practical consequences. The installation of a privately donated monument honoring those who died in a particular armed conflict waged on behalf of our Nation—of which there are thousands on federal parklands alone—could require the government to permit the installation of a monument suggesting that the cause in which those particular individuals died was unjust. The decision to accept and display a donated statue honoring a general who fought for the Union in the Civil War—of which there are at least three in Washington, D.C., alone—could require the government likewise to accept and display a privately funded statue honoring a general who fought for the Confederacy.

Second, even if most claims alleging viewpoint discrimination would ultimately fail, the threat of disruptive and time- consuming litigation would predictably deter many government entities from accepting and displaying privately donated objects in the first place. As in *Forbes*, "[t]hese concerns are more than speculative." The U.S. Army, for example, has already delayed deciding whether to accept a privately designed and funded monument honoring 41 American service members killed in a 1943 crash of a B-17 Flying Fortress for permanent display pending the resolution of this litigation. As this Court has recognized, First Amendment values are not well-served by doctrines that "result in less speech, not more."

Nor will applying the government speech doctrine in this context have any bearing on rules applicable in a true First Amendment forum. Traditional public forum status, and the rules that apply in one, are determined by reference to history and tradition. In *Forbes*, this Court recognized candidate debates as a "narrow exception" to its conclusion that "public broadcasting as a general matter does not lend itself to scrutiny under the forum doctrine," based on a functional assessment of the "design" and "very purpose" of such events. And in *Rosenberger*, the Court held that a public university had created a limited public forum with respect to the allocation of certain university funds because the university had "declared that the student groups eligible for its support were not the University's agents, were not subject to its control, and were not its responsibility." There is nothing remotely comparable in the government's selection of monuments for permanent display on the government's own property.

For the reasons stated above, the Court should hold that the City engaged in government speech in accepting and displaying on a permanent basis certain privately donated monuments and other objects in Pioneer Park (and in deciding which objects not to accept or display). Accordingly, because the government "is entitled to say what it wishes," in order "to ensure that its message is neither garbled nor distorted," and, like any other speaker, to decide "what not to say."[1]

Example 2

This excerpt is effective in its refutation of the contention that Guantanamo Bay detainees are entitled to greater procedural protections than the rest of the population. Observe the exemplary pace and organization of the argument.

The court of appeals found that Guantanamo Bay detainees are entitled to procedural protections greater than those afforded by the Constitution to U.S. citizens both in the criminal context and in the enemy-combatant context. Respondents have not disputed—and cannot dispute—that the court of appeals' conception of the record goes well beyond any known administrative or judicial context. Respondents attempt to justify that anomalous result by explaining that they deserve greater procedural protections than citizens because they believe Detainee Treatment Act (DTA) procedures are inadequate and they suspect Congress felt the same way. But respondents' repeated attacks on the DTA review process merely highlight the interconnection of this case with the *Boumediene* and *Al Odah* cases, and Congress surely did not intend that the review of Combatant Status Review Tribunal (CSRT) determinations would exceed any known judicial or administrative parallel.

Respondents devote much of their brief to protestations of innocence and distortion of the facts regarding the CSRT process provided. Limitations on the length of briefs prevent a full response to those misstatements. But two matters deserve mention here.

First, respondents' claims that they and the other detainees are innocent civilians are without basis. For example, in the recent merits briefing in *Parhat*, the government has explained that Parhat underwent military training at an al Qaeda- and Taliban-sponsored military training camp before he was captured by coalition forces. The classified brief (which will be made available to this Court upon request) details facts about the camp and persons trained there and about the organization of which Parhat was a member. The unclassified CSRT record likewise shows that Bismullah was a member of the Taliban; received AK-47s, vehicles, and communications devices from that group; was affiliated with Fidayan Islam, a terrorist group that targeted U.S. and coalition forces; and was directed by that group to identify and kill those Afghanis who supported U.S. forces.

Second, respondents are mistaken in contending that the government did not comply with CSRT procedures. Contrary to respondents' suggestion, recorders did not routinely with-hold relevant exculpatory information from the CSRTs. Admiral McGarrah unequivocally stated just the opposite, explaining that all identified exculpatory information was always presented to the CSRTs, unless that material was merely duplicative or was not relevant to an asserted basis of a detainee's enemy combat-ant status. Respondents are also mistaken in contending that identification and review of the Government Information was delegated to private contractors whose access to classified infor-mation was limited to portions of two databases. As the cited sources make clear, that role was performed by Defense Depart-ment personnel, including reservists. Only two contract analysts were used for a short period to perform limited tasks in assisting the recorder team. In addition, Admiral McGarrah explained that although Defense Department personnel initially turned to the two databases that were expected to contain the vast majority of rel-evant information, searches were not limited to the information contained in those databases.

In all events, these matters can be addressed more fully in the D.C. Circuit even if the Court holds this petition. The bottom line remains that the orderly manner of proceeding is for the Court to hold or grant and expedite this petition.[2]

Example 3

The following excerpt refutes the assertion that pregnancy leave taken before enactment of the Pregnancy Discrimina-tion Act must be treated like a temporary disability. Note the skillful use of case law in rebutting those contentions.

The court of appeals held that petitioner violated Title VII of the Civil Rights Act by failing to credit pregnancy leave before enactment of the Pregnancy Discrimination Act (PDA) when it cal-culated benefits owed to respondents. That holding is incorrect because it gives an unintended retroactive effect to the PDA. In addition, even assuming that petitioner violated Title VII by fail-ing to give pre-PDA pregnancy leave the same treatment as leave taken for temporary disabilities, such a violation occurred, at the latest, on the effective date of the PDA, and respondents' claims are accordingly time-barred.

The *en banc* Ninth Circuit held that, in calculating respondents' retirement benefits between 1994 and 2000, petitioner committed an unlawful employment practice under Title VII because the seniority system used to calculate those benefits does not treat pre-PDA pregnancy leave the same way as leave for temporary disabilities. The court of appeals reasoned that petitioner's seniority system was facially "discriminatory," emphasizing that petitioner, in making such post-PDA benefit decisions, did not adjust respondents' service date by treating pre-PDA pregnancy leave the same as post-PDA pregnancy leave. In a similar vein, respondents argue that calculating pension benefits in a manner that does not credit pre-PDA leave "perpetuates a facially discriminatory system which originated prior to the passage of the [PDA]."

That analysis is seriously flawed. When petitioner adopted its pre-PDA leave policies and applied those policies to respondents' pregnancy leaves, the law did not dictate that pregnancy leave be treated the same as leave for other temporary disabilities. As discussed, *Gilbert* explicitly held that an employer's disability plan did not violate Title VII's prohibition against sex discrimination because it denied benefits for disabilities arising from pregnancy. The PDA overruled the result reached in *Gilbert*, but it did not do so retroactively. Indeed, the PDA not only did not apply retroactively, but it did not even apply prospectively to benefits programs "until 180 days after the enactment of the Act." When the PDA became effective for existing programs, it required employers going forward to treat pregnancy leaves on the same terms as other temporary disabilities.

The PDA did not create an obligation to grant employees credit for pre-PDA leave that Title VII did not require employers to grant before the passage of the PDA. That result would have required employers to adjust the service dates of female employees reaching back decades. Such an affirmative undertaking is far different from and far more burdensome than the PDA's basic injunction to refrain from discrimination on the basis of pregnancy. Congress could not have envisioned such a massive undertaking without acknowledgment. This Court's decision in *Landgraf* forbids such a retroactive effect without a clear textual directive. Yet the Ninth Circuit's decision in this case gives the PDA precisely the kind of retroactive effect for bidden by Landgraf by subjecting employers to liability for not crediting leave that was taken before the PDA.

The Ninth Circuit erred in believing that it could circumvent that result by simply holding that petitioner was required to credit pre-PDA pregnancy leaves whenever an employee benefit was calculated post-PDA on the basis of a NCS date predicated in part on pre-PDA leave policies. To be sure, the calculation of respondents' benefits had the effect of perpetuating petitioner's pre-PDA pregnancy-leave policies, and those policies were "discriminatory" insofar as they distinguished between leave taken for pregnancies and for other temporary disabilities though before the PDA, that "discrimination" was not forbidden. That kind of perpetuation-of-past discrimination claim (even for discrimination that was unlawful when it occurred), however, is directly foreclosed by the *Evans-Ricks-Lorance-Ledbetter* line of precedents.

Those decisions—and in particular, *Evans*—dispose of respondents' Title VII claim. As noted, this case follows *a fortiori* from those decisions because the predicate act of discrimination here was not forbidden when it occurred. And even to the extent respondents believe (contrary to *Gilbert*) that petitioner violated Title VII when it denied full service credit for pre-PDA pregnancy leaves, that purported violation occurred when the credit was denied (or, if the violation is the failure to adjust service dates in light of the PDA, then upon passage of the PDA). Respondents could have, but did not, challenge the denial of such leave when it occurred decades ago. Thus, under *Evans*, petitioner "was entitled to treat that past act as lawful after respondent[s] failed to file a charge of discrimination" within the 300-day charging period.

Respondents attempt to distinguish *Evans* on the grounds that the seniority system in this case is "facially discriminatory," and that an employer who adopts a facially discriminatory seniority or pay policy can be regarded as engaging in intentional discrimination each time the policy is applied. But petitioner's seniority system is logically indistinguishable from the one in *Evans*, which this Court concluded was neutral and non-discriminatory because it did not "treat former employees who were discharged for a discriminatory reason any differently from former employees who resigned or were discharged for a nondiscriminatory reason." And in *Ledbetter* this Court reaffirmed *Evans* and explained that the fact that past discrimination "adversely affects the calculation of a neutral factor (like seniority) that is used in calculating benefits" {does not render the benefits system discriminatory on its face, or mean that "each new benefits decision constitutes a new violation."

Petitioner's seniority system is neutral and nondiscriminatory because the NCS date does not treat employees who used personal leave and were denied credit for a "discriminatory" reason any differently from employees who used personal leave and were denied credit for other reasons. The only way in which petitioner's seniority system could be characterized as discriminatory is that the system "gives present effect to a past act of discrimination" insofar as it does not make an affirmative adjustment for pregnancy leaves taken before the PDA. But the same was true in *Evans*: the plaintiff there was forced to resign under the employer's discriminatory no-marriage policy and the employer's seniority system gave present effect to that discrimination by not "crediting her with seniority for [her original hire period]."

The only relevant difference between this case and *Evans* is that, here, the past "discrimination" (i.e., not allowing full credit for pregnancy leave before the PDA) was not unlawful when it occurred, whereas the past discrimination in *Evans* (i.e., forcing female employees who married to resign) was unlawful when it occurred. *A fortiori*, petitioner's lawful pre-PDA discriminatory intent cannot be "shifted to a later act that was not performed with bias or discriminatory motive."

Respondents' reliance on *Bazemore v. Friday* is inapposite. In that case, the Court held that the employer violated Title VII by continuing—after Title VII was enacted—to pay black employees less than white employees even though the pay disparities resulted from a pay structure that pre-dated Title VII. The Court explained that "[a] pattern or practice that would have constituted a violation of Title VII, but for the fact that the statute had not yet become effective, became a violation upon Title VII's effective date, and to the extent an employer continued to engage in that act or practice, it is liable under that statute." As the Court emphasized in *Ledbetter*, "the focus in *Bazemore* was on a current violation [i.e., the continuation of a discriminatory pay structure], not the carrying forward of a past act of discrimination."

This case is the antithesis of *Bazemore*. This case does not involve the "mere continuation" of discriminatory practices after the PDA was enacted. To the contrary, as of the effective date of the PDA, petitioner changed its policy to eliminate its prior pregnancy leave policy and provide service credit for all prospective pregnancy leaves on the same basis as leave taken for other temporary disabilities. Unlike the plaintiffs in *Bazemore*, respondents here are seeking to impose liability retroactively on the employer for its policies before the pertinent statute was passed, and not for a present violation stemming from a continuation of such policies.

Nor can respondents escape the clear import of this Court's precedents simply by saying that they are challenging the denial of pension benefits as those benefits become due (because those benefits are calculated without granting credit for pre- PDA pregnancy leave), rather than the denial of pre-PDA leave. This Court repeatedly has rejected attempts to shift an earlier discriminatory intent onto a later non-discriminatory act that merely perpetuates and gives present effect to the earlier intent. Moreover, *Lorance* makes clear that the adoption of a discriminatory policy for accruing seniority constitutes a "concrete harm" even though at the time of adoption the effects of the policy are "by their nature speculative."[3]

Example 4

The proposition in this case—that the Solomon Amendment's obligation to post military recruiting literature on college campuses violates the Second Amendment—is countered here in a memorable argument that is notable for its precision.

Respondents argue that the Solomon Amendment, which provides for the Secretary of Defense to deny federal funding to institutions of higher learning if they prohibit military recruitment on campus, violates the First Amendment because it compels educational institutions to speak. In particular, respondents assert that the Solomon Amendment compels educational institutions to put the military's recruitment literature in student mailboxes, post the military's job announcements on bulletin boards, email students about the military's arrival on campus, arrange appointments for students, supply meeting rooms, and reserve spots at job fairs. Respondents argue that the Solomon Amendment violates their rights to be free from compelled speech, to protest government policy, and to associate for expressive purposes.

Those arguments are without merit. More fundamentally, respondents' arguments lose sight of the fact that the Solomon Amendment is not a free-standing requirement, but rather a common-sense condition on funds upon which any donor would insist. The United States makes available substantial federal funding that assists in the education of students, and in return seeks only the same opportunity to recruit those students that is extended to other employers.

Any speech under the Solomon Amendment is doubly uncompelled. Institutions can avoid the equal access requirement entirely by declining federal funds. The Solomon Amendment, moreover, does not require institutions to provide military recruiters with any particular type of access. Institutions covered by the Solomon Amendment are free to define the services they provide to recruiters in any way they choose. The Amendment merely requires that they provide military recruiters the same services that they deem appropriate for other recruiters.

Respondents contend that a requirement of equal access to a recruitment program is analogous to a requirement that a parade organizer include an unwanted message in its parade. As is true of all parades, the parade in *Hurley* was intended to express the collective views of its participants, and the parade organizer accordingly selected for inclusion in the parade messages it deemed worthy of presentation. The public therefore understood the messages to reflect the views of the organizer, and it was impractical for a moving parade to disclaim an unwanted message. In those circumstances, the message of any speaker in the parade became the speech of the parade organizer. That is why the Court invalidated as compelled speech a requirement that the parade organizer include an unwanted message in the parade.

An examination of the same factors leads to the opposite conclusion here. Educational institutions do not create recruitment programs as forums for the expression of their own ideological views; they create such programs to facilitate economic opportunities for their students with outside employers. Educational institutions do not approve the recruitment messages of employers that participate in their recruitment programs; they allow their students to judge the merit of the various employers' recruitment messages. And students and the public at large do not attribute to the educational institutions the recruitment messages of the participating outside employers. Nor is it impractical for educational institutions to disavow the military's recruitment messages to the extent they disagree with them. Educational institutions voice their criticisms of government policies all the time (including the policies of government agencies, like the Justice Department, to which they extend full access), and there is no reason why they cannot also effectively differentiate their own views from those of military recruiters.

Respondents argue that recruitment programs are like parades because institutions exclude some speakers based on conduct to which the institutions object. But that does not make the messages of participating recruiters those of the institution. In *Rosenberger*, the university excluded student organizations from an expressive forum based on discriminatory conduct it found objectionable, but that practice did not transform the views of the participating student organizations into those of the university. So too here, an institution that excludes some recruiters from its recruitment program based on conduct it finds objectionable does not transform the participating recruiters' speech into its own.

The other cases on which respondents rely take them further afield from the context of recruiting by outside employers and do not support their compelled speech claim. In *Miami Herald Publishing Co. v. Tornillo*, the Court invalidated a requirement that a newspaper publish a reply to its attacks on political candidates. The Court reasoned that newspapers make highly selective editorial judgments about what viewpoints most merit the public's consideration, and protection for those highly selective judgments lies at the core of the Free Press Clause. The Court also emphasized that if States could force newspapers to publish views opposing their own, newspapers would be deterred from voicing controversial views. Those considerations have no application here, which is far removed from the core of the Free Press Clause.

Contrary to respondents' contention, the government does not argue that attribution is an essential element of every compelled speech claim, or that the practical ability to disclaim a message always negates a compelled speech claim, or that the creation of a broadly inclusive forum for outside speakers who are not selected based on the merit of their messages is inherently incompatible with a compelled speech claim. Rather, the government's position is that a compelled speech claim depends on all the relevant circumstances, including those three significant factors, and that in this case the relevant circumstances show that there is no compelled speech violation. What is crucial here is that recruiting offices are involved in an inherently commercial activity, that none of the factors that the Court has identified as causing a compelled speech problem is present here, that institutions control the nature of access they extend to outside employers, and that the equal access requirement is not triggered to begin with unless the institution has agreed to accept federal funding.[4]

Notes

References to citations, transcripts, footnotes, and some authorities omitted for sake of clarity.

1. *Pleasant Grove City, Utah v. Summum*, No. 07-665.
2. *Gates v. Bismullah*, No. 07-1054.

3. *AT&T Corp. v. Hulteen*, No. 07-543.

4. *Rumsfeld v. Forum for Academic & Institutional Rights, Inc., et al.*, No. 04-11861.

Do Not Avoid Your Opponent's Arguments

You may think that your opponent's arguments are so weak that they do not deserve comment. The court, however, may find them persuasive after a first reading. If you ignore your opponent's arguments, the court may ultimately be persuaded by them.

13

■▬■▬

Policy Considerations:
They Often Count

Courts are increasingly receptive to public policy arguments—
which means that you must not only demonstrate that your client
deserves to win on a legal basis but that the result makes sense
from a policy standpoint. Judges want reassurance that the rights
of others will be protected.

If a court is forced to choose between competing rules of law,
your task is to persuade the bench that yours is the better outcome as a matter of policy. Even when the body of law is settled
and the issue is how it should be applied, a court is less likely to
decide in your favor if it's unconvinced that the result is a fair and
reasonable one.

These public policy arguments must, of course, be supported
with sufficient judicial or legislative authority. Some policies are
openly delineated in judicial decisions and statutes, but more
often they are implied. Only when overt authority is sparse should
policy arguments play the *predominant* role in your case. The
selection of arguments—policy-based and otherwise—is a strategic choice that you must carefully ponder.

The four examples demonstrating policy considerations
that are set forth here deal with a number of interesting issues:

(1) federal penalties prohibiting the sale of marijuana, (2) restrictions on casino gambling, (3) state legislation that arguably infringes on the exclusive domain of the federal government to conduct foreign affairs, and (4) the government's amnesty for price-fixing conspiracies. The public policies they espouse merited close attention from the courts that considered them.

Example 1

The policy argument presented here makes a strong case that federal penalties prohibiting the sale of marijuana are critical for suppressing its illegal use.

Respondents argue that penalties under California law for commercial or recreational activities involving marijuana would serve to mitigate the adverse consequences of holding that Congress may not apply the Controlled Substances Act (CSA) to respondents' activities. But the fact that California imposes penalties on the sale of marijuana and its cultivation or possession for recreational purposes does nothing to facilitate the effectiveness of the CSA's penalties for "simple possession," in order to eradicate the market in illicit drugs.

Those federal penalties are crucial both in suppressing the demand for marijuana and other Schedule I drugs and in decreasing the supply of drugs that can be sold. Such penalties also make enforcement of the ban on interstate commerce in such substances effective. If, as respondents urge, a possession or distribution charge could be defeated by an unrebutted claim that the marijuana was intended for personal "medical" use in compliance with state law, the government would have to rebut that claim in the context of a fungible commodity that, in light of its illicit nature, would not have any of the markings that lawful drugs are required to bear to indicate their proper manufacture, distribution, or dispensing.

Furthermore, while California law prohibits the sale of marijuana, it does not prohibit the purchase. As a result, a person who possesses marijuana for his own personal medical use would not be subject to prosecution even if he had purchased the marijuana from someone else. For the same reason, primary caregivers such as the Doe respondents presumably would not be subject to prosecution if they purchased marijuana to supply to someone else for personal medical use. And, significantly, a California Court of Appeal has held that caregivers may receive "*bona fide* reimbursement for their actual expense" in "cultivating or acquiring the medicinal marijuana." Thus, it is clear that there is a fundamental mismatch between what state law permits (which includes, for example, possession as a result of a commercial exchange) and conduct that respondents contend lies beyond the bounds of Congress's Commerce Clause authority.

The dramatic effects on marijuana commerce of exempting drug activity authorized by California law well illustrate how such a rule would significantly undermine the enforcement and effectiveness of the CSA. The California chapter of one of respondents' amici curiae "estimates that there are now more than 100,000 legal Prop. 215 patients in California." That is the number under a legal regime in which federal law criminalizes such activity. Were this Court to affirm the decision below, there would be no criminal prohibition against the manufacture, distribution, or possession of marijuana by the thirty-five million residents of California as long as they have a "written or oral recommendation or approval" of a physician that "marijuana provides relief " for "any illness."

Marijuana collectives pose even greater threats to the federal scheme. Marijuana "cultivation collectives or cooperatives" are currently proliferating in California under the apparent assumption that they are legal under state law as long as the marijuana is not sold outright. For example, in *County of Santa Cruz v. Ashcroft*, a district court held that the Ninth Circuit's decision in the instant case barred enforcement of the CSA against a cooperative of 250 members who manufactured and distributed marijuana because the cooperative did not charge its members for the marijuana but simply collected voluntary contributions.

The government's enforcement efforts would also be significantly hampered by the fact that there are no production, quality, or dose standards that could be relied upon to demonstrate that an amount of marijuana exceeds quantities appropriate for asserted medical purposes. For instance, in *Wright*, state court overturned a conviction of a person who possessed in his vehicle over a pound of marijuana packaged in six bags along with a scale. The court reasoned that the jury was entitled to believe the defendant's claim that "he needs relatively large quantities of the drug because he prefers to eat, rather than smoke," marijuana to alleviate physical pain and emotional stress.

Moreover, whatever the outer bounds of lawful possession in the State, California law clearly authorizes patients and primary caregivers to possess in excess of eight ounces of dried marijuana per patient and six mature or twelve immature plants per patient as long as the quantity is permitted by the city or county or the quantity is "consistent with the patient's needs." The relevant policy in the cities of Oakland and Santa Cruz and the counties of Sonoma and Tehama is to allow patients to possess up to three pounds of processed marijuana. Those amounts are astonishingly large, as three pounds of marijuana yields approximately 2,700 joints or cigarettes. The regime contemplated by respondents therefore would render it exceedingly unlikely that the federal government would be able to enforce the CSA as to persons manufacturing, distributing, or possessing even large quantities of marijuana without firm proof of a commercial transaction or purpose, despite Congress's specific finding that controlled substances typically have or will enter the stream of commerce.

It thus is highly implausible that existing state-law prohibitions against commercial or recreational marijuana activities would protect the regulatory scheme as envisioned by Congress. California law rests on fundamentally different assumptions about the risks and benefits of marijuana. Moreover, California law imposes none of the stringent production, order form, prescription, record-keeping, labeling, packaging, and diversion controls that the CSA places on controlled substances that (unlike marijuana) Congress has deemed to have an accepted and legitimate medical use. The regime urged by respondents and embraced by the Ninth Circuit's decision would therefore completely undermine the CSA's comprehensive, uniform, and closed system of regulation that is intended to protect both interstate commerce and the public health and safety, and would have a staggering effect on the interstate marijuana market and congressional control over that market.[1]

Example 2

The following excerpt is the expression of a policy argument that advocates the bolstering of restrictions on casino gambling.

Congress enacted the original federal anti-lottery statutes based on its judgment that lotteries and similar gambling activities impose pervasive and potentially destructive costs on society. In this Court's words, Congress concluded that "the widespread pestilence of lotteries infests the whole community; it enters every dwelling; it reaches every class; it preys upon the hard earnings of the poor; it plunders the ignorant and simple." Similarly, Section 1304 and related federal statutes today reflect Congress's considered and longstanding judgment that gambling contributes to corruption and the growth of organized crime; that it underwrites bribery, narcotics trafficking, and other crimes; that it imposes a regressive tax on the poor, the persons who are least able to bear that burden; and that it offers a false but sometimes irresistible hope of financial advancement.

Section 1304 is designed to reduce those social ills by discouraging public participation in casino gambling and other forms of "lotter[ies], gift enterprise[s], [and] similar schemes." When supporters of the casino gambling industry sought unsuccessfully to amend Section 1304 in 1988 to allow casino gambling advertising, the social costs of gambling, and the role of Section 1304 in limiting those costs, were specifically advanced as grounds for rejecting the proposed change.

Many of the social costs associated with casino gambling involve compulsive gambling, a recognized psychological disorder that is referred to clinically as "pathological gambling." The National Council on Problem Gambling has estimated that at least three million Americans are compulsive gamblers, and other estimates are comparable. Compulsive gambling behavior is primarily associated with forms of gambling that permit "continuous" play, such as slot machines and other forms of casino gambling. Although only a relatively small percentage of gamblers engage in compulsive gambling behavior, it has been estimated that compulsive gamblers account for a disproportionate share of casino revenues.

The incidence of compulsive gambling has grown in step with the nationwide expansion of legalized gambling. In Iowa, for example, the estimated percentage of compulsive gamblers among the adult population grew from 1.7 percent in 1989, before the State legalized riverboat gambling, to 5.4 percent in 1995. And the problem is at least as severe among youth: a review of nine studies of adolescent gambling in North America found a 5.4 percent rate of compulsive gambling.

Estimates of the purely economic costs of compulsive gambling amount to billions of dollars annually. Non-economic costs associated with compulsive gambling are, if anything, even more grave. For each compulsive gambler, an estimated 10 to 17 people are affected by the gambler's problems. For the compulsive gambler himself, the toll includes deteriorating relations with family, depression, and in some cases, suicide; for the compulsive gambler's family, the toll includes emotional turmoil, stress-related diseases, lack of financial support, neglect, abuse, and divorce. The children of compulsive gamblers are particularly vulnerable: they perform worse academically than their peers, are more likely to have alcohol, gambling, or eating disorders, and are more likely to be depressed and attempt suicide.

In addition to providing both a stimulus and an outlet for compulsive gambling, casinos have traditionally been a lure for organized crime and other kinds of criminal activity. As this Court noted, "the vast amount of money that flows daily through a casino operation and the large number of unrecorded transactions make the [casino] industry a particularly attractive and vulnerable target for organized crime." Congress has repeatedly noted the attraction of casino gambling for organized crime and has been presented with evidence documenting that relationship.

Casino gambling is also associated with other criminal activity, such as street crime and white collar crime. In *Posadas,* this Court held that the government interest in minimizing the social ills of gambling, particularly casino gambling, is a substantial one. In *Posadas,* the Puerto Rico legislature legalized casino gambling but prohibited casinos from directing gambling advertisements at residents of Puerto Rico. The Court held squarely that there is a substantial governmental interest in reducing demand for casino gambling:

As described, the costs of casino gambling fall not only on gamblers themselves, but also on their families, their employers, and their communities. As a result of those "negative externalities," the government's interest in discouraging public participation in casino gambling is not a mere exercise in "paternalism." Instead, the government has an interest in protecting society at large from the public harms caused by that private activity.[2]

Example 3

The effect of state legislation that arguably infringes upon the exclusive domain of the federal government to conduct foreign affairs is the subject of this persuasive policy argument.

This Court has recognized that state action may impermissibly infringe upon the national government's exclusive authority to conduct foreign affairs even in the absence of a treaty or an Act of Congress. The Massachusetts Burma Act, even if not preempted by federal law, is nonetheless invalid as inconsistent with the Constitution's assignment of the foreign-affairs power to the national government, not the States.

In *Zschernig,* the Court struck down a state probate law that prevented the distribution of an estate to a foreign heir if the proceeds of the estate were subject to confiscation by his government. The Court explained that such statutes, which required state courts to engage in "minute inquiries concerning the actual administration of foreign law [and] into the credibility of foreign diplomatic statements," had a "great potential for disruption or embarrassment" of the United States in the international arena. The Court concluded that such statutes therefore had "a direct impact upon foreign relations," and not merely "some incidental or indirect effect." Accordingly, even though the state statute involved a subject "traditionally regulated" by the States and was not affirmatively preempted by an Act of Congress, the statute was held to constitute "forbidden state activity."

The Massachusetts Burma Act, even more clearly than the state statute in *Zschernig,* is an impermissible "intrusion by the State into the field of foreign affairs which the Constitution entrusts to the President and the Congress." In its purpose, its operation, and its consequences, the Act has an impact on foreign relations that is "direct," not merely "incidental."

First, the Massachusetts Burma Act, as its sponsors declared, was designed as "foreign policy" legislation to "stop the violation of human rights" in Burma. The State acknowledged earlier in this case that the Act is part of a "growing effort to apply indirect economic pressure against the Burma regime for reform." The Act thus constitutes a deliberate attempt by a State to conduct its own foreign policy.

Second, by its structure and design, the Massachusetts Burma Act operates to apply pressure on the Burmese regime through third parties, i.e., companies, foreign and domestic alike, that seek to do business with the State, whether or not their business in Burma bears any relation to their business with State. Massachusetts does not suggest that the Act in any way advances its interests in procuring quality goods at a low price or in dealing only with responsible contractors. To the contrary, by eliminating qualified low bidders, the Act impairs the State's economic interests in order to advance its foreign-policy interests. Nor does the Act serve simply to disassociate Massachusetts from a direct relationship with the Burmese regime. Thus, the scope of the Act confirms that, as its sponsors stated, the Act is foreign-policy legislation.

Finally, as explained above, the Massachusetts Burma Act has adversely affected the United States' own foreign policy in several respects. Most significantly, the Act has undermined the development of "a comprehensive, multilateral strategy to bring democracy to and improve human rights practices and the quality of life in Burma." As senior U.S. officials have stated, the Massachusetts Burma Act, by antagonizing U.S. allies and trading partners, has diverted attention from Burma itself and complicated the implementation of such a multilateral strategy, which the United States views as the most effective means to seek reform in Burma. In addition, the Act is inconsistent with the choice of Congress and the President to permit some U.S. economic activity in Burma (short of "new investment"). The Act also has the potential to undermine the President's flexibility to adjust the economic sanctions against Burma based on the conduct of the Burmese regime, the actions of the international community, or other national security concerns.

In sum, whatever the outer limits of the foreign affairs doctrine applied in *Zschernig*, those three characteristics of the Massachusetts Burma Act render it plainly invalid. The Act, in its purpose and effect, has implemented a state foreign policy toward Burma, and the Act has interfered with the conduct of the United States' own foreign policy. The Act thus has the sort of "direct" and detrimental, not merely "incidental," impact on the national government's foreign-affairs power that renders state action impermissible under *Zschernig*.[3]

Example 4

The effectiveness of the government's amnesty program to enforce price-fixing conspiracies is the subject of the following policy argument.

The court of appeals' interpretation of the Foreign Trade Antitrust Improvements Act (FTAIA) would substantially interfere with the primary enforcement of the antitrust laws by the U.S. Government. Price-fixing conspiracies, including those operating globally, are inherently difficult to detect and prosecute. Cooperation by one of the conspirators, through provision of documents or testimony, is often vital to law enforcement.

In light of those practical realities, the Antitrust Division of the Department of Justice maintains a robust amnesty program that offers strong incentives to conspirators who voluntarily disclose their criminal conduct and cooperate with prosecutors. Since 1993, the program has offered: (1) automatic (i.e., not discretionary) amnesty to corporations that come forward prior to an investigation and meet the program's requirements; (2) the possibility of amnesty even if cooperation begins after an investigation is underway; and (3) if a corporation qualifies for automatic amnesty, all directors, officers, and employees who come forward and agree to cooperate also receive automatic amnesty. Critically, amnesty is available only to the first conspirator to break ranks with the cartel and come forward. The incentives, transparency, and certainty of treatment established by the program set up a "winner take all" dynamic that sows tension and mistrust among cartel members and encourages defection from the cartel.

The amnesty program has been extremely valuable to enforcement of the antitrust laws. The majority of the Antitrust Division's major international investigations, including the investigation of the vitamin cartel, have been advanced through cooperation of an amnesty applicant. The program has been responsible for cracking more international cartels than all of the Division's search warrants, secret audio or videotapes, and FBI interrogations combined. Since 1997, cooperation from amnesty applications has resulted in scores of criminal convictions and more than $1.5 billion in criminal fines.

The court of appeals' interpretation of Section 6a would undermine the effectiveness of the government's amnesty program. Even those conspirators who come forward and receive amnesty from criminal prosecution still face exposure to private treble damage actions under 15 U.S.C. 15(a). Potential amnesty applicants therefore weigh their civil liability exposure when deciding whether to avail themselves of the government's amnesty program. The court of appeals' interpretation would tilt the scale for conspirators against seeking amnesty by expanding the scope of their potential civil liability. Faced with joint and several liability for co-conspirators' illegal acts all over the world, a conspirator could not readily quantify its potential liability. The prospect of civil liability to all global victims would provide a significant disincentive to seek amnesty from the government.

From a practical standpoint, moreover, the court of appeals' analysis of deterrence is unsound because its focus is on private lawsuits that often follow the exposure of a cartel by the government. Such lawsuits are possible, of course, only if the cartel is discovered in the first place. A private action "supplements government enforcement of the antitrust laws; but it is the Attorney General and the U.S. district attorneys who are primarily charged by Congress with the duty of protecting the public interest under these laws."

In the government's judgment, the amnesty program, by creating a high risk of defection and exposure, deters cartel behavior more effectively than an increase in private litigation after the cartel has been exposed. It follows that deterrence is best maximized, and U.S. consumers are best protected, not by maximizing the potential number of private lawsuits, but by encouraging conspirators to seek amnesty and thus expose cartels in the first place.

The court of appeals' holding would also present a risk of undermining the foreign relations of the United States. Germany, a major trading partner of the United States, expressed the view in its *amicus* brief at the petition stage that, "[b]y applying the United States' antitrust laws in cases where neither the plaintiff nor the alleged harm has direct effects on United States commerce, the court of appeals' decision fails to respect the fundamental right of foreign sovereigns to regulate their own markets and industries." We understand that other countries share that view. A scheme in which U.S. courts would adjudicate treble damages actions arising out of transactions that occur wholly in foreign countries and that have no meaningful connection to the United States would be likely to result in tension with our trading partners and attempts by foreign countries to enact statutory counter-reactions to any judgments entered in such suits. It is for reasons such as these that the Court declined to apply U.S. law to transactions in foreign countries in *Arabian American Oil Co.* and *Foley Brothers*.[4]

Notes

References to citations, transcripts, footnotes, and some authorities omitted for sake of clarity.

1. *Ashcroft v. Raich*, No. 03-1454.
2. *Greater New Orleans Broadcasting Association, Inc. v. United States*, No. 98-387.
3. *Natsios v. National Foreign Trade Council*, No. 99-474.
4. *F. Hoffmann-LaRoche, Ltd., et al. v. Empagran*, No. 03-724.

14

Obsessive Compulsive:
Organization Is Key

A judge will immediately recognize a well-organized argument. Issues in such an argument are logically set forth, and each is neatly resolved before the next one is discussed. The court is given just the right amount of analysis to quickly and confidently come to the advocate's conclusion.

Likewise, legal contentions are discussed in the order of their logical importance, not necessarily in chronological sequence. Paragraphs are effectively used to reflect the structure of the analysis, and the organization is apparent throughout the document. The judge is always aware of how the argument fits together. These organizational structure springs from sound architecture— a wisely chosen building plan that the proponent has carefully considered.

In general, the most effective sequence is to first present the issues on which you are most likely to win. Within those issues, you should present your strongest points first. And within those points you should correspondingly cite your best authority first. The overall goal should be to focus the judge's thoughts on the most appealing theory.

An effective legal argument is not just a collection of stray thoughts, so you cannot afford to let the judge lose sight of how your propositions are related to one another. You must enable the judge to clearly see your train of thought. Soon after you begin to discuss each issue, you must remind the judge exactly what your theory is.

Important points of argument should be placed where they will be noticed—at the beginning of the sentence, paragraph, or passage. If the points are related, they should be presented in logical order, so that the second follows naturally from the first. In the case of complex arguments, you should consider whether certain points should be developed as sub-points under one major point, instead of a series of separate points.

Headings for the points of argument are important because they inform the judge what the legal issues are and how the brief is organized. This allows the judge to follow your train of thought and focus on those portions that appear most critical. The easier you make matters for the judge, the more likely he will concentrate on the substance of your discussion.

The four examples demonstrating well-organized arguments that are set forth next deal with a number of interesting issues: (1) the Federal Election Commission, (2) political activities of unions, (3) racial classifications of students in a public school, and (4) allegations of extortion against governmental employees. All are exceptional models of the kind of well-organized legal argumentation that judges find persuasive.

Example 1

This well-organized example deals with issues surrounding the Federal Election Commission. Note how in this truncated version the argument progresses in a logical and coherent fashion.

I. THIS CASE IS MOOT

A. Appellant's complaint in this case was filed on June 28, 2006, and alleged that appellant had declared his candidacy for the 2006 House election approximately three months earlier . . .

The district court issued its opinion in this case on August 9, 2007 ...

B. The Constitution's case-or-controversy limitation on federal judicial authority, Art. III, § 2, underpins this Court's mootness jurisprudence ...

This Court has recognized an exception to mootness principles for situations that are "capable of repetition, yet evading review" ...

C. Typically mootness problems are alleviated in the election context when the plaintiff alleges that he plans to participate in future campaigns and therefore will be subject to the same challenged laws ...

1. The FEC's finding of probable cause to believe that appellant violated Section 319 during the 2004 campaign, with the consequent prospect that the Commission will pursue an enforcement action pursuant to 2 U.S.C. 437g(a)(6) if appellant declines to enter into the proposed conciliation agreement, provides no sound basis for this Court to decide the instant appeal on the merits ...

In short, the prospect of such an enforcement action cannot provide a sufficient stake to bring this case within the "capable of repetition, yet evading review" exception to mootness principles because the enforcement action has a built-in mechanism to ensure that review is provided, not evaded ...

2. In arguing that the FEC's probable-cause determination gives him a continuing stake in the question whether Section 319 is constitutional, appellant seeks in essence to use the judicial-review provisions of BCRA § 403(a), 116 Stat. 113, as a mechanism for pretermitting a possible Commission enforcement action ...

Appellant's effort to derail the FEC's possible enforcement action is also in tension with established principles governing judicial review of Executive Branch action ...

It is also significant that, while the FEC has found probable cause to believe that appellant violated Section 319 during the 2004 campaign, appellant's brief does not concede that such a violation occurred ...

If appellant had not been a candidate in the 2006 election, but had instead premised his claim of standing on the possibility of an FEC enforcement action concerning his conduct in 2004, the instant suit would have been subject to dismissal *ab initio* under the principles set forth above . . .

II. APPELLANT LACKS STANDING TO CHALLENGE THE INCREASED CONTRIBUTION LIMITS ESTABLISHED BY SECTION 319, AND THOSE LIMITS ARE IN ANY EVENT CONSTITUTIONAL ON THEIR FACE

A. Appellant Cannot Establish Any Actual Or Imminent Injury Resulting From The Increased Contribution Limits

1. In order to satisfy the "irreducible constitutional minimum" of Article III standing, appellant must establish

(1) an injury-in-fact that is "concrete and particularized," not "conjectural" or "hypothetical"; (2) a causal connection between the injury and the challenged con duct of the defendant; and

(3) a likelihood that the injury will be redressed by a favorable decision of the court . . .

During the 2006 election campaign, appellant's opponent received no contributions, and the opponent's political party made no coordinated expenditures, in excess of the generally applicable FECA limits . . . Even if appellant could demonstrate that the "capable of repetition, yet evading review" exception to mootness principles applies to this case, appellant could not pursue his constitutional challenge to the aspects of Section 319 that caused him no injury during the 2006 campaign . . .

2. Appellant contends that "the injuries imposed by Section 319's disclosure regime are sufficient to confer standing on appellant to challenge the statute in its entirety" . . .

3. In a related vein, appellant contends that he has standing to challenge Section 319's expanded contribution limits, notwithstanding his opponent's failure to invoke those limits in the 2006 campaign, because those limits cannot be severed from Section 319's disclosure requirements . . .

Moreover, this Court has not viewed disclosure requirements and substantive financing limits as standing or falling together . . .

B. Section 319's Enhanced Contribution Limits Are Consistent With The First Amendment

Section 319's modified limits on financial support for the opponents of self-financing candidates do not violate the First Amendment and certainly do not do so on their face.

1. Appellant repeatedly describes Section 319 as "regulating," "burdening," or "punishing" a self-financing candidate's campaign-related speech . . .

In short, as the district court explained, Section 319 "does not limit in any way the use of a candidate's personal wealth in his run for office" . . .

2. The principal thrust of appellant's First Amendment argument is that (i) because appellant has a constitutional right to make unlimited expenditures in support of his own campaign, he cannot be penalized for exercising that right; and (ii) because an election can have only one winner, any benefit provided to his opponent should be regarded for constitutional purposes as a penalty imposed on appellant . . . The Court held in *Buckley* that, although the First Amendment precludes Congress from placing binding limits on a candidate's independent campaign expenditures, Congress "may condition acceptance of public funds on an agreement by the candidate to abide by specified expenditure limitations" . . .

This case follows *a fortiori* from *Buckley* because the disadvantage to which self-financing presidential candidates are subjected—i.e., the denial of federal funds that would otherwise be paid to the candidate himself—is much more direct and immediate than the competitive injury that appellant claims he would suffer if an opponent were enabled to raise greater amounts of money . . .

Appellant seeks to distinguish *Buckley* on the ground that, unlike a presidential candidate who receives public funds in exchange for his agreement to comply with statutory spending limits, appellant would have "received no countervailing benefits" if he had decided to forgo self-financing . . .

The fundamental premise of appellant's First Amendment challenge is that, in a zero-sum game like a candidate election, any benefit to one candidate is for constitutional purposes a burden on the other . . .

Appellant contends that, "in the context of the campaign finance system, imposition of the standard contribution limits on one's opponents—limits that are uniformly applied to all other candidates—confers no benefit; it simply preserves the status quo" . . .

3. As the district court recognized, Congress enacted Section 319 to reduce the natural advantage that wealthy individuals possess in campaigns for federal office . . .

The Court in *Buckley* also noted, however, that in light of the Court's invalidation of expenditure limits, the "normal relationship" between a candidate's financial resources and the level of popular support for his candidacy "may not apply where the candidate devotes a large amount of his personal resources to his campaign" . . . Although appellant repeatedly contends that attempting to level electoral opportunities for candidates of different personal wealth is an illegitimate governmental objective, this Court's decisions do not support that assertion . . .

In a related vein, appellant contends that the Court's decisions identify the prevention of actual or apparent corruption as the only government interest that can support campaign-finance regulation . . .

Moreover, in upholding BCRA's disclosure requirements, the Court relied not only on the government's interest in "deterring actual corruption and avoiding any appearance thereof," but also on the separate interests in "providing the electorate with information" and "gathering the data necessary to enforce more substantive electioneering restrictions" . . .

The core rationale for Section 319—i.e., the public interest in diminishing the importance of personal wealth as a criterion for election to federal office (and the related interest in diminishing the perception that wealth has become an essential prerequisite for federal elective office)—was not specifically identified in *Buckley* and is not identical to the interests that public financing of presidential campaigns is intended to serve . . .

Appellant also argues that Section 319 fails to achieve its equalization objective because it ignores (or discounts the significance of) other sources of funding, such as incumbents' "war chests" . . .

4. Appellant contends that, because Section 319 permits opponents of self-financing candidates to accept contributions in
excess of the generally applicable FECA limit, it is inconsistent
with the anti-corruption rationale on which those limits have been
sustained . . .

In setting and later adjusting the FECA limit on individual
contributions, Congress has sought to prevent the actual or
apparent corruption that large contributions might engender,
while ensuring that candidates can obtain the resources needed
to run effective campaigns . . . The modified contribution and
coordinated-expenditure limits contained in Section 319 do not
reflect congressional abandonment of FECA's anti-corruption
purpose. . . .

Specifically, Congress determined that, for elections in which a
self-financing candidate's expenditures threaten to sever the usual
link between a candidate's financial resources and the level of his
actual public support, the fundraising limits applicable to opposing candidates should be recalibrated to account for the fact that
one candidate's spending is enhanced based on factors not tied to
any indication of popular support . . .

Nothing in this Court's decisions suggests that Congress is
foreclosed from recalibrating the statutory limits for particular
elections in which one candidate's large expenditures of personal
wealth implicate a government interest distinct from those that
inform the generally applicable caps . . .

5. Appellant's repeated assertions that Section 319 favors incumbents over challengers is unsupported by the statutory text or by
record evidence . . .

The record evidence concerning Section 319's actual implementation also does not support appellant's characterization of
Section 319 as an incumbent-protective measure . . .

Appellant's reliance on the plurality opinion in *Randall*, is
therefore misplaced . . .

C. Appellant's Equal Protection Challenge To Section 319's
Expanded Contribution Limits Lacks Merit

Appellant contends that "Section 319 violates the equal protection component of the due process clause of the Fifth Amendment

because it subjects opposing candidates in the same election to different fund raising obligations" . . .

The Court in *Buckley* held that "the Constitution does not require Congress to treat all declared candidates the same for public financing purposes" . . .

Appellant further contends that Section 319 violates equal protection principles because (a) the equalization of electoral opportunities for wealthy and non-wealthy candidates is not a legitimate government interest, and (b) the statute treats accumulated personal wealth differently from funds raised from private donors under BCRA's contribution limits . . .

III. SECTION 319's DISCLOSURE REQUIREMENTS ARE CONSTITUTIONAL ON THEIR FACE

Section 319 creates three new reporting requirements for self-financing candidates: a declaration of intent to self-finance, an initial notification that the candidate has spent more than $350,000 of personal funds, and additional notifications within 24 hours of each $10,000 in aggregate expenditures of personal funds . . .

On the merits, however, appellant has identified no colorable basis for holding that the challenged disclosure requirements are unconstitutional on their face. . . .

A. The provisions at issue in *Buckley* required disclosure by candidate committees and other political committees of the contributions of any person who had given in excess of $100 in a calendar year, as well as disclosures by any person making an independent expenditure of over $100 . . .

The disclosure requirements at issue here are significantly less intrusive than the requirements this Court has previously upheld. Disclosure of a self-financing candidate's spending does not reveal the names of supporters and therefore does not implicate the privacy interests of persons other than the candidate himself . . .

B. Since *Buckley*, FECA has subjected all federal candidates to disclosure requirements similar to those imposed by Section 319 . . .

1. Although Section 319's "declaration of intent" requirement has no close analog in pre-BCRA law, that requirement places no significant burden on self-financing candidates . . .

The requirement that a declaration of intent be filed does not violate the First Amendment rights of any candidate . . .

Appellant's constitutional challenge to Section 319's "declaration of intent" requirement is further undermined by the fact that appellant actively publicized the same information that he now characterizes as sensitive strategic data . . .

2. Section 319 further provides that a self-financing candidate must file (a) an initial notification within 24 hours after making or obligating aggregate campaign-related expenditures from personal funds of more than $350,000 and

(b) an additional notification whenever the candidate spends a further increment of more than $10,000 of personal funds on his campaign.

As the district court correctly concluded, Section 319's timing requirements do not impair appellant's rights under the First Amendment, particularly because those requirements "are no more burdensome than other BCRA reporting deadlines that were upheld in *McConnell* " . . .

3. The district court also correctly explained that "any burden that Section 319's reporting provisions may hypothetically impose is not 'unilateral'" because "the opponent of a self-financing candidate also faces additional reporting requirements, which are similar to those of the self-financed candidate" . . .

Moreover, if the opponent of a self-financing candidate accepts increased contributions from individuals under Section 319, these contributions must be reported in the same format as all contributions above $200, in mandatory periodic reports, with an indication that the particular contribution was permitted pursuant to Section 319.17 . . .[1]

Example 2

The political activity of unions is the subject of this well-organized excerpt. Observe how fluidly the argument progresses in this abbreviated version.

This Court long ago established that the First Amendment prohibits unions from using for political purposes fees collected under a state-imposed union-shop or agency-shop arrangement from nonmembers who object to the union's political activities. In many States, that constitutional prohibition is given effect by permitting nonmembers to opt out of any regime in which their dues are used for political purposes . . .

I. WASHINGTON'S AFFIRMATIVE-AUTHORIZATION REQUIREMENT PROMOTES THE LEGITIMATE FIRST AMENDMENT INTERESTS OF NONMEMBERS AND THE INTEGRITY OF THE ELECTION PROCESS

A. Union-shop and agency-shop arrangements directly impact the First Amendment interests of workers who are compelled by state law to pay dues or fees to the union . . .

If the government authorizes a union or agency shop, employees may be required to pay only their fair share of "the work of the union in the realm of collective bar gaining," work from which all employees benefit . . .

B. The federal and state governments have adopted various approaches to balancing their interest in promoting labor peace with their interest in protecting workers who would prefer not to associate with a union . . .

Federal and state governments have also adopted a variety of approaches to union and agency shops in the context of public-sector employment . . .

In the statute at issue here, Washington mitigated the impact of the agency-shop arrangement on nonmembers' freedom of association and speech by requiring unions to obtain nonmembers' affirmative authorization before using their fees for political purposes . . .

Washington thereby struck a reasonable balance between the two competing government interests . . .

C. As the Washington Supreme Court recognized, the affirmative-authorization requirement also "protects the integrity of the election process from the perception that elected officials are improperly influenced by monetary contributions and the perception that individuals have an insignificant role to play" . . .

II. THE AFFIRMATIVE-AUTHORIZATION REQUIREMENT DOES NOT ABRIDGE FREEDOM OF SPEECH OR ASSOCIATION, BUT INSTEAD PROMOTES IT

The Washington law at issue in no way impedes the First Amendment rights of unions. Indeed, unions receive preferential treatment under Washington law compared with other speakers . . .

A. The Washington Law Does Not Infringe Union Members' Freedom Of Speech Or Association

1. The Washington Supreme Court held that Washington's affirmative-authorization requirement must satisfy strict scrutiny because "regulation of First Amendment rights is always subject to exacting judicial scrutiny" . . .

That affirmative-authorization requirement imposes no restriction on the First Amendment rights of unions, and furthers First Amendment values overall . . .

2. Nor is union members' freedom of association meaningfully implicated, much less violated . . .

The opt-in requirement only restricts the unions' unique and state-enabled ability to compel fees from nonmembers and then use them for political purposes . . .

B. The Administrative Cost Of Obtaining Nonmembers' Authorization Is Not An Unconstitutional Burden

The Washington Supreme Court nonetheless held that the affirmative-authorization requirement is subject to strict scrutiny because the administrative costs of securing nonmembers' authorization "significantly burden the union's expressive activity" . . .

1. The negligible administrative costs imposed by the Washington law do not approach a constitutional dimension . . .

The Washington Supreme Court expressed concern that "the lack of access to those funds could impact the timeliness of the union's political speech" while the union sought authorization . . .

That is particularly true because the challenged provision is better understood as a minor reduction in the unique advantages the State gives unions when it comes to nonmembers' political contributions in the agency-shop context, rather than the imposition of a burden, however small . . .

Any remaining doubt is dispelled by this Court's decisions holding that far more serious burdens do not abridge union members' freedom of association . . .

2. Citing this Court's decision in *Dale, supra*, the Washington court concluded that it must "give deference to the union's view of what would impair its political expression" . . .

3. The Washington Supreme Court's conclusion that the affirmative-authorization requirement "violates the First Amendment rights of nonmembers" is inexplicable . .

C. The Constitutional Floor For Protecting Nonmembers' First Amendment Rights Is Not Also A Constitutional Ceiling On Such Protections

The Washington Supreme Court's decision is premised on its erroneous belief that the constitutional floor that this Court has established for protecting the First Amendment rights of nonmembers against being compelled to pay for union political activities with which they disagree also establishes a constitutional ceiling on how far States can go in protecting those rights.

As discussed, unions have no constitutional right to compel membership or to collect agency shop fees from nonmembers . . .

In outlining that constitutionally sufficient remedy, this Court did not so much as suggest that greater protection of nonmembers' First Amendment rights would violate unions' First Amendment rights . . .

The Washington Supreme Court reached a contrary conclusion only by overreading statements in this Court's decisions to the effect that "dissent is not to be presumed it must affirmatively be made known to the union by the dissenting employee" . . .

To the contrary, the State's discretion to permit or prohibit agency shops logically entitles it to condition the statutory benefit to the union of an agency shop on greater protection for nonmembers than the Constitution requires . . .

III. THIS COURT'S CAMPAIGN-FINANCE DECISIONS UNDERSCORE THE CONSTITUTIONALITY OF THE AFFIRMATIVE-AUTHORIZA-TION REQUIREMENT

The Washington Supreme Court's decision invalidating the State's opt-in requirement is also fundamentally out of step with this Court's decisions upholding more burdensome campaign-finance laws against First Amendment challenges ...

A. Under the Federal Election Campaign Act of 1971 (FECA), 2 U.S.C. 431 *et seq.*, it is unlawful for a union or corporation "to make a contribution or expenditure in connection with any election" for federal office ...

Moreover, in addition to that opt-in requirement, it is generally unlawful for a union or its SSF to "solicit contributions ...

Such solicitations are carefully regulated to ensure that contributions are voluntary. Solicitations of a nonmember must be made by mail to the person's residence, and must be designed to prevent the labor organization or corporation conducting the solicitation from determining which recipients do not contribute or contribute $50 or less ...

To protect the voluntariness and anonymity of contributions, the Commission has also forbidden the use of payroll deductions to collect contributions from nonmembers ...

Like the Washington statute, Section 441b therefore permits a union to use a nonmember's wages for political purposes only if the nonmember has affirmatively authorized that use ...

B. Significantly, the constitutionality of Section 441b is well-settled ...

Although NRWC involved a corporation without capital stock rather than a union, this Court drew no distinction between the different types of organizations in upholding Section 441b's solicitation limits in light of the long history of congressional regulation of unions' and corporations' political contributions and expenditures ...

This Court later drew on NRWC in upholding Section 441b's ban on political contributions, noting that the statute protects "individuals who have paid money into a corporation or union for non-political purposes" while also "permitting some participation of unions and corporations in the federal election process by allowing them to establish and pay the administrative expenses" of SSFs . . .

The Washington Supreme Court's decision in this case is irreconcilable with those cases. For example, because this Court recognized in NRWC that the government may limit solicitations of voluntary contributions, it follows that the government may condition the use of involuntary fees on nonmembers' consent . . .

C. Respondent errs in arguing that NRWC is distinguishable because it involved a contribution limit, as opposed to an expenditure limit . . .

The Washington law directly regulates neither contributions nor expenditures, but instead regulates the means by which the union solicits the subset of contributions facilitated by the State's agency-shop laws . . .

In *McConnell*, this Court analyzed as a contribution limit FECA's prohibition against political parties' spending of soft money . . .

D. Respondent also errs in arguing that Washington's affirmative-authorization requirement is unconstitutional because it applies to ballot initiatives as well as candidate elections . . .

More fundamentally, the type of political expenditure (candidate or ballot initiative) has never mattered for purposes of the right not to have coerced fees used for political purposes and is of no moment here . . .

As discussed, Washington's affirmative-authorization requirement does not restrict unions' spending on ballot initiatives or, for that matter, on any particular political topics . . .[2]

Example 3

This excerpt deals with racial classifications of students in a public school. Notice the effective progression of the argument in this condensed rendition.

In *Brown v. Board of Education*, this Court held that state laws that intentionally segregate public school students on the basis of race violate the Equal Protection Clause . . .

This case, like *Parents Involved In Community Schools v. Seattle School District*, involves the use of a racial classification to achieve a predetermined racial balance rather than to eliminate the lingering effects of any *de jure* segregation . . .

I. JCPS'S RACE-BASED STUDENT ASSIGNMENT PLAN MUST SATISFY STRICT JUDICIAL SCRUTINY

The central purpose of the Equal Protection Clause is to guarantee "racial neutrality in governmental decisionmaking". . .

The right to equal protection is "personal" and "guaranteed to the individual" . . .

II. JCPS'S RACE-BASED ASSIGNMENT PLAN IS NOT BASED ON A COMPELLING GOVERNMENTAL INTEREST

A. The Government's Unquestioned Interest In Using Race-Based Measures To Eliminate The Vestiges Of Past Discrimination Is Not Implicated Here

The prototypical government interest that warrants the use of race-based measures is remedying a finding of *de jure* segregation . . .

Like the *Seattle* case, however, this case does not implicate that unquestioned remedial interest . . .

B. The *Grutter* Interest In Obtaining A Genuinely Diverse Student Body With A Critical Mass Of Minority Students Is Not Implicated Here

Three years ago, this Court recognized a second compelling interest that permits the limited consideration of race to attain a genuinely diverse student body, including a critical mass of minority students, at universities and graduate schools . . .

1. In *Grutter* and *Gratz*, the Court upheld the goal of assembling a "broadly diverse" class as compelling because "attaining a diverse student body is at the heart of [a law school's] proper institutional mission" . . .

The Court emphasized that such individualized consideration of each student's "background, experiences, and characteristics" is necessary to assess a student's "individual 'potential contribution to diversity'" . . .

Unlike the law school in *Grutter*, JCPS does not seek a genuinely diverse student body in its elementary schools whereby "all factors that may contribute to student body diversity are meaningfully considered alongside race" . . .

In light of the absence of any individualized consideration under the aspects of the plan at issue here, affirming the Sixth Circuit's decision would remove the critical requirement that individuals be considered as individuals and open the way for the wholesale consideration of race in which students are labeled solely on the basis of their race and then granted or denied admission based on that label in order to achieve a pre-set racial balance among students . . .

C. JCPS's Objective Amounts To "Outright Racial Balancing," Which This Court Has Repeatedly Admonished Does Not Justify Race-Based Decisionmaking

1. Absent the need to remedy a prior constitutional violation or the specialized kind of diversity objective identified in *Grutter*, a goal of "assuring within a student body some specified percentage of a particular group merely because of its race" cannot justify the use of race in making student placement decisions . . .

As discussed, JCPS's racial guidelines cannot be justified as an effort to remedy any constitutional violation . . .

That means that the plan requires, *inter alia*, that students such as petitioner's son, who desire to transfer from one elementary school to another, may do so only if the transfer will not cause either the student's current school or the proposed transfer school to fall outside the required racial range . . .

As explained above, JCPS does not base its rigid race-based range on a finding that a certain percentage is necessary to achieve particular educational benefits associated with broadly diverse student bodies . . .

2. The district court concluded that JCPS is not seeking a pre-set racial balance "for its own sake," but rather to achieve the educational and social benefits of racially diverse schools . . .

The district court also pointed to the County's interest in avoiding racially concentrated schools as a potential compelling interest justifying the County's rigid racial guidelines . . .

To be sure, the government has a compelling interest in eliminating or reducing minority group isolation that is the product of *de jure* segregation . . .

And this Court "has consistently held that the Constitution is not violated by racial imbalance in the schools, without more" . . .

III. JCPS'S RACE-BASED STUDENT ASSIGNMENT PLAN IS NOT NARROWLY TAILORED

Like the plan at issue in the Seattle case, JCPS's race-based student assignment plan is also not narrowly tailored because it fails to meet any of the "hallmarks" of a constitutionally permissible race-conscious program . . .

A. JCPS's Plan Treats Students Solely As Members Of Racial Groups And Denies Them Individualized, Holistic Consideration

As this Court stressed in *Grutter*, individualized consideration is "paramount" in any race-conscious admissions program, because "the Fourteenth Amendment protects persons, not groups" . . .

Wholly unlike the admissions plan upheld in *Grutter*, JCPS's plan considers a student's race in an "inflexible, mechanical way" to achieve a pre-set racial balance of students in each of its schools . . .

Although the district court described JCPS's target racial balance as "flexible," the consideration of a student's race in administering the plan is not . . .

The district court mistakenly characterized the County's plan as providing individualized review because, in addition to race, the plan also considers "the individual characteristics of a student's application, such as place of residence and student choice of school or program" . . .

Similarly unavailing is the district court's attempt to rely on contextual differences between public high schools and selective graduate programs . . .

First, while it is true that student assignments in the elementary and secondary school context are typically not subject to the type of selective consideration common in the university admissions process, that does not mean that individualized consideration is inherently infeasible in the elementary and secondary school admissions context . . .

More fundamentally, regardless of the relative feasibility of individualized consideration in this context, adopting the district court's reasoning that individualized consideration is less relevant here and therefore optional wholly undermines the narrow-tailoring analysis and would mean that individualized consideration is no longer "paramount" in a race-conscious admissions program . . .

To the extent that the district court was suggesting that the requirements of *Grutter* are inapplicable on the theory that educational opportunities within JCPS are fungible, that argument also should be rejected . . .

B. JCPS's Plan Operates As A Quota

The County's plan is indistinguishable from a quota because it imposes "a fixed . . . percentage which must be attained, or which cannot be exceeded," in its schools . . .

JCPS's plan "requires each school to seek a Black student enrollment of at least 15 percent and no more than 50 percent," and provides school administrators with the authority "to maintain schools within the 15-50 percent range" . . .

That the plan determines black and nonblack student enrollment in accordance with a fixed numeric range, rather than a single fixed number, makes no difference . . .

The County's goal of enrolling a pre-set balance of students differs substantially from the Michigan law school's goal of enrolling a "critical mass" of underrepresented minority students . . .

JCPS's plan also operates as a quota because it "insulates a category of applicants with certain desired qualifications from competition with other applicants" . . .

C. JCPS Failed To Pursue Race-Neutral Means of Achieving Racially Integrated Schools

The County's plan is also not narrowly tailored because its goal of achieving racially integrated schools can be achieved effectively through race-neutral alternative . . .

Moreover, school districts have a strong interest in providing a high-quality education to all students, and should continue to seek innovative solutions to improve educational opportunities for all children, including race-neutral choice and open enrollment programs. The County here, however, failed adequately to consider race-neutral alternatives.

D. The County's Plan Unfairly Burdens Innocent Third Parties

While JCPS's plan does not deny any student the opportunity to attend a public school, it does deny those students whose race would negatively affect a school's racial balance the opportunity to attend the school of their choice, including the ability to attend the most sought-after schools and programs in the school district solely because of their race . . .

E. The County's Plan Is Not Limited In Time

Race-based policies in an educational setting "must be limited in time" and "have a logical end point" . . .

The promise of *Brown* and its progeny was "to effectuate a transition to a racially nondiscriminatory school system," and thus "achieve a system of determining admission to the public schools on a nonracial basis" . . .[3]

Example 4

This excerpt deals with allegations of extortion against government employees. Notice in this truncated excerpt how well the argument is executed.

I. THE COURT OF APPEALS ERRED IN REJECTING PETITIONERS' QUALIFIED IMMUNITY DEFENSE TO RESPONDENT'S RICO CLAIM

RICO provides civil remedies for "[a]ny person injured in his business or property by reason of a violation of 18 U.S.C. 1962" . . .

The court of appeals held that a RICO predicate act of extortion under the Hobbs Act or state law may be shown by allegations that government officials, whose actions were authorized by law, had an extortionate intent to obtain property for the sole benefit of the government and the public, with no allegation that they sought any private gain for themselves or another . . .

A. Government Officials Do Not Become Racketeers Or Extortionists Merely By Taking Overzealous Regulatory Actions

The court of appeals' RICO decision underscores the growing concern that civil RICO has evolved far beyond its animating concern-combating organized crime . . .

The predicate act of extortion under color of official right addresses the classic situation of abuse of public office for private gain . . .

It is not surprising, therefore, that the one court of appeals that has addressed the application of RICO to a claim of overzealous regulation found such an application to be "ludicrous on its face" . . .

By holding otherwise, the court of appeals below has exposed BLM and Forest Service officials like petitioners who regulate intermingled public lands; bank regulators like the defendants in *Sinclair*; and potentially countless other government officials who negotiate with private parties on behalf of the government to extortion charges under RICO, along with the prospect of personal liability and treble damages, for taking tough regulatory actions or driving hard bargains, even if the officials have no personal interest in the property they seek on behalf of the government . . .

B. Extortion Requires Showing Both That Government Officials Acted With "Wrongful" Intent And That They "Obtained" A Private Benefit For Themselves Or Others

1. Extortion under color of official right requires a showing that "a public official has obtained a payment to which he was not entitled, knowing that the payment was made in return for official acts" . . .

2. Another critical difference between an overzealous regulator and an extortionist is that an extortionist must actually "obtain" the victim's property for himself or another private party . . .

The case law does not always require that the official himself benefit from the extortion; there may be extortion if payments are made to a third party at the official's direction . . .

C. Petitioners Did Not Act With A "Wrongful" Or Extortionate Intent And Did Not "Obtain" Any Property For The Private Benefit Of Themselves Or Others

1. Petitioners did not take any action based on a "wrongful" intent to obtain property not due to them in exchange for official actions . . .

That is particularly true in the context of this case, where, as authorized by regulation, the government sought to obtain reciprocal treatment of interlocking parcels of land . . .

The government, no less than a typical property owner, may seek through lawful means to encourage a neighboring property owner to agree to a reciprocal property right . . .

Petitioners, therefore, are even further removed from the plain terms and purposes of RICO and the Hobbs Act than the petitioners in *Scheidler*, who the Court recognized personally exercised some degree of control over the abortion clinic's business as a result of their illegal and violent acts, even if they did not "obtain" property within the meaning of the Hobbs Act . . .

D. The Regulatory Actions At Issue Cannot Support A Claim Of Extortion In Any Event

The specific regulatory actions respondent alleges do not support his claim of extortion for additional reasons . . .

Respondent also alleges that petitioners caused a false criminal charge to be filed against him . . .

The central harm that respondent alleges in his RICO and *Bivens* claims stems from BLM's administrative decisions to cancel his right-of-way on interlocking government lands and his grazing and special use permits on government land . . .

E. At A Minimum, Petitioners Did Not Violate Any Clearly Established RICO Right

For the foregoing reasons, petitioners did not violate respondent's rights under RICO . . .

Accordingly, petitioners had no reason to believe that they were violating RICO or any clearly established right against extortion in attempting to obtain a reciprocal easement for the United States through the exercise of their lawful regulatory authority . . .

II. THE COURT OF APPEALS ERRED IN REJECTING PETITIONERS' QUALIFIED IMMUNITY DEFENSE TO RESPONDENT'S BIVENS CLAIM

A. The Fifth Amendment, Tucker Act, And APA Preclude A *Bivens* Cause Of Action In This Context

Respondent's *Bivens* claim under the Fifth Amendment is precluded by the availability of judicial review under the APA and the Tucker Act, and by the nature of the Fifth Amendment right itself . . .
1. A *Bivens* action is inconsistent with claims under the Fifth Amendment's Just Compensation Clause *Bivens* is fundamentally ill-suited for claims, like respondent's, founded on the Just Compensation Clause of the Fifth Amendment . . .

A damages remedy against individual federal officials, moreover, is fundamentally inconsistent with the nature of the Fifth Amendment right to just compensation, which this Court has repeatedly held is a right that is owed by (and can be violated only by) the government itself, not by federal officials in their individual capacity . . .

That Fifth Amendment claims cannot be brought against individual officials necessarily follows from the fact that the Fifth Amendment does not prohibit the government from taking property but simply requires the government to pay just compensation if it does . . .

It is clear, therefore, that no *Bivens* action would be appropriate for an actual taking of property under the Fifth Amendment. The fact that respondent cannot even allege that any actual property has been taken in this case does not make his novel attempt to import a *Bivens* remedy into the Fifth Amendment's Just Compensation Clause context any more appropriate.
2. The APA precludes respondent's *Bivens* action in its entirety
In recent years, this Court has "consistently refused to extend *Bivens* liability to any new context or new category of defendants" . . .

Thus, for example, in *Bush v. Lucas* the Court refused to create a *Bivens* cause of action for federal employees seeking to challenge personnel decisions even though "existing remedies did not provide complete relief," and there was no remedy at all for certain personnel actions against probationary employees . . .

The reasoning of *Bush*, *Chilicky*, and *Malesko* compels the conclusion that the APA's comprehensive scheme for challenging agency action precludes a *Bivens* remedy with respect to agency actions like those at issue here . . .

Similarly, in the Section 1983 context, this Court has generally declined to hold that a federal statute is actionable under Section 1983 if the statute may be enforced through a "private judicial remedy" or "even a private administrative remedy" . . .

Although it acknowledged that the APA generally precludes a *Bivens* action arising out of final agency action, the court of appeals purported to carve up respondent's *Bivens* claim into two separate categories: (1) allegations of final agency action (which the court held had to be pursued under the APA) and (2) allegations it deemed insufficiently related to final agency action (for which, it held, a *Bivens* action was appropriate) . . .

Moreover, all of respondent's arguments against the regulatory actions he now alleges as the basis for his RICO and *Bivens* claims were either raised and resolved against him during his administrative challenges to those actions, or could have been raised in those or similar challenges . . .

Similarly, in challenging BLM's proposed cancellation of his grazing permit, respondent expressly argued that BLM's actions constituted an uncompensated taking under the Fifth Amendment and this Court's decisions in *Nollan v. California Coastal Commission* . . .

Respondent cannot contend, on the one hand, that "all" of the actions alleged in his complaint "were taken as part of an ongoing scheme to coerce him to grant the BLM an easement," and simultaneously maintain, on the other, that certain of those acts (those not leading to final agency action) are unrelated to the final agency actions (the cancelling of his right-of-way and permits) that he claims primarily caused his injuries . . .

3. None of the limitations of the APA warrant the extension of a *Bivens* remedy in this context

The fact that the APA provides no remedy for certain agency action i.e., that involving acts "unrelated to final agency action," does not mean that a *Bivens* action may be inferred with respect to that conduct . . .

Similarly, the fact that the APA does not permit an award of damages does not justify extending *Bivens* to this context . . .

Furthermore, when a comprehensive statutory remedial scheme exists, it does not matter whether a particular plaintiff will have any remedy under that scheme . . .

Accordingly, extending *Bivens* to this context would radically expand *Bivens* in direct contravention of this Court's precedents and principles of judicial restraint . . .

B. There Is No Fifth Amendment Right Against Retaliation For The Exercise Of Property Rights

Even assuming a *Bivens* action might be inferred under the Just Compensation Clause in certain circumstances, respondent's claim here is without merit, because not only has he failed to show a substantive violation of the Fifth Amendment (as explained below), but the Fifth Amendment does not embody the novel anti-retaliation right conceived of by the court below . . .

This Court's constitutional retaliation doctrine is limited to suits alleging retaliation for the exercise of First Amendment rights . . .

Neither this Court nor any circuit court other than the court below has held that other constitutional provisions include an anti-retaliation component . . .

While the Fifth Amendment is of course entitled to equal footing with the First, the concerns about chilling protected activity that motivate the anti-retaliation doctrine in the First Amendment context are not present, or at least are greatly reduced, in the Fifth Amendment takings context . . .

Furthermore, the Fifth Amendment, which requires the availability of just compensation in order for a taking to be valid, presupposes a degree of permissible governmental interference with property rights that is wholly alien in the context of First Amendment speech rights . . .

That conclusion is particularly true in the present context of interlocking properties and reciprocal easements that are common in public land management in the West . . .

Finally, any practical value of creating a separate Fifth Amendment right against retaliation is severely diminished by the fact that the well-established First Amendment right against retaliation protects citizens seeking to invoke their Fifth Amendment pro-tections by petitioning the government for just compensation or other administrative means of redress . . .

C. Respondent Has Not Alleged The Violation Of Any Right Pro-tected By The Fifth Amendment

Respondent does not allege that any of his property rights were actually taken by the government, or that the right to just compensation guaranteed by the Fifth Amendment has otherwise been triggered by any of the regulatory actions about which he complains . . .

1. The Fifth Amendment guarantees only the right to just compensation

By its terms, respondent's *Bivens*-based retaliation claim is predicated entirely on the Fifth Amendment . . .

Because the only guarantee of the Fifth Amendment is the availability of just compensation(which is presumptively available under the Tucker Act), respondent has no Fifth Amendment right to preclude the government from taking his property (or under his theory, from seeking to coerce him to grant property to the government) . . .

In *Williamson County*, the Court declared that "[t]he Fifth Amendment does not proscribe the taking of property; it pro-scribes taking without just compensation" . . .

In addition, this Court has long held that takings may occur outside of the eminent-domain process . . .

Kaiser Aetna—the principal case on which the court of appeals relied is not to the contrary . . .

2. Respondent cannot claim that petitioners imposed an uncon-stitutional condition on either his property rights or his right to access public lands

As indicated, respondent does not allege that any of his prop-erty was actually taken, but that BLM tried to take his property by pressuring him to give the government a reciprocal right-of-way over his property . . .

Relying, *inter alia*, on this Court's decisions in *Nollan* and *Dolan*, respondent asserts that "the Constitution forbade petitioners from conditioning respondent's right to other government benefits (e.g., grazing permits, road maintenance, etc.) on his waiver of his Fifth Amendment rights," because "the denial of those benefits had no relationship to the BLM's legitimate regulatory interests relating to grazing, road maintenance, etc., and was nothing more than an 'out-and-out plan of extortion'" . . .

First, the only regulatory action BLM took that can be fairly characterized as being based on respondent's refusal to grant the United States a reciprocal easement on his land was the cancellation of the right-of-way the government had granted to respondent—which was conditioned on the receipt of the reciprocal easement . . .

Indeed, seeking to obtain such reciprocal property rights is a reasonable and commonplace feature of federal land management, just as it is for private landowners . . .

The reciprocal easement at issue in this case simply represents a logical consequence of the considerations discussed in this Court's decision in *Leo Sheep Co. v. United States*, which also arose because of the interlocking nature of public and private lands in Wyoming . . .

Second, respondent is precluded from claiming in this *Bivens* action that petitioners impermissibly conditioned other regulatory benefits, such as his grazing and special recreation permits, on his granting a reciprocal easement to the government . . .

Third, in the *Nollan* line of cases, there was an actual interference with property owned by the private citizen . . .

Here, in stark contrast, respondent alleges—at most—that petitioners placed an improper condition on an asserted right to use public lands . . .

D. At a Minimum, Petitioners Did Not Violate Any Clearly Established Fifth Amendment Right

Finally, even if this Court were to adopt a theory of constitutional retaliation that for the first time extended to rights under the Fifth Amendment, petitioners in this case still would be entitled to qualified immunity . . .[4]

Notes

References to citations, transcripts, footnotes, and some authorities omitted for sake of clarity.

1. *Davis v. FEC*, No. 07-320.
2. *State of Washington v. Washington Educational Association*, No. 05-1657 and 05-1589.
3. *Meredith v. Jefferson County Board of Education, et al.*, No. 05-915.
4. *Wilkie, et al. v. Robbins*, No. 06-219.

15

A Word About Trial and Appellate Briefs

The legal advocate must first try to think like the judge who will hear and decide the case. The practitioner should ask, "If I were the judge, how would I view the facts and law of this case?"

Too many briefs, judges say, are the work of those who start writing without a plan. This is like taking a journey without a map: You may never find your final destination, and if you do, you will have consumed a lot of needless energy and tested your passengers' patience along the way.

Failing to Filter the Issues

Judges find it tedious to read briefs in which the lawyer failed to hone the arguments. Some of these arguments are trivial, and others actually weaken the case.

Some attorneys suggest that you never know exactly which arguments might appeal to a judge, so they include all the possibilities, just in case. But an overwhelming litany of arguments more often than not convinces judges that there is *no* merit to the case. Even when you put your strongest point first, judges can grow weary if the brief goes on and on, and the impact of the strong argument may be lost in the clutter.

Clear and Simple

You must communicate with the court in terms as simple and as easily understood as the subject matter permits. This means you must write and talk to judges in the clearest way possible. All judges want to understand, and understanding is the condition precedent to persuasion. You should also speak to the court in conversational tones. Arguing a case is more of a Socratic dialogue than an oration.

Telling the Whole Truth

Every advocate must state the facts and the law candidly and accurately. This is an absolute. Every sentence must stand firm for truth. The court will typically find the correct path anyway, and an attorney who is inaccurate or less than candid will reap the consequences.

Professional Courtesies

Your brief should reflect your dignity and professional competence. Casting aspersions on your adversary reflects poorly on you and the strength of your presentation.

Working on the Reader's Mind

How the facts and law are unfurled in the brief is important in and of itself. Like the initial summary, subject headings should work on the reader's mind. It is impossible to measure the impact of such subtleties—they are often small, but ultimately decisive.

Conveying a Sense of Justice

Judges like to think of themselves as performing a service for those who appear before them. Behind every lawsuit is a story involving real people. Therefore, you must humanize your client. You must tell your story so that a fair-minded and reasonably intelligent reader would instinctively think your client was right if there were no law.

Finally, the judge will recognize the effort you put into preparing your brief. Briefing, when artfully done, is an intense intellectual endeavor that requires careful crafting.

The Art of Skillful Briefing

Good appellate briefs are characterized by what appellate judges call the ABC's of legal writing:

- *Is the writing Accurate?* Embellishment and exaggeration will not get an advocate anywhere but in trouble.
- *Is the writing Brief?* You must be precise in what you say. The only way to achieve brevity is through painstaking, careful work.
- *Is the writing Clear?* A brief is supposed to assist—not confuse—the court regarding the issues.

16

■■■───────────────────────────────

A Word About
Oral Arguments

Oral argument is never a substitute for a well-written brief, but it can be important in having the case heard in an open forum.

Oral argument of a motion or appeal is a unique opportunity to discuss the critical issues of your case with the court. Many judges believe that oral argument can influence the decision in a case. The bench may also have questions about an opinion that you can satisfactorily explain, but that was not addressed in your brief. Oral argument also ensures that there is a period of time in which the judges are focused on the case without distraction.

Know the Record Well

There is one indispensable requisite for effective oral argument—complete mastery of the case. To be effective, you must know, in detail, the record, the procedural history, and the various arguments made throughout the case.

First Things First

The cardinal rule for successful argument is that the strongest and best argument should be presented first and clearly identified. If you have several alternative arguments, do not make the mistake of discussing them before leading up to the real point. Your primary point may never be reached because of time constraints, or it may become obscured in the process.

You must choose the most persuasive points. There is no need for reciting case and transcript citations unless one of the judges asks for them. If such citations are not readily at hand, counsel should remind the court that they are in the brief and readily available by consulting the table of authorities.

The Legal Argument

Most judges will tell you that in oral argument, skill is at a premium. Unless a lawyer is capable of analyzing a case at a sophisticated level and has devoted time and effort doing so, oral argument can be a disaster. There is inevitably a limited amount of time in which the lawyer can control the content of the argument. The question is what to say and how to say it.

Most controlling issues are not pure questions of law. Therefore, you should devote time to the facts central to the appeal so that the court can get a clear understanding of them and the legal premises. You should spend the rest of your time arguing the law of the case as though the case were one of first impression. Explain why as a matter of principle your client should win. Then reason by analogy to other settled premises of law, and show that your client's victory would be consistent with established law. You should cite very few cases in oral argument since they are already included in the brief.

Presentation Is Everything

The worst thing a lawyer can do at oral argument is read his presentation. If the court has read the briefs (and most have), there is nothing worse than having a lawyer read a digest of his brief. Because this practice is so annoying, some judges suggest that lawyers bring very few notes, as they invariably become a crutch and detract from the presentation.

Reliance on notes can also prevent a lawyer from doing the most important part of the job—listening to the court. Listening carefully to what the judges ask is absolutely critical. Judges express astonishment at how often counsel fail to detect those issues that are troubling the court. It is simply because they are not listening to the court's questions.

This failure may be a result of inadequate preparation. A lawyer must review the hard questions beforehand, anticipate the hypotheticals that push the analysis to its logical limits, and be ready to answer damaging questions. To do this, you must know the case inside and out. When judges believe that an attorney has mastered the legal issues, that advocate's credibility is established, and this goes a long way toward successful persuasion.

Nothing undermines confidence in a lawyer faster than an evasive answer. It is exasperating enough when a lawyer provides an answer that misses the point. It is even more disturbing when a lawyer tries to obscure or evade an issue.

Another suggestion from judges, especially for young lawyers, is to learn to overcome your fear. A bit of nervousness may keep you alert, but fear can also detract from what would otherwise be an effective presentation.

Welcome Interruptions

Oral argument is the opportunity for judges to probe the logical limits of the argument and examine holes in that logic. Most experienced advocates understand this principle and welcome questions from the bench. They know how to capitalize on them. The advocate should try to leave some parting impression fixed in the minds of the judges who have read and listened to his argument.

Ending Well

You have done your best to put your client's case to the court as cleanly and crisply as possible, with an absolute minimum of distractions. Neither your client nor the judge could ask for more.

The Substance of Oral Argument

An oral argument can be more effectively presented by:

- *Focusing on a few points.* You cannot possibly make more than a few good points in such a limited period of time. You must leave the rest of your discussion to your brief.
- *Outlining the dispositive issues.* This is the time when you can lay out the framework of your argument in a crystal-clear fashion.
- *Making it compelling.* This will give the court an overview of your argument and a framework with which to analyze the case.
- *Checking for current authority.* This will save you any embarrassment.
- *Knowing the record.* An attorney should be able to respond to any question a judge may have about the facts. The facts of the case are important, and judges are put off by a lawyer who has not mastered them.

17

■ ■ ■

Stellar Examples

At long last, the argument finally comes together, building from all of the elements discussed in the previous examples. Following are two arguments in their entirety. These controversial cases have been chosen not for their subject matter but for the range of argumentative tools used in their construction. This is legal argumentation at the top of its art.

The two examples demonstrating stellar argumentative skills that are set forth next deal with (1) possible violation of the Establishment Clause when requiring participation in the Pledge of Allegiance and (2) the constitutionality of the Partial Birth Abortion Ban Act. A lawyer could do much worse than emulate the skills of argumentation demonstrated here.

Example 1

This excerpt deals with whether requiring participation in the Pledge of Allegiance in a public school violates the Establishment Clause.

QUESTION PRESENTED

1. Whether respondent Newdow has standing to challenge as unconstitutional a public school district policy that requires teachers to lead willing students in reciting the Pledge of Allegiance.

2. Whether a public school district policy that requires teachers to lead willing students in reciting the Pledge of Allegiance, which includes the words "under God," violates the Establishment Clause of the First Amendment, as applicable through the Fourteenth Amendment.

STATEMENT

1.a. In 1942, as part of an overall effort to "codify and emphasize the existing rules and customs pertaining to the display and use of the flag of the United States of America," Congress enacted a Pledge of Allegiance to the United States flag. It read: "I pledge allegiance to the flag of the United States of America and to the Republic for which it stands, one Nation indivisible, with liberty and justice for all."

Twelve years later, Congress amended the Pledge of Allegiance by adding the words "under God" after the word "Nation." Accordingly, the Pledge of Allegiance now reads: "I pledge allegiance to the Flag of the United States of America, and to the Republic for which it stands, one Nation under God, indivisible, with liberty and justice for all." Both the Senate and House Reports expressed the view that, under this Court's precedent, the amendment "is not an act establishing a religion or one interfering with the 'free exercise' of religion."

Following the decision below, Congress passed legislation that (i) made extensive findings about the historic role of religion in the political development of the Nation, (ii) reaffirmed the text of the Pledge as it has "appeared for decades", and (iii) repeated Congress's judgment that the legislation is constitutional both facially and as applied by school districts whose teachers lead willing students in its recitation.

b. California law requires that each public elementary school in the State "conduct appropriate patriotic exercises" at the beginning of the school day, and that "the giving of the Pledge of Allegiance to the Flag of the United States of America shall satisfy the requirements of this section." To satisfy that requirement, petitioners adopted a policy that requires "each elementary school class to recite the pledge of allegiance to the flag once each day." No child is compelled to join in reciting the Pledge.

2. Respondent Michael Newdow (Newdow) is the non-custodial father of a child who is enrolled in a public elementary school within the jurisdiction of petitioner Elk Grove Unified School District. The child's teacher leads willing students in reciting the Pledge of Allegiance daily. The child's mother, who was never married to Newdow, has "sole legal custody as to the rights and responsibilities to make decisions relating to the health, education and welfare of" the child. Newdow retains limited visitation rights, a right of access to the child's school and medical records, and the right to "consult" on "substantial" decisions pertaining to the child's "educational needs," but if the parents disagree, the child's mother "may exercise legal control of" the child as long as it "is not specifically prohibited or inconsistent with the physical custody order."

   In March 2000, Newdow filed suit, on behalf of himself and as next friend of his child, against the U.S. Congress, the United States of America, the President of the United States, the State of California, and two California school districts and their superintendents, seeking a declaration that the 1954 statute adding the words "under God" to the Pledge of Allegiance is "facially unconstitutional" under the Establishment and Free Exercise Clauses of the First Amendment, and requesting injunctive relief. Newdow asserts that recitation of the Pledge in the child's school "results in the daily indoctrination" of his child "with religious dogma," which "infringes" upon Newdow's asserted "unrestricted right to inculcate in his daughter—free from governmental interference—the atheistic beliefs he finds persuasive." The district court dismissed the complaint for failure to state a claim, relying on numerous decisions of this Court expressly addressing the Pledge and describing it as consistent with the Establishment Clause.

3. A divided panel of the Ninth Circuit affirmed in part and reversed in part. The court first held that Newdow has standing to challenge petitioners' policy of reciting the Pledge "because his daughter is currently enrolled in elementary school" in Elk Grove. The majority then ruled that the addition of the phrase "under God" to the Pledge of Allegiance violates the Establishment Clause. The majority determined that the "sole purpose" of the 1954 Act was to "advance religion," and characterized the Pledge as "a profession of a religious belief, namely, a belief in monotheism," which "impermissibly takes a position with respect to the purely religious question of the existence and identity of God." The majority then concluded that "the mere fact that a pupil is required to listen every day to the statement 'one nation under God' has a coercive effect."

   Judge Fernandez dissented. In his view, phrases like "'In God We Trust,' or 'under God' have no tendency to establish a religion in this country or to suppress anyone's exercise, or non-exercise, of religion, except in the fevered eye of persons who most fervently would like to drive all tincture of religion out of the public life of our polity."

4. While the case was pending on rehearing, the mother of Newdow's child notified the court that Newdow lacked legal custody of the child and legal control over the child's educational and religious upbringing. She further advised that, as the parent with legal custody and control of the daughter, she "wishes for her to be able to recite the Pledge at school exactly as it stands."

   The court of appeals then issued a separate decision reaffirming that Newdow has standing to prosecute his challenge to the Pledge. The court concluded that Newdow no longer could prosecute the action on behalf of his child, nor could he "disrupt the mother's choice of schools for their daughter." The court concluded, however, that Newdow continues to have standing in his own right to challenge, "unconstitutional government action affecting his child." The court reasoned that, because non-custodial parents have a right to "expose" their children to their beliefs and values, Newdow was injured because state law "surely does not permit official state indoctrination of an impressionable child on a daily basis with an official view of religion contrary to the express wishes of either a custodial or noncustodial parent."

5.a. The court issued an amended opinion on rehearing, in which the court limited its Establishment Clause holding to petitioners' policy of leading willing students in the recitation of the Pledge. The court repeated its view that the reference to God in the Pledge "is a profession of a religious belief, namely, a belief in monotheism," and ruled that its daily recitation in school classrooms has a "coercive effect" because it "places students in the untenable position of choosing between participating in an exercise with religious content or protesting." The court stressed its view that the Pledge "is a performative statement."

Judge Fernandez again dissented, noting that, although the majority "now formally limits itself to holding that it is unconstitutional to recite the Pledge in public classrooms, its message that something is constitutionally infirm about the Pledge itself abides and remains a clear and present danger to all similar public expressions of reverence."

b. Judge O'Scannlain, joined by Judges Kleinfeld, Gould, Tallman, Rawlinson, and Clifton, filed a lengthy dissent from the court of appeals' denial of rehearing en banc. He described the panel opinion as wrong, very wrong-wrong because reciting the Pledge of Allegiance is simply not "a religious act" as the two-judge majority asserts, wrong as a matter of Supreme Court precedent properly understood, wrong because it set up a direct conflict with the law of another circuit, and wrong as a matter of common sense.

SUMMARY OF ARGUMENT

I. Respondent Newdow lacks standing to challenge petitioners' policy concerning recitation of the Pledge of Allegiance because he lacks the legal authority to direct and control his child's educational and religious upbringing. While state law affords him a right to expose his daughter to his own atheistic views, he does not have a corresponding right to exclude other influences—especially those that the mother has chosen for the child. His asserted interest in not having his viewpoint countered by governmental speech with which he disagrees is too generalized an interest to support standing. Finally, Newdow's constitutional challenge is, in its practical effect, a collateral attack on ongoing state custody proceedings. That proceeding provides an adequate forum for Newdow to press any argument that his or the child's interests are being harmed. Federal court litigation should not become a vehicle for obtaining a measure of legal control over the child's upbringing that the state court has denied him.

II. Two decisions of this Court have said without qualification that the Pledge of Allegiance is constitutional. Numerous other opinions, joined in by nine Justices of this Court, have likewise expressly addressed and affirmed the constitutionality of the Pledge of Allegiance with its reference to God. No Justice has expressed the view that the Pledge violates the Establishment Clause. Those consistent and oft-repeated statements stand as a fixed lodestar in this Court's Establishment Clause jurisprudence, demarcating a constitutional baseline that has informed and directed the resolution of a number of the Court's Establishment Clause cases. Whatever else the Establishment Clause may prohibit, this Court's precedents make clear that it does not forbid the government from officially acknowledging the religious heritage, foundation, and character of this Nation. That is precisely what the Pledge of Allegiance does.

That conclusion does not change when the Pledge is said by willing students in a public elementary school classroom. Reciting the Pledge of Allegiance is a patriotic exercise, not a religious testimonial. The reference to God permissibly acknowledges the role that faith in God has played in the formation, political foundation, and continuing development of this Country. Children may be taught about that heritage in their History classes; acknowledging the same in the Pledge is equally permissible.

ARGUMENT

I. RESPONDENT NEWDOW LACKS STANDING BECAUSE HE HAS NO LEGALLY PROTECTED INTEREST IN PREVENTING HIS CHILD'S EXPOSURE TO THE PLEDGE

Article III of the Constitution confines the judicial power to the resolution of actual "Cases" and "Controversies," and one "essential and unchanging" component of the case-or- controversy requirement is the rule that a plaintiff invoking the jurisdiction of the federal courts must have standing. Because standing goes to the power of the Court to adjudicate a case, resolution of the standing question is necessarily antecedent to any decision on the merits.

The "irreducible constitutional minimum of standing" requires that the plaintiff (1) "have suffered an 'injury in fact'" in the form of the "invasion of a legally protected interest," that is both "concrete and particularized" and "actual or imminent, not conjectural or hypothetical"; (2) identify a "causal connection between the injury and the conduct" of which he complains, such that the alleged injury is "fairly traceable]to the challenged action of the defendant, and not .the result of the independent action of some third party not before the court"; and (3) show that it is "likely, as opposed to merely speculative, that the injury will be redressed by a favorable decision." Standing must exist at every stage of the litigation, and the party invoking the jurisdiction of the federal courts bears the burden of establishing standing. Newdow has a "substantially more difficult" burden because he challenges not petitioners' regulation of his own activities, but the "allegedly unlawful regulation of someone else" his child.

Newdow has not met that burden. He has no legally protected interest that has been invaded by petitioners' Pledge of Allegiance policy. Furthermore, both the cause of the alleged harm and the ability of the court to redress it depend upon, "the unfettered choices made by an independent actor" the child's mother-who is "not before the court and whose exercise of broad and legitimate discretion the court cannot presume either to control or to predict." Finally, the lower courts lacked jurisdiction because this litigation is, at its core, a collateral attack on orders entered by the state court in the ongoing child custody dispute between Newdow and the child's mother.

A. Newdow Has Not Suffered The Invasion Of Any Legally Protected Interest

Newdow has not suffered an "injury in fact" because the School District's policy does not trench upon any "legally protected interest" that he has concerning the education of his child.

1. A number of this Court's Establishment Clause cases have involved lawsuits by parents challenging practices or policies in the public schools that their children attend. In all of those cases, however, it was undisputed that the parents had the legal right to sue as next friend to vindicate their children's interests and to protect the parents' own constitutional right to direct and control the religious and educational upbringing of their children.

   Newdow has neither right. Under California law, which is controlling on this fundamental question of state law, the prerogative of suing to enforce the child's rights rests exclusively with the mother because, in this case, she has the legal authority to make final and binding decisions concerning the child's "health, education and welfare."

   Nor does Newdow enjoy any right to direct the education of his daughter. Under California law, the parent with legal custody alone "directs the child's activities and makes decisions regarding the child's education and religion." In this case, the mother has selected Elk Grove School District as "the environment in which she as the child's sole legal custodian wishes to have her educated," and she specifically endorses petitioners' policy under which her child may daily "recite the Pledge of Allegiance as it currently stands, including the portion stating that we are 'one Nation under God.'" The mother's legal control specifically encompasses the right to decide, over the non-custodial parent's objections, whether the child should salute the flag of the United States.

With respect to the child's religious upbringing, the mother has chosen to raise the child as a "Christian who regularly attends church, and believes in God." Under California law, moreover, the mother would be free to place the child in a pervasively religious private school in which daily prayer is an integral aspect of the educational environment.

2. Notwithstanding the clarity of that state law, which leaves Newdow no "legally cognizable right," affected by petitioners' policy, the court of appeals discerned three potential sources of injury to Newdow's legal interests. But none of them is sufficient to confer standing. First, the court of appeals noted that Newdow retains the right to "consult" with the mother on educational decisions and to "inspect" the child's educational records. That is true, but irrelevant. Petitioners' policy concerning recitation of the Pledge in school classrooms does not implicate either of those rights.

    Second, the court of appeals relied heavily upon Newdow's residual right, under California law, to "expose" his child to his views. But, again, petitioners' policy does not prevent or preclude Newdow from exposing his child to his particular viewpoints. The court of appeals was able to discern an injury to Newdow's legal interests only by transmogrifying Newdow's limited right to expose his child to his views into a right to exclude other viewpoints, including those specifically chosen by the parent with controlling legal custody. But Newdow has no such right of exclusion. The court of appeals cited no state law authority for such a right. The court simply reasoned that it must "surely" follow from the right of exposure. But it surely does not: any such right of exclusion is flatly inconsistent with the custody determination. The very essence of the mother's legal custody is the right to expose the child to pedagogical practices or viewpoints with which the non-custodial parent disagrees.

Indeed, the Ninth Circuit vested Newdow with rights that even a custodial parent does not enjoy. Public schools routinely instruct students about evolution, war, racial integration, gender equality, and other matters with which some parents may disagree on religious, political, or moral grounds, and thus schools may convey indirectly to children that the parent's views "are those of an outsider." What the Constitution protects, in those circumstances, is the parents' right to instill their own views in their children and to place them in a private school that is more consonant with their beliefs. Petitioners have not interfered with Newdow's right or ability to instill his own views. And a parent like Newdow who lacks the power to move the child because of a state custody determination can have no greater power to dictate the curriculum in the school of the custodial parent's choice.

Because Newdow lacks the necessary control over the child's education, his interest in not having his viewpoint diluted by the government's educational practices is the same generalized interest that could be asserted by a grandparent, nanny, or proselytizing friend. Frustration and dissatisfaction with having another person witness or hear messages with which one disagrees is too diffuse an injury to confer Article III standing.

Third, the court of appeals erroneously couched Newdow's Article III injury in terms of a legal right not to have his daughter "subjected to unconstitutional state action." The court thus attempted to transform Newdow's right to expose his child to his views into a right to prevent her exposure to unconstitutional conduct. That approach to standing is flawed at multiple levels.

As an initial matter, that approach conflates the standing inquiry and the ultimate question on the merits. Newdow, just like concerned grandparents or neighbors, does not have a greater claim to standing if the state action he challenges is ultimately proven to be unconstitutional. Standing "in no way depends on the merits of the plaintiff's contention that particular conduct is illegal." Rather, the plaintiff must identify some action by the opposing party that affects his particularized legal rights concretely and imminently—regardless of whether that action ultimately is found to be lawful or not. "The requirement of standing 'focuses on the party seeking to get his complaint before a federal court and not on the issues he wishes to have adjudicated.'" Newdow simply has no right to seclude the child from viewpoints that the custodial mother endorses, and that fact does not change just because he alleges that the views are unconstitutional.

Furthermore, by focusing on the mother's supposed lack of a legal right to "consent to unconstitutional government action" the court of appeals asked the wrong question. Standing turns not upon the absence of a legal right in the mother, but on the presence of a legal injury to Newdow. Once again, the logic of the Ninth Circuit's approach to standing would confer standing not just on the non-custodial parent, but also on any concerned individual who disagreed with the custodial parent's failure to object. Beyond that, the court's supposition that a parent with controlling legal custody cannot permit a child to endure unlawful state action is wrong. The court of appeals again cited no state law supporting its proposition. And, as a matter of common sense, custodial parents have no obligation to resist through litigation every potential playground tort or constitutional affiront (such as locker searches or procedural missteps in disciplinary procedures) that befalls their children.

B. Because Of The Mother's Independent Control Over Education, Newdow Cannot Demonstrate Causation Or Redressability

Even if Newdow has suffered an injury in fact, that injury derives from the independent actions of the mother and cannot fairly be attributed to petitioners' Pledge of Allegiance policy. The court of appeals defined the harm to Newdow's interests as having his daughter taught that "her father's beliefs are those of an outsider, and necessarily inferior to what she is exposed to in the classroom." To establish standing, however, Newdow must show that it is petitioners' Pledge policy, rather than the "independent action" of the mother in raising the child, that caused that harm.

The mother, the parent with whom the child spends the vast majority of her time, is raising the child as a "Christian who regularly attends church, and [who] believes in God." Given those substantial and weighty influences, it is "purely speculative," whether any perception on the part of the child that her father's atheistic viewpoint is "inferior" or "outside" the mainstream, is the product of reciting the Pledge of Allegiance, rather than of the daily Christian influence of the mother and the child's consistent exposure to church activities. The "remote possibility" that the child's receptivity to Newdow's atheistic beliefs "might have been better" if the child did not say the Pledge is insufficient to confer standing.

For similar reasons, Newdow cannot show that it is "likely," that his injury will be redressed by a favorable court ruling in a "tangible" way. The mother has made clear her intention that her daughter recite the Pledge of Allegiance daily during her elementary school years. A ruling in Newdow's favor would not prevent the mother from placing the child in a private school where the official governmental Pledge, with its reference to God, could be said daily. Indeed, the mother retains the right to transfer her daughter to a pervasively sectarian institution that begins the day not just with the Pledge, but also with a prayer and Bible reading. That right, conferred on the mother by a state-court custody determination, demonstrates that Newdow's asserted injury is neither traceable to the petitioners' Pledge policy nor redressable by the policy's invalidation. The child also remains subject to exposure to the Pledge and similar official acknowledgments of the Nation's religious heritage in a wide variety of other settings, public or private. In short, unless the Establishment Clause compels courts to root out every reference to religion in public life, the relief ordered by the court here is incapable of inoculating Newdow's message of atheism against any perceived dilution.

C. The Lawsuit Is A Collateral Attack On The Pending State Court Child Custody Proceedings

For well over a century, this Court has acknowledged that "the whole subject of the domestic relations of husband and wife, parent and child, belongs to the laws of the States and not to the laws of the United States." In this case, orders entered in the pending state child custody proceeding establish that, where the two parents disagree on an educational practice, such as whether the child should be exposed to the Pledge of Allegiance, the mother's decision controls and Newdow has no right to overturn it. If Newdow believes the mother's educational decisions are causing harm to the child, the proper remedy is for him to seek a modification of the custody agreement from the family court. Newdow cannot use federal litigation to circumvent that state-law process or to modify indirectly a state-law custody judgment.

Under the Rooker-Feldman doctrine, federal district courts lack subject-matter jurisdiction over any action that "in essence, would be an attempt to obtain direct review of the state court's judicial decision in the lower federal courts." The issues presented in state and federal court need not be identical. The Rooker- Feldman doctrine applies as long as the issues are "inextricably intertwined." Numerous courts of appeals have invoked the Rooker-Feldman doctrine to bar relitigation of claims related to state divorce and child custody proceedings in the federal courts.

Newdow's challenge to petitioners' Pledge policy likewise should be barred because it is inextricably intertwined with the pending child custody proceedings. At bottom, Newdow's challenge reflects a fundamental disagreement with the state court's assignment to the mother of the legal authority to control the child's educational and religious upbringing and to the attendant limitations on his own rights. To the extent that Newdow believes his own rights as a parent or the interests of his child are being harmed, the pending state custody proceedings provide an appropriate forum for those claims. By the same token, a federal court could not enter relief in this case without disrupting the state court's division of decisionmaking authority and control between the two parents. Indeed, disputes over Newdow's conduct of the present litigation and its impact on the child's well-being have already surfaced as part of the child custody proceedings. He specifically cites as error the family court's assessment of (i) the harm to his child of "being inculcated with religious dogma in the public schools," and (ii) the benefit of ensuring that the child does not view atheists as "outsider[s]." He then argues that the "Pledge of Allegiance litigation" is but one example of "arbitrary risk analyses" made by the family court that should be overturned. In short,

Rooker-Feldman bars this action because it represents Newdow's effort to obtain from the federal courts a measure of control over his child's upbringing that the state court has withheld and the state appeals court is currently reviewing.

II. PETITIONERS' POLICY OF LEADING WILLING ELEMENTARY SCHOOL STUDENTS IN THE DAILY RECITATION OF THE PLEDGE OF ALLEGIANCE IS CONSISTENT WITH THE ESTABLISHMENT CLAUSE

A. Religious Faith Has Played A Defining Role In The History Of The United States

1. Religious beliefs inspired settlement of the colonies and influenced the formation of the government

"Religion has been closely identified with our history and government." Many of the Country's earliest European settlers came to these shores seeking a haven from religious persecution and a home where their faith could flourish. In 1620, before embarking for America, the Pilgrims signed the Mayflower Compact in which they announced that their voyage was undertaken "for the Glory of God." Settlers established many of the original thirteen colonies, including Massachusetts, Rhode Island, Connecticut, Pennsylvania, Delaware, and Maryland, for the specific purpose of securing religious liberty for their inhabitants. The Constitutions or Declarations of Rights of almost all of the original States expressly guaranteed the free exercise of religion. It thus was no surprise that the very first rights enshrined in the Bill of Rights included the free exercise of religion and protection against federal laws respecting an establishment of religion.

The Framers' deep-seated faith also laid the philosophical groundwork for the unique governmental structure they adopted. The Framers, "in perhaps their most important contribution, conceived of a Federal Government directly responsible to the people and chosen directly by the people." In the Framers' view, government was instituted by individuals for the purpose of protecting and cultivating the exercise of their inalienable rights. Central to that political order was the Framers' conception of the individual as the source (rather than the object) of governmental power. That view of the political sovereignty of the individual, in turn, was a direct outgrowth of their conviction that each individual was entitled to certain fundamental rights, as most famously expressed in the Declaration of Independence: "We hold these truths to be self-evident, that all men are created equal, that they are endowed by their Creator with certain unalienable Rights, that among these are Life, Liberty and the pursuit of Happiness." Indeed, "the fact that the Founding Fathers believed devotedly that there was a God and that the unalienable rights of man were rooted in Him is clearly evidenced in their writings, from the Mayflower Compact to the Constitution itself."

Indeed, religious faith was so central to the formation and organization of the Republic as to cause Alexis de Tocqueville to remark that "I do not know if all Americans have faith in their religion-for who can read to the bottom of hearts?-but I am sure that they believe it necessary to the maintenance of republican institutions."

2. The Framers considered official acknowledgments of religion's role in the formation of the Nation to be appropriate

Many Framers attributed the survival and success of the foundling Nation to the providential hand of God. The Continental Congress itself announced to the nation in 1778 that the Nation's successes in the Revolutionary War had been "so peculiarly marked, almost by direct interposition of Providence, that not to feel and acknowledge his protection would be the height of impious ingratitude." Likewise, in his first inaugural address, President Washington proclaimed that "no people can be bound to acknowledge and adore the Invisible Hand which conducts the affairs of men more than those of the United States," because "every step by which they have advanced to the character of an independent nation seems to have been distinguished by some token of providential agency."

Against that backdrop, from the Nation's earliest days, the Framers considered references to God in official documents and official acknowledgments of the role of religion in the history and public life of the Country to be consistent with the principles of religious autonomy embodied in the First Amendment. Indeed,

two documents that this Court has looked to in its Establishment Clause cases—James Madison's *Memorial and Remonstrance
Against Religious Assessments* (1785), and Thomas Jefferson's *Bill
for Establishing Religious Freedom* (1779)—repeatedly acknowledge the Creator. The Constitution itself refers to the "Year of our
Lord" and excepts Sundays from the ten-day period for exercise of
the presidential veto.

The First Congress—the same Congress that drafted the Establishment Clause—adopted a policy of selecting a paid chaplain to
open each session of Congress with prayer. That same Congress,
the day after the Establishment Clause was proposed, also urged
President Washington "to proclaim 'a day of public thanksgiving
and prayer, to be observed by acknowledging with grateful hearts
the many and signal favours of Almighty God.'" President Washington responded by proclaiming November 26, 1789, a day of thanksgiving to "offer our prayers and supplications to the Great Lord
and Ruler of Nations, and beseech Him to pardon our national and
other transgressions." President Washington also included a reference to God in his first inaugural address: "It would be peculiarly
improper to omit in this first official act my fervent supplications
to that Almighty Being who rules over the universe, who presides
in the council of nations, and whose providential aids can supply
every human defect, that His benediction may consecrate to the
liberties and happiness of the people of the United States a Government instituted by themselves for these essential purposes."

Later generations have followed suit. Since the time of Chief
Justice Marshall, this Court has opened its sessions with "God
save the United States and this Honorable Court." President Abra-
ham Lincoln referred to a "Nation under God" in the historic Gettysburg Address (1863): "That we here highly resolve that these
dead shall not have died in vain; that this Nation, under God, shall
have a new birth of freedom, and that government of the people,
by the people, for the people shall not perish from the earth."
Every President that has delivered an inaugural address has
referred to God or a Higher Power, and every President, except
Thomas Jefferson, has declared a Thanksgiving Day holiday. In

1865, Congress authorized the inscription of "In God we trust" on United States coins. In 1931, Congress adopted as the National Anthem "The Star-Spangled Banner," the fourth verse of which reads: "Blest with victory and peace, may the heav'n rescued land Praise the Pow'r that hath made and preserved us a nation! Then conquer we must, when our cause it is just, And this be our motto "'In God is our Trust.'" In 1956, Congress passed legislation to make "In God we trust" the National Motto, and provided that it be inscribed on all United States currency, above the main door of the Senate, and behind the Chair of the Speaker of the House of Representatives. The Constitutions of all 50 States, moreover, include express references to God. There thus "is an unbroken history of official acknowledgment by all three branches of government," as well as the States, "of the role of religion in American life from at least 1789."

B. The Establishment Clause Permits Official Acknowledgment Of The Nation's Religious Heritage And Character

That uninterrupted pattern of official acknowledgment of the role that religion has played in the foundation of the Country, the formation of its governmental institutions, and the cultural heritage of its people, counsels strongly against construing the Establishment Clause to forbid such practices. "If a thing has been practised for two hundred years by common consent, it will need a strong case for the Fourteenth Amendment to affect it." In fact, this Court's Establishment Clause cases have stated time and again that such official acknowledgments of the Nation's religious history and enduring religious character pass constitutional muster.

At its core, the Establishment Clause forbids "sponsorship, financial support, and active involvement of the sovereign in religious activity." Beyond that, the Court has long refused to construe the Establishment Clause in a manner that "presses the concept of separation of Church and State to extremes" and that thus would condemn as unconstitutional the "references to the Almighty that run through our laws, our public rituals, and our ceremonies." That is because "the purpose" of the Establishment Clause "was to state an objective, not to write a statute." That objective was not to "sweep away all government recognition and acknowledgment of the role of religion in the lives of our citizens," or to compel the type of official disregard of or stilted indifference to the Nation's religious heritage and enduring religious character that the Ninth Circuit endorsed. "It is far too late in the day to impose that crabbed reading of the Clause on the country."

Indeed, this Court itself has "asserted pointedly" on five different occasions that "[w]e are a religious people whose institutions presuppose a Supreme Being." The Establishment Clause thus does not deny the Judicial Branch the ability to acknowledge officially both the religious character of the people of the United States and the pivotal role that religion has played in developing the Nation's governmental institutions.

Neither does it compel the Executive and Legislative Branches to ignore that tradition. In *Marsh v. Chambers, supra,* the Court upheld the historic practice of legislative prayer as "a tolerable acknowledgment of beliefs widely held among the people of this country." In so holding, the Court discussed numerous other examples of constitutionally permissible religious references in official life "that form 'part of the fabric of our society,'" such as "God save the United States and this Honorable Court." Similarly, in *Schempp,* the Court explained, in the course of invalidating laws requiring Bible-reading in public schools, that the Establishment Clause does not proscribe the numerous public references to God that appear in historical documents and ceremonial practices, such as oaths ending with "So help me God."

The opinions of individual Justices have further reinforced the proposition that acknowledgments of the Nation's religious heritage and character, are constitutionally permissible. Such official acknowledgments of religion are consistent with the Establishment Clause because they do not "establish a religion or religious faith, or tend to do so."

Indeed, even the stalwart separationist Thomas Jefferson found no constitutional impediment to such official acknowledgments of religion. Jefferson, along with Benjamin Franklin, proposed, in a "transparent allegory for America's ordeal," that the

Great Seal of the United States depict the scene of God intervening to save the people of Israel by drowning Pharaoh and his armies in the Red Sea, ringed by the motto, "Rebellion to Tyrants is Obedience to God." Thus, even Jefferson's view of the separation between church and State left ample room for official references to God and the Nation's religious heritage. That is because such official acknowledgments reflect the nationally defining and nationally unifying understanding of the Country's history and the role that religion has played in it. To insist that government must studiously ignore that one significant aspect of the Nation's history and character solely because of its religious basis—while freely acknowledging the other political, philosophical, and sociological influences on American history—would transform the Establishment Clause from a principle of neutrality into a mandate that religion be shunned. But the First Amendment prohibits only the "establishment" of religion; it does not command complete estrangement.

C. The Pledge Of Allegiance, With Its Reference To A Nation "Under God," Is A Constitutionally Permissible Acknowledgment Of The Nation's Religious History And Character

For four decades, opinions of this Court and of individual Justices have spoken with unparalleled unanimity in affirming the constitutionality of the Pledge of Allegiance, characterizing its reference to God as a permissible acknowledgment of the Nation's religious heritage and character. That settled understanding has informed the Court's Establishment Clause jurisprudence and is entitled to respect.

In *Lynch v. Donnelly*, the Court held that the Establishment Clause permits a city to include a nativity scene as part of its Christmas display. The Court reasoned that the creche permissibly "depicts the historical origins of this traditional event long recognized as a National Holiday," and noted that similar "examples of reference to our religious heritage are found," among other places, "in the language 'One nation under God,' as part of the Pledge of Allegiance to the American flag," which "is recited by many thousands of public school children—and adults—every year." The words "under God" in the Pledge, the Court explained, are an "acknowledgment of our religious heritage" similar to the "official references to the value and invocation of Divine guidance in deliberations and pronouncements of the Founding Fathers" that are "replete" in our nation's history.

Likewise, in *County of Allegheny*, the Court sustained the inclusion of a Menorah as part of a holiday display, but invalidated the isolated display of a creche at a county courthouse. In so holding, the Court reaffirmed *Lynch*'s approval of the reference to God in the Pledge, noting that all the Justices in *Lynch* viewed the Pledge as "consistent with the proposition that government may not communicate an endorsement of religious belief." The Court then used the Pledge and the general holiday display approved in *Lynch* as benchmarks for what the Establishment Clause permits, and concluded that the display of the creche by itself was unconstitutional because, unlike the Pledge, it gave "praise to God in sectarian Christian terms."

The individual opinions of nine Justices have likewise specifically endorsed the constitutionality of the Pledge, finding it consistent with the Establishment Clause. As those opinions illustrate, the reference to God in the Pledge is not reasonably and objectively understood as endorsing or coercing individuals into silent assent to any particular religious doctrine. Rather, the Pledge is "consistent with the proposition that government may not communicate an endorsement of religious belief," because the reference to God acknowledges the undeniable historical facts that the Nation was founded by individuals who believed in God, that the Constitution's protection of individual rights and autonomy reflects those religious convictions, and that the Nation continues as a matter of demographic and cultural fact to be "a religious people whose institutions presuppose a Supreme Being."

While none of those cases involved direct challenges to the Pledge, the court of appeals fundamentally erred in disregarding this Court's consistent statements over nearly three decades validating the Pledge. That is because, "when an opinion issues for the Court, it is not only the result but also those portions of the opinion necessary to that result by which we are bound." The Court's analysis of the Pledge and similar official acknowledgments of religion in *Lynch* and *County of Allegheny* were not "mere *obiter dicta*" that the court of appeals was free to disregard. They were components of the "well-established rationale upon which the Court based the results of its earlier decisions." Those references articulated the constitutional baseline for permissible official acknowledgments of religion under the Establishment Clause against which the governmental practices at issue in each of those cases were then measured. Indeed, for decades, the Court and individual Justices "have grounded their decisions in the oft-repeated understanding," that the Pledge of Allegiance, and similar references, are constitutional.

D. The Pledge Of Allegiance, With Its Reference To God, May Be Recited In Public School Classrooms

The Establishment Clause inquiry is sensitive to context, and the Court "has been particularly vigilant in monitoring compliance with the Establishment Clause in public elementary and secondary schools," Nevertheless, this Court's Establishment Clause precedent does not require public schools to expunge any and all references to God and religion from the classroom. Rather, in *Engel v. Vitale*, in the course of invalidating official school prayers, the Court took pains to stress:

> There is of course nothing in the decision reached here that is inconsistent with the fact that school children and others are officially encouraged to express love for our country by reciting historical documents such as the Declaration of Independence which contain references to the Deity or by singing officially espoused anthems which include the composer's professions of faith in a Supreme Being, or with the fact that there are many manifestations in our public life of belief in God. Such patriotic or ceremonial occasions bear no true resemblance to the unquestioned religious exercise [official prayer] that the State of New York has sponsored in this instance.

In determining whether recitation of the Pledge in public school classrooms comports with the Establishment Clause, the

Court "asks whether the government acted with the purpose of advancing or inhibiting religion" and whether recitation of the Pledge has the "'effect' of advancing or inhibiting religion." Recitation of the Pledge in petitioners' public school classrooms has no such impermissible purpose or effect.

1. The purpose of reciting the Pledge is to promote patriotism and national unity

A statute or rule runs afoul of the Establishment Clause's purpose inquiry only if it is "entirely motivated by a purpose to advance religion." Petitioners adopted their policy of having teachers lead willing students in the daily recitation of the Pledge for the avowed purpose of promoting patriotism, not advancing religion. The single-sentence policy, which directs that "each elementary school class recite the pledge of allegiance to the flag once each day," falls right below the heading "Patriotic Observances." Petitioners adopted the policy, moreover, to comply with California law, which requires that each public elementary school "conduct appropriate patriotic exercises" at the beginning of the school day. The law provides that "the giving of the Pledge of Allegiance to the Flag of the United States of America shall satisfy the requirements of this section." The promotion of patriotism and instillation of "a broad but common ground" of shared values in the children attending public schools, is a "clearly secular purpose."

"Newdow concedes the school district had the secular purpose of fostering patriotism in enacting the policy," and the court of appeals did not find otherwise. Newdow's complaint, however, emphasizes certain statements from the 1954 legislative history accompanying Congress's amendment of the Pledge to include the phrase "under God." That analysis is wrong as a matter of both fact and law.

First, as a matter of fact, the 1954 amendment adding the phrase "under God" to the Pledge did not have the single-minded purpose of advancing religion that Newdow portrays. The Committee Reports viewed the amendment as a permissible acknowledgment that, "from the time of our earliest history our peoples and our institutions have reflected the traditional concept that our

Nation was founded on a fundamental belief in God." Both Reports traced the numerous references to God in historical documents central to the founding and preservation of the United States, from the Mayflower Compact to the Declaration of Independence to President Lincoln's Gettysburg Address, with the latter having employed the same reference to a "Nation under God."

The Reports further identified a political purpose for the amendment—it would highlight a foundational difference between the United States and Communist nations: "Our American Government is founded on the concept of the individuality and the dignity of the human being" and "underlying this concept is the belief that the human person is important because he was created by God and endowed by Him with certain inalienable rights which no civil authority may usurp." Congress thus added "under God" to highlight the Framers' political philosophy concerning the sovereignty of the individual—a philosophy with roots in 1954, as in 1787, in religious belief-to serve the political end of textually rejecting the "communist" philosophy "with its attendant subservience of the individual."

The House Report further underscored the vital role the amended Pledge would play in educating children about the foundational values underlying the American system of government. Through "daily recitation of the pledge in school," "the children of our land will be daily impressed with a true understanding of our way of life and its origins," so that "as they grow and advance in this understanding, they will assume the responsibilities of self-government equipped to carry on the traditions that have been given to us."

No doubt some Members of Congress might have been motivated, in part, to amend the Pledge because of their religious beliefs. But "what motivates one legislator to make a speech about a statute is not necessarily what motivates scores of others to enact it." In any event, the Establishment Clause focuses on "the legislative purpose of the statute, not the possibly religious motives of the legislators who enacted the law."

Second, as a matter of law, because Newdow's suit challenges contemporary practices—petitioners' Pledge—recitation policy and the federal government's continued use of and refusal to amend the Pledge, the purpose inquiry focuses on petitioners' current policy of reciting the Pledge and the federal government's modern-day purpose for retaining it intact. In *McGowan*, the Court acknowledged that Sunday closing laws originally "were motivated by religious forces," but nevertheless sustained those laws against Establishment Clause challenge because modern-day retention of the laws advanced secular purposes, The Court reasoned that, to proscribe laws that advanced valid secular goals "solely" because they "had their genesis in religion would give a constitutional interpretation of hostility to the public welfare rather than one of mere separation of church and State."

2. The Pledge has the valid secular effect of promoting patriotism and national unity

Petitioners' policy of leading willing students in recitation of the Pledge of Allegiance serves the secular values of promoting national unity, patriotism, and an appreciation for the values that define the Nation. "National unity as an end which officials may foster by persuasion and example is not in question."

The "relevant question" in analyzing whether recitation of the Pledge also has the effect of endorsing religion is "whether an objective observer, acquainted with the text, legislative history, and implementation of the policy, would perceive it as a state endorsement of prayer" or religion "in public schools." There is no reasonable basis for perceiving such religious endorsement in the Pledge. The Pledge is not a "profession of a religious belief," but a statement of allegiance and loyalty to the Flag of the United States, as a representative of the Republic itself. By its common understanding, a "pledge" of "allegiance" is a "promise or agreement" of "devotion or loyalty" "owed by a subject or citizen to his sovereign or government."

The court of appeals, however, trained its focus on the two-word phrase "under God" and concluded that uttering that phrase amounted to "swearing allegiance to monotheism." That conclusion is wrong in three fundamental respects.

a. The Pledge must be considered as a whole

In divorcing the phrase "under God" from its larger context, the court of appeals "plainly erred." In *Lynch*, this Court stressed that the Establishment Clause analysis looks at religious symbols and references in their broader setting, rather than "focusing almost exclusively on the" religious symbol alone. The *Lynch* Court accordingly did not ask whether the government's display of a crèche—a clearly sectarian symbol—was permissible. The Court analyzed whether the overall message conveyed by a display that included both that religious and other secular symbols of the holiday season conveyed a message of endorsement, and concluded that it did not.

Likewise, in *County of Allegheny*, the Court analyzed and upheld the "combined display" during the winter holiday season of a Christmas tree, Liberty sign, and Menorah. The Court thus looked at the content of the display as a whole, rather than focusing on the presence of the Menorah and the religious message that the Menorah would convey in isolation. That Congress added the phrase "under God" to a preexisting Pledge does not change this analysis. The city government in *County of Allegheny* had likewise added the Menorah, after the fact, to a preexisting holiday display. Yet this Court focused its constitutional analysis on the display as a whole, rather than scrutinizing the message conveyed by each component as it was added *seriatim*.

Read as a whole, the Pledge is much more than an isolated reference to God. Congress did not enact a pledge to a religious symbol, a pledge to God, or a pledge of "belief in God." Individuals pledge allegiance to "the Flag of the United States of America," and "to the Republic for which it stands." The remainder of the Pledge is descriptive, not "normative"—delineating the culture and character of that Republic as a unified Country, composed of individual States yet indivisible as a Nation, established for the purposes of promoting liberty and justice for all, and founded by individuals whose belief in God gave rise to the governmental institutions and political order they adopted and continues to inspire the quest for "liberty and justice" for each individual. The Pledge's reference to a "Nation under God," in short, is a statement about the Nation's historical origins, its enduring political philosophy centered on the sovereignty of the individual, and its continuing demographic character—a statement that itself is simply one component of a larger, more comprehensive patriotic message.

b. Reciting the Pledge is not a religious exercise

The court of appeals' decision proceeds from the faulty premise that reciting the Pledge's acknowledgment of the Nation's religious heritage is tantamount to praying or Bible reading. The decisions of this Court and individual Justices outlined above, however, repeatedly admonish that not every reference to God amounts to an impermissible government-endorsed religious exercise, and they expressly refer to the Pledge and similar ceremonial references in contradistinction to formal religious exercises like prayer and Bible reading. Prayer is a medium for calling upon, invoking, or speaking to God or a divine entity, conveying reverence, thankfulness, or praise to God, and seeking the Deity's blessings, favor, assistance, or forgiveness. Prayer, in short, is an interactive relationship between the person and a Higher Being.

This Court's decisions have long understood the difference between a prayer and a patriotic or ceremonial reference to God. In *Engel*, the Court struck down the New York public school system's practice of reciting a nondenominational Regents prayer because that formal "invocation of God's blessings" was a religious activity, "a solemn avowal of divine faith and supplication for the blessings of the Almighty." The Court contrasted the Regents prayer with the "recitation of historical documents such as the Declaration of Independence which contain references to the Deity," concluding that "such patriotic or ceremonial occasions bear no true resemblance to the unquestioned religious exercise that the State of New York has sponsored." Thus, while the official prayer transgressed the boundary between church and state, no Justice questioned New York's practice of preceding the prayer with recitation of the Pledge.

Likewise, in the course of striking down school prayer in *Schempp*, the Court noted, without a hint of disapproval, that the students also recited the Pledge of Allegiance immediately after the invalidated prayer. That is because, as the concurrence explained, "daily recitation of the Pledge of Allegiance serves the solely secular purposes of the devotional activities without jeopardizing either the religious liberties of any members of the community or the proper degree of separation between the spheres of religion and government." "The reference to divinity in the revised pledge of allegiance," the concurrence continued, "may merely recognize the historical fact that our Nation was believed to have been founded 'under God.'" Its recitation thus is "no more of a religious exercise than the reading aloud of Lincoln's Gettysburg Address, which contains an allusion to the same historical fact."

As those cases recognize, describing the Republic as a Nation "under God" is not the functional equivalent of prayer. No communication with or call upon the Divine is attempted. The phrase is not addressed to God or a call for His presence, guidance, or intervention. Nor can it plausibly be argued that reciting the Pledge is comparable to reading sacred text, like the Bible, or engaging in an act of religious worship. The phrase "Nation under God" has no such established religious usage as a matter of history, culture, or practice.

The court of appeals attempted to distinguish the Pledge from other references to God in public life on the ground that the Pledge is "a performative statement," rather than simply "a reflection of [an] author's profession of faith." It is true that the Pledge is a "declaration of a belief," but the belief declared is not monotheism; it is a belief in allegiance and loyalty to the United States Flag and the Republic that it represents. That's a politically performative statement, not a religious one. A reasonable observer, reading the text of the Pledge as a whole, cognizant of its purpose, and familiar with (even if not personally subscribing to) the Nation's religious heritage, would understand that the reference to God is not an approbation of monotheism, but a patriotic and

unifying acknowledgment of the role of religious faith in form-
ing and defining the unique political and social character of the
Nation.

Beyond that, the attempted distinction of the Pledge from
other permissible acknowledgments of religion in public life
makes no sense. With respect to "impressionable young schoolchildren," there simply is no coherent or discernible "performative" difference between having them say the Pledge, rather than
sing the "officially espoused" National Anthem Trust."), or having them memorize and recite the National Motto ("In God we
trust"), the Declaration of Independence ("We hold these truths
to be self-evident, that all men are endowed by their Creator with
certain unalienable Rights."), or the Gettysburg Address. Indeed,
the court of appeals' approach leads to the curious conclusion
that the recitation of Bible passages or long-established prayers
in public schools, where students "merely repeat the words of
an historical document," would trench less upon Establishment
Clause principles than the Pledge's two-word acknowledgment of
the Nation's religious heritage.

c. The Pledge recital policy is not coercive

The court of appeals ultimately rested its determination that
recital of the Pledge by willing students violates the Establishment
Clause on the ground that the practice has a "coercive effect,"
because it forces students to choose between "participating in an
exercise with religious content or protesting." That test has no
basis in Establishment Clause jurisprudence and is unworkable in
the public school environment.

First, the court of appeals' "coercion" analysis fails because
it is based on the false premise that reciting the Pledge is a
religious exercise. The test for unconstitutional coercion is not
whether some aspect of the public school curriculum has "religious content", but whether the government itself has become
pervasively involved in or effectively coerced a religious exercise. In *Lee*—the case on which the court of appeals placed
critical reliance—the Court held that the Establishment Clause
proscribes prayer at secondary school graduations. What made

those prayers unconstitutionally coercive, however, was their character as a pure "religious exercise" and the government's "pervasive" involvement in institutionalizing the prayer, to the point of making it a "state-sponsored and state-directed religious exercise." Coercion thus arose because (1) the exercise was so profoundly religious that even quiet acquiescence in the practice would exact a toll on conscience, and (2) the force with which the government endorsed the religious exercise sent a signal that dissent would put the individual at odds not just with peers, but with school officials as well.

Those concerns have little relevance here. Reciting the Pledge or listening to others recite it is a patriotic exercise. It is not a religious exercise at all, let alone a core component of worship like prayer. Nor has the government, by simply acknowledging the Nation's religious heritage, so intruded itself into religious matters as to pressure or intimidate schoolchildren into violating the demands of conscience. Classroom "exposure to something does not constitute teaching, indoctrination, opposition or promotion of any particular value or religion." Government does not make "religion relevant to standing in the political community simply because a particular viewer of a display might feel uncomfortable." Whatever "incidental" benefit might befall religion from government's acknowledgment of the Nation's religious heritage is not of constitutional moment. The Establishment Clause is not violated just because a governmental practice "happens to coincide or harmonize with the tenets of some or all religions."

Second, any analysis of the coercive effect of voluntary recital of the Pledge must take into account this Court's repeated assurances that the "many manifestations in our public life of belief in God," far from violating the Constitution, have become "part of the fabric of our society," including in public school classrooms. In particular, over the last half century, the text of the Pledge of Allegiance, with its reference to God, "has become embedded" in the American consciousness and "become part of our national culture." Public familiarity with the Pledge's use as a patriotic exercise and a solemnizing ceremony for public events ensures both that the reasonable observer, familiar with the context and historic use of the Pledge, will not perceive governmental endorsement of religion at the mere utterance of the phrase "under God," and that petitioners' Pledge policy has no more coercive effect than the use of currency that bears the National Motto "In God we trust." Moreover, the text of the Pledge has become so engrained in the national psyche that declaring it unconstitutional would have its own Establishment Clause costs, as a generation of school children would struggle to unlearn the Pledge they have recited for years and, under the direction of public school teachers, would labor to banish the reference to God from their memory. That would bespeak a level of hostility to religion that is antithetical to the very purpose of the Establishment Clause.

Finally, the public schools cannot perform their job of educating the next generation of citizens and teaching those values that are "essential to a democratic society," if they have to expunge all pedagogical "exercises with religious content," because they would perforce compel students to choose "between participating or protesting." The Declaration of Independence has "religious content"; the Gettysburg Address has "religious content"; many famous works of art, literature, and music have "religious content." To those whose faith demands a purely domestic role for women or opposes racial integration, history lessons about the women's suffrage and civil rights movements have "religious content." "Many political issues have theological roots." The reality is that the Nation's history and culture have religious content, and "if we are to eliminate everything that is objectionable to any of these warring sects or inconsistent with any of their doctrines, we will leave public education in shreds."

Thus, public schools may teach not just that the Pilgrims came to this country, but also why they came. They may teach not just that the Framers conceived of a governmental system in which power and inalienable rights resided in the individual, but also why they thought that way. They may teach not just that abolitionists opposed slavery, but also why they did. The reference to a "Nation under God" in the Pledge of Allegiance is an official and patriotic acknowledgment of what all students—Jewish, Christian, Muslim, or atheist—may properly be taught in the public schools. Recitation of the Pledge by willing students thus comports with the Establishment Clause.

CONCLUSION

The judgment of the court of appeals should be vacated with directions to dismiss the complaint for lack of standing or lack of jurisdiction. In the alternative, the judgment of the court of appeals should be reversed.[1]

Example 2

This excerpt deals with the Partial-Birth Abortion Ban Act.

QUESTION PRESENTED

The Partial-Birth Abortion Ban Act of 2003 (the Act) prohibits a physician from knowingly performing a "partial-birth abortion" (as defined in the statute) in or affecting interstate commerce. The Act contains an exception for cases in which the abortion is necessary to preserve the life of the mother, but no corresponding exception for the health of the mother. Congress, however, made extensive factual findings, including a finding that "partial-birth abortion is never medically indicated to preserve the health of the mother." The question presented is as follows:

Whether, notwithstanding Congress's determination that a health exception was unnecessary to preserve the health of the mother, the Partial-Birth Abortion Ban Act of 2003 is invalid because it lacks a health exception or is otherwise un constitutional on its face.

STATEMENT

This case concerns the constitutionality of the federal Partial-Birth Abortion Ban Act of 2003. That Act prohibits a physician from knowingly performing a partial-birth abortion—a particular abortion procedure that Congress found to be "gruesome and inhumane" and to "blur the line between abortion and infanticide in the killing of a partially-born child just inches from birth." Congress passed the Act after conducting nine years of hearings and debates, after carefully considering this Court's precedents, and after making extensive findings based on the substantial testimony that it had received. Because Congress found, *inter alia*, that partial-birth abortion is "never medically indicated to preserve the health of the mother," it did not adopt a statutory exception for cases in which the abortion is necessary to preserve the mother's health. The court of appeals held that, under this Court's decision in *Stenberg v. Carhart*, the statute was facially invalid because it lacked a health exception, and permanently enjoined the Act's enforcement. That decision should be reversed by this Court.

1. The phrase "partial-birth abortion" refers to a particularly gruesome, late-term abortion procedure known as dilation and extraction (D&X) or intact dilation and evacuation (intact D&E). In that procedure, a physician partially delivers the fetus intact and then intentionally kills it, typically by puncturing its skull and vacuuming out its brain. "The vast majority of babies killed during such partial-birth abortions are alive until the end of the procedure" and "will fully experience the pain associated with piercing his or her skull and sucking out his or her brain." The D&X procedure differs from a more frequently used late-term abortion procedure known as standard dilation and evacuation (D&E), in which the physician typically dismembers the fetus while most of the fetus is still inside the womb. A consensus exists that "D&X is distinct from D&E and is a more serious concern for medical ethics and the morality of the larger society." Indeed, Congress has found that "the disturbing similarity of partial-birth abortion to the killing of a newborn infant promotes a complete disregard for infant human life," and that partial-birth abortion "blurs the line between abortion and infanticide."

2. Congress, like the majority of the States, has enacted legislation banning partial-birth abortions. It first began considering proposals to prohibit partial-birth abortion in 1995. In the following years, Congress held numerous hearings and received expert testimony that partial-birth abortions were not necessary to preserve the health of the mother in any

circumstances; claims that partial-birth abortions were safer than standard D&E abortions were either incorrect or speculative; and, indeed, partial-birth abortions posed safety risks that D&E abortions did not. In 1996 and 1997, Congress passed bills that would have prohibited partial-birth abortion, but the President vetoed them. In addition, between 1992 and 2000, some 30 States enacted prohibitions on partial-birth abortion of their own.

3. In 2000, this Court invalidated a Nebraska statute that banned "partial birth abortion" (as defined in that statute) unless the procedure was necessary to preserve the life of the mother. The Court held that the Nebraska statute was invalid for two independent reasons. First, the Court held that the statute was facially invalid because it lacked an exception for cases implicating the health of the mother. Second, the Court held that the statute was invalid because it defined "partial birth abortion" in such a way as to reach not only D&X abortions, but also standard D&E abortions, and thereby imposed an "undue burden" on a woman's access to an abortion.

4. In 2003, after more hearings and debate and by wide margins in both Houses, Congress passed, and the President signed, the Partial-Birth Abortion Ban Act of 2003 (the Act). The Act was predicated on numerous findings concerning the nature of partial-birth abortions and was expressly designed to avoid the deficiencies identified by this Court in the Nebraska statute at issue in *Stenberg*.

First, based on "the testimony received during extensive legislative hearings during the 104th, 105th, 107th, and 108th Congresses," the Act contains detailed factual findings with respect to the medical necessity of partial-birth abortion. Congress found, *inter alia*, that "partial-birth abortion poses serious risks to the health of a woman undergoing the procedure," that "there is no credible medical evidence that partial-birth abortions are safe or are safer than other abortion procedures," and that "the physician credited with developing the partial-birth abortion procedure has testified that he has never encountered a situation where a partial-birth abortion was medically necessary to achieve the desired outcome." Based on those and other findings, Congress ultimately found that "partial-birth abortion is never medically indicated to preserve the health of the mother." In the Act's operative provisions, therefore, Congress did not include an express statutory exception for cases in which the abortion is necessary to preserve the mother's health.

Second, the Act contains the following, more specific definition of "partial-birth abortion":

> an abortion in which the person performing the abortion (A) deliberately and intentionally vaginally delivers a living fetus until, in the case of a head-first presentation, the entire fetal head is outside the body of the mother, or, in the case of breech presentation, any part of the fetal trunk past the navel is outside the body of the mother, for the purpose of performing an overt act that the person knows will kill the partially delivered living fetus; and (B) performs the overt act, other than completion of delivery, that kills the partially delivered living fetus.

Act § 3, 117 Stat. 1206-1207 (18 U.S.C. 1531(b)(1) (Supp. III 2003)).

That definition is tailored to exclude the more common standard D&E abortion procedure that this Court found was reached by the Nebraska statute invalidated in *Stenberg*. The Act imposes criminal and civil sanctions only on a physician who "knowingly" performs a partial-birth abortion.

5. Respondents, four physicians who perform late-term abortions, brought suit against the Attorney General, seeking a permanent injunction against enforcement of the Act. After a bench trial, the district court granted judgment to respondents, and enjoined the Attorney General from enforcing the Act against respondents "in all of its applications when the fetus is not viable or when there is a doubt about the viability of the fetus in the appropriate medical judgment of the doctor performing the abortion."

The district court first held that the Act was invalid because it lacked a health exception. The court refused to defer to Congress's findings, including its ultimate finding that partial- birth abortion was never medically indicated to preserve the health of the mother. The court recognized that, under *Turner Broadcasting System, Inc. v. FCC*, Congress's findings were entitled to "binding deference" as long as the findings were reasonable and supported by substantial evidence. However, the court stated that, in its view, the "case-deciding question" was whether "there was substantial evidence from which a reasonable person could conclude that there is no substantial medical authority supporting the proposition that banning 'partial-birth abortions' could endanger women's health." Under that standard, the court concluded, Congress's findings were not entitled to deference.

The district court also held that the Act was invalid because it reached certain standard D&E abortions, as well as D&X abortions. The court, however, ultimately rejected respondents' contention that the Act was unconstitutionally vague.

6. The court of appeals affirmed, holding that the Act was facially invalid because it lacked a health exception. The court first determined that the appropriate standard for reviewing respondents' facial challenge was not the "no set of circumstances" standard articulated in *United States v. Salerno*, but rather "the test from *Stenberg*." The court then reasoned that *Stenberg* required a health exception when "'substantial medical authority' supports the medical necessity of the regulated procedure in some instances." "In effect," the court continued, "we believe when a lack of consensus exists in the medical community, the Constitution requires legislatures to err on the side of protecting women's health by including a health exception."

The court of appeals, like the district court, refused to defer to Congress's factual findings concerning the medical necessity of partial-birth abortion. Unlike the district court, however, the court of appeals ultimately concluded that "the government's argument regarding *Turner* deference is irrelevant to the case at hand." The court explained that, while "whether a partial-birth abortion is medically necessary in a given instance would be a question of fact," "whether the record in a particular lawsuit reflects the existence of 'substantial medical authority' supporting the medical necessity of such procedures is a question that is different in kind." The court reasoned that "*Stenberg* created a standard in which the ultimate factual conclusion is irrelevant," and concluded that, "under the 'substantial medical authority' standard, our review of the record is effectively limited to determining whether substantial evidence exists to support the medical necessity of partial-birth abortions without regard to the factual conclusions drawn from the record by the lower court (or, in this case, Congress)."

The court of appeals then asserted that the medical necessity of a particular abortion procedure was a question of "legislative" fact. The court observed that, in *Stenberg*, this Court had determined that "substantial medical authority" supported the need for a health exception in a statute regulating partial-birth abortion. The court asserted that "neither we, nor Congress, are free to disagree with the Supreme Court's determination because the Court's conclusions are final on matters of constitutional law." Although the court conceded that *Stenberg* did not stand for the proposition that "legislatures are forever constitutionally barred from enacting partial-birth abortion bans," it asserted that legislatures could enact such bans only if, "at some point (either through an advance in knowledge or the development of new techniques, for example), the procedures prohibited by the Act will be rendered obsolete." While the court recognized that "there is some evidence in the present record indicating each of the advantages discussed in *Stenberg* are incorrect and the banned procedures are never medically necessary," it held that the government had failed to "demonstrate that relevant evidentiary circumstances (such as the presence of a newfound medical consensus or medical studies) have in fact changed over time."

7. Since the court of appeals' decision, two other courts of appeals have passed on the constitutionality of the Act.

a. The Ninth Circuit held that the Act was facially invalid because it lacked a health exception, covered certain D&E abortions, and was unconstitutionally vague. Based on that holding, the Ninth Circuit concluded that it could not craft a narrower injunction under the approach outlined in *Ayotte v. Planned Parenthood of Northern New England*, and therefore permanently enjoined enforcement of the Act in its entirety.

b.   A divided Second Circuit panel held that the Act was facially invalid because it lacked a health exception. Chief Judge Walker concurred. He stated that it was his "duty to follow this Court's precedent in *Stenberg*," but that in his view *Stenberg* was "flawed" in "at least three respects." First, *Stenberg* "equates the denial of a potential health benefit (in the eyes of some doctors) with the imposition of a health risk and, in the process, promotes marginal safety above all other values." Second, *Stenberg* "endorses a rule that permits the lower courts to hold a statute facially invalid upon a speculative showing of harm." Third, *Stenberg* "establishes an evidentiary standard that all but removes the legislature from the field of abortion policy." Judge Straub dissented. He explained that *Stenberg* is distinguishable in important respects and concluded that the "fundamental error" with the majority's approach was "to collapse the inquiry into whether a 'division of medical opinion' exists and thereby discard any role for congressional findings about the actual necessity of the procedure."

SUMMARY OF ARGUMENT

The court of appeals erred in invalidating the Partial-Birth Abortion Ban Act of 2003. Congress's decision to ban the particularly gruesome partial-birth abortion procedure advances vital state interests and does not impose an "undue burden" on a woman's access to an abortion. Indeed, far from placing a substantial obstacle in the path of any woman seeking an abortion, the Act simply eliminates a disfavored and rarely used late-term abortion procedure that, as Congress found, is medically unnecessary. No precedent of this Court requires the judicial invalidation of that legislative measure.

I.   The absence of a health exception to the Act's ban on a particular procedure does not impose an undue burden. Under this Court's precedents, the relevant inquiry in this context is whether a statute regulating an abortion procedure would create significant health risks, such that it would place a substantial obstacle in the path of a woman seeking an abortion, in a large fraction of its applications. The court of appeals erred by reading *Stenberg v. Carhart* as holding that the relevant inquiry was instead whether there is merely a division of medical opinion on whether the statute would create substantial health risks. Such a reading would delegate the authority over constitutional decision-making to a minority of medical professionals and put *Stenberg* into conflict with this Court's earlier decisions, including *Planned Parenthood of Southeastern Pennsylvania v. Casey*, which require a plaintiff to do more than merely demonstrate the existence of conflicting opinions about health risks in order to negate the government's compelling interests in proscribing or limiting an abortion procedure. There is no reason for this Court to construe *Stenberg* in a manner that would *sub silentio* override its prior precedents.

Viewed in the proper light, the Act readily passes muster. In the Act, Congress made numerous factual findings, culminating in the ultimate finding that partial-birth abortion is never medically indicated to preserve the health of the mother. Those findings are supported by substantial evidence and entitled to deference under the long-standing principle that Congress is better equipped than courts to make factual findings that inform the constitutionality of federal statutes, including findings about complex medical judgments. There is no justification to disregard that principle here, where Congress has made express statutory findings on an issue of medical judgment based on testimony and other evidence received in extensive legislative hearings. This Court's decision in *Stenberg* focused on the trial record and the district court's factual findings concerning the medical necessity of partial-birth abortion. It did not purport to foreclose Congress from subsequently making findings on the same issue, based on a more recent, and more complete, evidentiary record.

Even if the Court were to decline to defer to Congress's findings concerning the absence of any significant health risks, the evidence presented by respondents at trial at most suggests that partial-birth abortion may be marginally safer than more common abortion procedures in some narrow circumstances. Given the critical state interests in proscribing that procedure, that cannot be sufficient to demonstrate that a statute prohibiting partial-birth abortion imposes an undue burden on a woman's access to an abortion. The Act directly advances not only the government's compelling interest in protecting potential life, but also its specific, and equally compelling, interest in prohibiting a particular type of abortion procedure that bears a "disturbing similarity to the killing of a newborn infant." Indeed, one of the express purposes of the Act is to "draw a bright line that clearly distinguishes abortion and infanticide." In light of the relative strength of the government's interests, the Act is constitutional under the undue-burden standard. Any different understanding would be at odds with one of the central objectives of the joint opinion in *Casey*: i.e., to accommodate more fully the government's paramount interest in protecting potential human life.

This case is distinguishable from *Stenberg* in several important respects, and, as explained, under a proper reading of *Stenberg*, respondents' facial challenge to the constitutionality of the Act fails. To the extent that the Court concludes that *Stenberg* compels the conclusion that the Act is facially in valid, however, *Stenberg* should be overruled.

II. The Act readily passes muster under overbreadth and vagueness principles as well. Unlike the statute at issue in *Stenberg*, the Act does not reach standard D&E abortions, but instead is limited to abortions in which the physician delivers the fetus beyond a specified anatomical "landmark" and then performs a discrete "overt act" that kills the living fetus (and delivers the fetus with the purpose of performing that act). The Act therefore does not cover any abortion that does not qualify as a "partial-birth abortion" under any reasonable understanding of that concept. Nor is the Act void for vagueness. It provides ample notice of the conduct that it prohibits and contains no ambiguous terms or phrases. Moreover, because this case, unlike *Stenberg*, involves a federal statute, there is no obstacle to this Court's construing the statute to avoid any perceived overbreadth or vagueness difficulties.

III. Because the Act suffers from no constitutional defect, the Court need not fashion any remedy. If the Court nevertheless concludes that the Act is unconstitutional in any respect, it may be possible to craft narrower injunctive relief under *Ayotte v. Planned Parenthood of Northern New England*. Because that inquiry necessarily entails a statute-specific consideration of legislative intent, in light of an identified constitutional difficulty with the statute, it would be appropriate for the Court to leave that issue for remand, as it did in *Ayotte*. In any event, because the statute is in fact facially constitutional, no remedial question arises in this case, and the judgment below should be reversed.

ARGUMENT

THE PARTIAL-BIRTH ABORTION BAN ACT OF 2003 IS CONSTITUTIONAL ON ITS FACE

In *Planned Parenthood of Southeastern Pennsylvania v. Casey*, the controlling joint opinion surveyed the Court's abortion jurisprudence since *Roe v. Wade*, and concluded that the portion of *Roe* recognizing "the State's 'important and legitimate interest in potential life' has been given too little acknowledgment and implementation by the Court in its subsequent cases." Thus, while the joint opinion reaffirmed "the central holding of *Roe*," it abandoned *Roe*'s strict-scrutiny approach in favor of an "undue burden" standard that would provide a more "appropriate means of reconciling the State's interest with the woman's constitutionally protected liberty." Under that framework, an abortion regulation is constitutional unless it places a "substantial obstacle" in the way of a woman's access to an abortion.

Since *Casey*, Congress and some 30 States have passed laws banning partial-birth abortion—a gruesome and rarely used procedure that, as Congress found, legislatures have a "compelling interest in prohibiting," not only to promote the government's paramount interest in protecting human life, but also to "promote maternal health" and "draw a bright line that clearly distinguishes abortion and infanticide." In *Stenberg v. Carhart*, this Court held that a State's partial-birth abortion statute was unconstitutional under *Casey*'s undue-burden standard. The question in *Stenberg* divided even the Justices who jointly wrote the controlling opinion in *Casey*, with Justice Kennedy concluding that the majority was undervaluing "critical state interests" and thus ignoring the central lesson of *Casey*.

This case differs from *Stenberg* in critical respects. For example, this case involves an Act of Congress that is accompanied by extensive findings; the Act contains a more targeted definition of partial-birth abortion and, as a federal statute, can be construed by the Court to avoid difficulties; and this case reaches the Court on a different, and more extensive, trial record. Recognizing those differences, giving proper weight to Congress's findings, and acknowledging the government's compelling interests, should yield only one conclusion-that the Act is constitutional on its face.

I. THE ABSENCE OF A HEALTH EXCEPTION DOES NOT RENDER THE ACT FACIALLY INVALID

The court of appeals held that the Partial-Birth Abortion Ban Act of 2003 was facially invalid because it lacked a health exception. That holding was based on the fallacious premise that a statute regulating an abortion procedure must contain a health exception as long as there is a division of medical opinion on whether the statute would create substantial health risks. This Court's decisions, however, hold that such a statute is facially invalid only where it would create significant health risks, such that it would create an undue burden by imposing a substantial obstacle in the path of a woman seeking an abortion, in a large fraction of its applications. Viewed in the proper light, the Act readily survives scrutiny because the record—including Congress's considered findings, which are entitled to deference—overwhelmingly demonstrates that the partial-birth abortion procedure at issue is never medically indicated to preserve the health of the mother. Moreover, even if partial-birth abortion had marginal health benefits in some cases, that still would not be sufficient to overcome Congress's compelling interests in protecting potential human life, drawing a bright line between abortion and infanticide, and prohibiting a rarely used, late-term abortion procedure that is inhumane.

A. A Statute That Regulates Abortion, But Lacks A Health Exception, Is Not Facially Invalid Unless It Would Create Significant Health Risks, And Thereby Impose An Undue Burden, In A Large Fraction Of Its Applications

1. This Court has held that "a State may not restrict access to abortions that are necessary, in appropriate medical judgment, for preservation of the life or health of the mother." That proposition originates from the Court's decision in *Roe v. Wade*. After determining that a State's interest in potential life became compelling at the point of viability, the Court concluded that, "subsequent to viability, the State may, if it chooses, regulate, and even proscribe, abortion except where it is necessary, in appropriate medical judgment, for the preservation of the life or health of the mother."

In *Planned Parenthood of Southeastern Pennsylvania v. Casey*, the joint opinion concluded that regulations that imposed an "undue burden" on a woman's access to an abortion were unconstitutional, explaining that "an undue burden exists, and therefore a provision of law is invalid, if its purpose or effect is to place a substantial obstacle in the path of a woman seeking an abortion before the fetus attains viability." Applying that standard, the Court sustained all of the regulations at issue in *Casey* (except for a spousal-notification provision), including a blanket statutory exception for cases involving medical emergencies. As a factual matter, the Court rejected the contention that the statutory exception for medical emergencies "foreclosed the possibility of an immediate abortion despite some significant health risks" and was thus too narrow. In so doing, the Court stated that "the essential holding of *Roe* forbids a State to interfere with a woman's choice to undergo an abortion procedure if continuing her pregnancy would constitute a threat to her health."

2. a.   In *Stenberg*, the Court "applied" the "legal principles" from *Roe* and *Casey* "to the circumstances" of a specific Nebraska statute based on a particular factual record. The Court held that a statute prohibiting a particular abortion procedure without an express health exception would be unconstitutional if the statute would "create significant health risks": i.e., health risks significant enough to constitute an undue burden. The Court appeared to recognize that, unlike a statute entirely prohibiting abortion (which would create significant health risks where "the pregnancy itself creates a threat to health"), a statute prohibiting a particular abortion procedure would create significant health risks by prohibiting a procedure that is substantially safer than other procedures, either more generally or in specific circumstances (e.g., where the mother has a particular health-threatening condition).

Applying that standard, the Court, pointing to the district court's findings and evidence, held that the plaintiff had demonstrated that the statute at issue would create significant health risks. The Court noted that the district court had found that "the D&X method was significantly safer in certain circumstances." The Court also noted that the State had "failed to demonstrate that banning D&X without a health exception may not create significant health risks for women." Having concluded, on the discrete record before it, that "a statute that altogether forbids D&X creates a significant health risk," the Court held the statute unconstitutional because it lacked a health exception.

b. To be sure, some language in the Court's opinion in *Stenberg* could be read, in isolation, to suggest that a statute prohibiting a particular abortion procedure would be unconstitutional as long as there is conflicting evidence as to whether the statute at issue would create significant health risks.

In *Stenberg*, however, the Court did not hold that the appropriate constitutional test was whether the plaintiff had established a division of medical opinion concerning the health risks of a ban on partial-birth abortion. As the principal dissenting opinions in *Stenberg* noted, such a test would effectively render it impossible to sustain a statute prohibiting a particular method of abortion against a facial challenge, insofar as "there will always be some support for a procedure and there will always be some doctors who conclude that the procedure is preferable." The Court responded that it was not suggesting that "a State is prohibited from proscribing an abortion procedure whenever a particular physician deems the procedure preferable." *Stenberg* therefore did not establish a rule that a plaintiff need only identify a division of opinion among medical experts on the existence of significant health risks.

A contrary reading of *Stenberg*, moreover, would be inconsistent with this Court's previous abortion decisions. In *Casey*, for example, the Court held only that it would be unconstitutional for a State to prohibit or restrict abortion where the regulation at issue would "interfere with a woman's choice to undergo an abortion procedure if continuing her pregnancy would constitute a threat to her health," without any suggestion that it would be sufficient for the plaintiff to demonstrate merely that there were conflicting medical opinions on whether "continuing her pregnancy would constitute a threat to her health." Because the Court emphasized in *Stenberg* that it was merely applying, and not modifying, *Casey*, there is no reason to attribute such a substantial doctrinal shift to *Stenberg*.

In addition, a contrary reading of *Stenberg* would be at odds with traditional standards of proof. Whereas a plaintiff who identified a dispute on a constitutionally relevant question of fact would ordinarily be entitled only to survive a motion for summary judgment, a plaintiff who demonstrated the existence of a dispute on the medical necessity for a particular abortion procedure would be entitled to prevail on the merits. If *Stenberg* meant to introduce such an innovation in civil procedure in the abortion context, it presumably would have made that intent far more manifest.

In short, the proper understanding of *Stenberg*, and the one that best squares with this Court's precedents, is that a plaintiff challenging an abortion regulation that lacks a health exception must actually prove that the regulation at issue would create significant health risks for women, such that the absence of a health exception would impose an undue burden.

3. Like this case, *Stenberg* involved a facial challenge to an abortion regulation that lacked a health exception. In *Stenberg*, however, the Court did not expressly address the question whether a plaintiff bringing such a facial challenge must demonstrate that the statute is unconstitutional—i.e., that the statute would create significant health risks—in all, or merely most or many, of its applications. For the reasons discussed at greater length in the government's brief in *Ayotte*, the better view is that a plaintiff bringing a facial challenge must show that the statute is in valid in all its applications. At most, however, *Stenberg* stands only for the proposition that a plaintiff bringing a facial challenge to an abortion regulation that lacks a health exception must demonstrate that the statute would create significant health risks for at least a "large fraction" of women covered by the statute. And because the federal Act is facially constitutional under the "large fraction" test, there is no occasion in this case for the Court to choose between that test and *Salerno*'s "no set of circumstances" test.

Respondents suggest that *Stenberg* adopted a more permissive standard for facial challenges than either the "no set of circumstances" standard from *Salerno* or the "large fraction" standard from *Casey*, and instead held that a plaintiff bringing a facial challenge to an abortion regulation that lacks a health exception need only demonstrate that the statute would create significant health risks in a small percentage of its applications. That reading of *Stenberg*, however, not only would belie the Court's assertion that the requirement of a health exception constituted "simply a straightforward application of *Casey*'s holding," but would entirely subvert the *Salerno* standard by allowing a plaintiff to obtain facial invalidation of a statute simply by showing that the statute had a few unconstitutional applications. Such a virtual presumption of facial invalidity would be difficult to reconcile with this Court's other abortion decisions, which have upheld applications of abortion regulations while acknowledging the potential for other, unconstitutional applications, and with this Court's decisions in other contexts, even the unique context of the First Amendment. Indeed, if the absence of a health exception suffices to invalidate a statute on its face, then this Court's decision in *Ayotte* to vacate, rather than affirm, the injunction of the New Hampshire parental-notification statute at issue in its entirety is difficult to understand. Instead, *Stenberg*, as properly understood, teaches that a statute that regulates a particular abortion procedure, but lacks a health exception, is not facially invalid unless, at a minimum, the statute would create significant health risks in a large fraction of its applications.

B. When Analyzed Under The Proper Standard, The Record Over-whelmingly Supports Congress's Judgment That No Health Exception Was Required

In enacting the Partial-Birth Abortion Ban Act of 2003, Congress made numerous findings, culminating in the ultimate finding that partial-birth abortion is never medically indicated to preserve the health of the mother. Consistent with the constitutional rule established by this Court's precedents, Congress therefore was entitled to conclude not only that a health exception was not constitutionally required, but that a health exception would effectively undermine the critical state interests that Congress sought to advance. The court of appeals, however, refused to defer to Congress's findings on the assumption that *Stenberg* effectively foreclosed Congress from making them. That was error.

1. Congressional Findings On Constitutionally Relevant Factual Issues Are Entitled To Great Deference

This Court has long held that courts should afford a high degree of deference to congressional factual findings that inform the constitutionality of federal statutes. In *Turner Broadcasting System, Inc. v. FCC*, the Court set out the principles governing judicial review of congressional findings. The Court held that, "in reviewing the constitutionality of a statute, 'courts must accord substantial deference to the predictive judgments of Congress.'" The Court further noted that "the sole obligation of a court is 'to assure that, in

formulating its judgments, Congress has drawn reasonable inferences based on substantial evidence.'" The Court stressed that,
where congressional fact-finding is at issue, "substantiality is to
be measured by a standard more deferential" than even the standard applicable to agency fact-finding. That deference is appropriate, the Court explained, both because "Congress is far better
equipped than the judiciary to amass and evaluate data bearing
upon legislative questions," and because "the Constitution gives
to Congress the role of weighing conflicting evidence in the legislative process."

This Court has deferred to congressional factual findings in a
wide variety of contexts and with regard to a wide variety of constitutional claims. In *Turner*, for example, in rejecting a Free Speech
Clause challenge to statutory provisions requiring cable-television
systems to carry local television stations, the Court deferred to
express statutory findings, including Congress's ultimate finding
that the provisions were necessary to preserve those stations.
The Court reasoned that, "even in the realm of First Amendment
questions," deference was due to "Congress's findings as to the
harm to be avoided and to the remedial measures adopted for
that end."

Congressional findings on medical or scientific issues are not
subject to a different rule. In *Jones v. United States*, for example,
in rejecting a due process challenge to a statute providing for the
indefinite civil commitment of certain individuals acquitted by reason of insanity, the Court deferred to a congressional finding that
those individuals were likely to be dangerous. The Court rejected
the plaintiff's contention that there was conflicting psychiatric
research on the issue, concluding that "the lesson we have drawn
is not that government may not act in the face of this uncertainty,
but rather that courts should pay particular deference to reasonable legislative judgments." And in *Lambert v. Yellowley*, in rejecting a contention that physicians were constitutionally entitled
to prescribe alcohol for patients for whom they believed it to be
medically necessary, the Court deferred to an "implicit congressional finding" that alcohol had no medicinal uses. The Court

recognized that "practicing physicians differed about the value" of using alcohol for medicinal purposes, but reasoned that Congress could permissibly conclude that it had no medicinal uses in the absence of any consensus to the contrary.

Congress's findings in enacting the Partial-Birth Abortion Ban Act of 2003 including its ultimate finding that partial-birth abortion "is never medically necessary" are based on an extensive legislative record. They concern complex medical matters as to which courts lack any particular institutional expertise. And they are entitled to the same degree of respect as other congressional findings to which this Court has traditionally deferred.

2. Congress's Findings On The Medical Necessity Of Partial-Birth Abortion Are Entitled To Deference

a. Respondents contend that, although this Court has generally deferred to congressional findings of fact that bear on the constitutionality of federal statutes, that principle is inapplicable here. That contention should be rejected.

i. Respondents assert that congressional findings are not entitled to deference unless the findings at issue are "predictive." As a preliminary matter, and contrary to respondents' suggestion, Congress was in fact "making predictions about the future impact of legislation" in this case: namely, predictions about the likely health effects of prohibiting a particular type of abortion procedure. More fundamentally, however, where Congress makes a predictive judgment about the effects of proposed legislation, it inevitably relies on data concerning the *status quo* in making that judgment. Thus, in *Turner*, Congress's finding that the "must-carry" provisions at issue would be necessary to preserve local television stations was predicated on its assessment of then-existing conditions in the local broadcasting industry. So too in this case, Congress's finding that the abortion procedure at issue was never (and thus would never be) necessary to preserve the mother's health was concededly based on evidence concerning the "current state of medicine": namely, evidence concerning the current use of the procedure.

Nor would it be logical to defer to "predictive" congressional findings only when they are based wholly on conjecture, and not when they are grounded in empirical data. To the contrary, a fundamental rationale for deference to congressional findings is that Congress "is far better equipped than the judiciary to amass and evaluate data bearing upon legislative questions." It is thus unsurprising that this Court has deferred to Congress's predictive judgments on medical and scientific issues, even (or especially) where those judgments were based on the "current state" of the evidence.

ii. Respondents alternatively suggest that congressional findings are not entitled to deference in cases "involving a burden on a constitutional right, infringement of which is subject to heightened scrutiny." That contention, however, is refuted by *Turner*, which involved a content-neutral regulation subject to intermediate scrutiny under *United States v. O'Brien*. As courts have noted, the undue-burden standard applicable to abortion regulations under the joint opinion in *Casey* closely resembles an intermediate-scrutiny standard. Moreover, this Court has deferred to congressional findings in a number of other cases involving fundamental constitutional rights and different levels of scrutiny. There is therefore no principled basis for holding that the degree of deference owed to congressional findings depends on the level of scrutiny applicable to the right at issue.

iii. Respondents contend that, in several of the cases cited above involving issues of medical or scientific judgment, Congress did not defer to "legislative findings" at all. It is true that, in a number of those cases, Congress did not make express findings in the text of the statute, but instead made implicit findings about a disputed question of fact that was relevant to the constitutional claim at issue. Other cases, including *Turner*, involved express statutory findings. In any event, the Court's willingness to defer even to implied findings by Congress only strengthens the case for deference where, as here, Congress deliberately and unambiguously made explicit findings based on testimony and other evidence received in extensive legislative hearings.

b. The court of appeals took a different approach. It reasoned that Congress was not "free to disagree with the Supreme Court's determination concerning the medical necessity of partial-birth abortion because the Court's conclusions are final on matters of constitutional law." That reasoning is deeply flawed. In passing the Act, Congress did not attempt to supersede the constitutional rule applied in *Stenberg*—i.e., the rule that a statute prohibiting a particular abortion procedure would be unconstitutional where the statute would create significant health risks. To the contrary, Congress expressly took into account the constitutional rule of *Stenberg* and proceeded to make findings on a factual issue (indeed, the central factual issue) relevant to the application of that constitutional rule—*viz.*, whether partial-birth abortion was in fact medically necessary. In *Stenberg*, the Court expressly characterized that issue as a "factual question" (and ultimately concluded that the plaintiff had demonstrated that the statute at issue would in fact create significant health risks). This case is therefore crucially different from cases in which Congress either sought to supersede a constitutional ruling of this Court, or made findings that were simply insufficient to sustain a statute's constitutionality.

The court of appeals also suggested that, even if the medical necessity of partial-birth abortion were a question of fact, it was a question of "legislative" fact, and *Stenberg* thus foreclosed Congress from making findings on that question. As a preliminary matter, in *Stenberg*, no federal statute was at issue, and there were no congressional findings on the necessity for a health exception. Accordingly, nothing in *Stenberg* suggests that the Court intended to bar Congress from deliberating on the issue and making its own findings, and thus to carve out an "abortion-only" exception to the customary rule that congressional findings concerning the constitutionality of federal statutes are entitled to deference. Indeed, the lower court's conclusion that *Stenberg* estopped it from giving deference to Congress's findings is analogous to the error this Court corrected in *National Cable & Telecommunications Ass'n v. Brand X Internet Services*. Just as a prior judicial determination about the meaning of an ambiguous statute does not deprive a later administrative construction of the deference that it would otherwise be due, an earlier judicial finding of fact likewise does not deprive a later congressional finding of deference. Indeed, the error here is much more obvious. In *Brand X*, the statute to be construed was the same, while here, Congress passed the statute at issue based on a different, and more extensive, record.

Even assuming that the medical necessity of partial-birth abortion is accurately labeled a "legislative" fact, moreover, it does not follow that this Court's determination on a question of "legislative" fact somehow forecloses Congress from subsequently making contrary findings on the same question. After all, the very concept of "legislative" facts is premised on the assumption that such facts are ones that the legislature is uniquely well- equipped to find, in light of the legislature's superior capacity to "amass and evaluate the vast amounts of data" relevant to such fact-finding. At most, to the extent that this Court's decision in *Stenberg* could be read as treating the medical necessity of partial-birth abortion as a question of "legislative" fact, its resolution of that factual issue would merely foreclose lower courts from making contrary findings, in order to ensure that those courts do not reach inconsistent results on the constitutionality of materially identical legislation. It would not permanently fore close Congress from making contrary findings.

In any event, the better reading of *Stenberg* is that it did not treat the medical necessity of partial-birth abortion as a question of "legislative" fact at all. Although the Court noted that other district courts had generally "reached similar factual conclusions" to that reached by the district court in *Stenberg*, and quoted at some length from statements made by a physician group in an *amicus* brief, the Court primarily relied on the evidence presented to, and the factual findings made by, the district court. The district court, in turn, made clear that it was considering partial-birth abortion only as it was performed by the plaintiff in that case—perhaps not surprisingly, given that the court appeared to view the plaintiff's claim as an as-applied challenge.

The practical consequence of the court of appeals' approach would thus be to treat the factual findings of the district court in *Stenberg*, based on the particular circumstances of the plaintiff before it and made following a trial that lasted only one day, as binding nationwide and effectively foreclosing Congress from making contrary findings on the same topic—despite the fact that Congress made its findings based on a more recent, and more robust, evidentiary record. Because *Stenberg* did not foreclose Congress from making factual findings on the necessity of partial-birth abortion, but instead merely upheld the district court's findings in that case on the particular record before it, the court of appeals clearly erred by refusing to defer to Congress's findings.

3. Congress's Findings On The Medical Necessity Of Partial-Birth Abortion Are Supported By Substantial Evidence

While the court of appeals refused to defer to Congress's factual findings at all, the district court seemingly recognized that Congress's findings were entitled to deference, but instead held that Congress's findings were not supported by substantial evidence. In analyzing Congress's findings, however, the district court asked the wrong question: namely, whether substantial evidence supported the proposition that no substantial medical authority supported the proposition that partial-birth abortion was ever necessary to preserve the mother's health. The relevant question is instead whether substantial evidence supported Congress's ultimate finding that "partial-birth abortion is never medically indicated to preserve the health of the mother." Because substantial evidence plainly supported that finding, it is entitled to deference, and respondents' contention that the Act is facially invalid because it lacks a health exception should be rejected.

a. In engaging in "substantial evidence" review, a reviewing court should not "reweigh the evidence *de novo*, or replace Congress' factual predictions with its own." Instead, a reviewing court is required to defer to a congressional finding even if the "evidence is in conflict" and inconsistent conclusions could thus be drawn from that evidence. Although a reviewing court may consider not only the evidence that was before Congress, but also any evidence adduced at trial, in engaging in "substantial evidence" review, the critical inquiry is whether there is sufficient evidence to suggest that Congress's determination was reasonable—not whether the reviewing court would reach the same determination as Congress on the basis of the record that Congress had before it (as supplemented by any evidence adduced at trial).

b. Substantial evidence supported Congress's finding that partial-birth abortion is never necessary to preserve the mother's health.

i. Testimony from physicians. As the district court acknowledged, most of the physicians who appeared before Congress testified in favor of the Act. Their testimony strongly supported Congress's findings concerning the medical necessity of partial-birth abortion.

Dr. Kathi Aultman, a fellow of the American College of Obstetricians and Gynecologists (ACOG), testified that "the ban on partial-birth abortion would not endanger a woman's health because it isn't medically necessary and there are standard alternative methods available at every gestational age." She stated that "there does not appear to be any identified situation in which intact D&X is the only appropriate abortion procedure." She suggested that, because lengthy dilation is required before a partial-birth abortion can be performed, partial-birth abortion could not be used where a woman required an immediate abortion because of a medical emergency. And she noted that D&X abortions may pose greater health risks than D&E abortions: namely, an increased risk of cervical incompetence and similar or greater risks of hemorrhaging, infection, and other complications.

Dr. Curtis Cook, an assistant professor of medicine at Michigan State University and ACOG fellow specializing in maternal-fetal medicine, testified that, in 10 years, he had never "experienced a single clinical situation where partial-birth abortion has ever been required or even considered a superior option clinically" to other types of abortion. He further testified that he had consulted with his colleagues and had "yet to find a single individual who has experienced a clinical situation that would require this procedure." He suggested that partial-birth abortion presented various safety risks, including "potential cervical complications" from the placement of multiple dilators into the cervix; additional risks from the internal rotation of the fetus to a feet-first position, a practice that "has been largely abandoned in modern obstetrics"; and other risks, including hemorrhaging and infection. He stated that he had been contacted by women who had suffered "subsequent pregnancy complications" after undergoing partial-birth abortions.

Dr. Mark Neerhof, an associate professor of obstetrics and gynecology at Northwestern University specializing in maternal-fetal medicine, testified that partial-birth abortion "poses serious medical risks to the mother." He contended that the rotation of the fetus "carries risks of uterine rupture, abruption, amniotic fluid embolus, and trauma to the uterus," and that the use of a sharp object to puncture the skull of the fetus presents "the risk of iatrogenic laceration and secondary hemorrhage." He added that "none of these risks are medically necessary because other procedures are available" for late-term abortions.

Dr. Nancy Romer, a professor of obstetrics and gynecology at Wright State University and ACOG fellow, testified that, "if partial-birth abortion truly were superior to other methods of second-trimester termination, there would be more physicians using it; there would be more physicians trained in it; and it would be described in the medical literature." She asserted that partial-birth abortion "offers no advantage in safety nor efficacy over other methods of termination," and that physicians at her hospital "have never found it necessary to perform this procedure to save the life of a woman" and "have found alternatives that we feel are equally efficacious and safe."

Finally, Dr. Pamela Smith, director of medical education in the obstetrics and gynecology department at Mount Sinai Hospital in

Chicago and ACOG member, testified that "there are absolutely no obstetrical situations encountered in this country which require a partially delivered human fetus to be destroyed to preserve the life or health of the mother." She added that the extended dilation of the cervix during partial-birth abortions could lead to cervical incompetence, threatening the future fertility of the patient; that the rotation of the fetus risks trauma to the mother; and that the use of a sharp instrument makes it "very easy to accidentally poke a hole" in the uterus or cervix. She concluded that partial-birth abortion is "too lengthy" and "too risky" and that "there are too many other alternatives."

ii. Other evidence. In addition to the testimony of physicians who appeared before Congress, other evidence in the legislative record-including statements from leading physician groups, articles in medical journals, and written statements from other physicians-supported Congress's findings.

In making its findings, Congress expressly credited the conclusion of the American Medical Association (AMA) that partial-birth abortion is "never the only appropriate abortion procedure." The AMA expressed that conclusion in a variety of different ways. The AMA's board of trustees issued a report in which it stated that, "according to the scientific literature, there does not appear to be any identified situation in which intact D&X is the only appropriate procedure to induce abortion." In a separate fact sheet concerning the AMA's support for an earlier version of the Act, the board of trustees noted that "AMA's expert panel could not find any identified circumstance where D&X was the only appropriate alternative." And in a press release, the AMA noted that partial-birth abortion is "broadly disfavored both by experts and by the public," and added that "it is a procedure which is never the only appropriate procedure and has no history in peer re viewed medical literature or in accepted medical practice development."

Although ACOG, unlike the AMA, opposed earlier versions of the Act, it reached a similar conclusion about the medical necessity of partial-birth abortion. In a formal policy statement issued in 1997 and then reaffirmed in 2000, ACOG conceded that "a select panel convened by ACOG could identify no circumstances under which partial-birth abortion would be the only option to save the life or preserve the health of the woman." Although ACOG proceeded to suggest that partial-birth abortion "may be the best or most appropriate procedure in a particular circumstance to save the life or preserve the health of the woman", ACOG did not identify any circumstance in which that would be true. While ACOG's vice president likewise asserted in a letter that "there are rare occasions when intact D&X is the most appropriate procedure" and "is medically necessary," he also failed to elaborate on that assertion.

Moreover, Congress considered various articles in medical journals which expressed similar doubts about the medical necessity of partial-birth abortion. For example, in an article published in the *Journal of the American Medical Association*, Dr. LeRoy Sprang and Dr. Neerhof stated that "there exist no credible studies on intact D&X that evaluate or attest to its safety"; that the procedure may increase the risk of uterine rupture because of the necessity of rotating the fetus into a feet-first position; that the procedure "could result in severe bleeding and the threat of shock or even maternal death" from the use of a sharp object to puncture the skull of the fetus; and that none of those risks is "medically necessary," because "other procedures are available" for late-term abortions.

Finally, in addition to the physicians who appeared before Congress, numerous other physicians submitted written statements attesting that partial-birth abortion is never medical necessary. For example, Dr. Camilla Hersh, an assistant professor of obstetrics and gynecology at Georgetown University and ACOG fellow, wrote that partial-birth abortion presents risks of cervical incompetence, serious infection, and hemorrhaging. She also rejected the argument that partial-birth abortion was necessary in cases involving various specific maternal or fetal conditions.

iii. Trial evidence. At trial, still other physicians testified that partial-birth abortion was never medically necessary, thereby confirming the reasonableness of Congress's findings. Dr.

Watson Bowes, a professor emeritus of obstetrics and gynecology at the University of North Carolina specializing in maternal-fetal medicine, testified that he had never seen a situation in which, in his view, there would be any advantage to using partial-birth abortion over any other type of abortion.

Dr. Steven Clark, a professor of obstetrics and gynecology at the University of Utah and ACOG member specializing in maternal-fetal medicine, testified that "under no circumstance is D&X abortion necessary to preserve the life or health of the mother" and that "there are in fact grave concerns regarding the long-term safety of this procedure." He explained that it was "very rare" that an abortion would ever be necessary to preserve the health of the mother, and that D&E was an "in credibly safe procedure with negligible risk of serious complications in skilled hands." He then reviewed each of the various specific conditions for which partial-birth abortion was allegedly the safest abortion method and explained that the asserted safety advantages were either hypothetical or non-existent. He concluded that he could not "imagine any medical condition in which this D&X procedure might be helpful" at any gestational age.

Dr. Charles Lockwood, chairman of the department of obstetrics and gynecology at Yale University, testified that he was unaware of any medical evidence "that the D&X offers any safety advantage over D&E or medical induction," and that partial-birth abortion itself posed a potential long-term risk to maternal health. He explained in detail why partial-birth abortion would not be the safest method of abortion in cases involving various specific conditions, and concluded that he "really can't conceive of any specific condition that would specifically warrant a D&X." Notably, he so testified despite the fact that he was personally opposed to the Act.

Dr. Elizabeth Shadigian, an associate professor of obstetrics and gynecology at the University of Michigan and ACOG fellow, testified, "There is no basis to say the D&X is safer than any other procedure." She stated that she could not "think of a situation" in which partial-birth abortion would be necessary "because of a particular type of health condition that the mother is facing in the pregnancy."

Finally, Dr. LeRoy Sprang, an ACOG fellow, testified that he had "never seen a situation where a D&X would be the safest, the best, or the only procedure to use to protect the health of the mother." He added that other physicians had been unable to identify a single situation in which partial-birth abortion would be the best method to preserve the mother's health.

c. To be sure, respondents presented evidence at trial suggesting that partial-birth abortion may be marginally safer than other types of abortion in specific circumstances (e.g., where the mother has *preeclampsia* or *placenta previa*) or as a more categorical matter (e.g., because a partial-birth abortion requires fewer instrument passes in the uterus than a standard D&E abortion). As noted above, however, the mere existence of conflicting evidence does not render Congress's factual findings invalid. Indeed, to the extent that the district court concluded that there was a division of medical opinion on the medical necessity of partial-birth abortion, the necessary implication is that substantial evidence would support the conclusion that partial-birth abortion was never medically necessary.

At various points in its opinion, the district court suggested that deference to Congress's factual findings was inappropriate because the physicians who testified that partial-birth abortion was never medically necessary did not carry out partial-birth abortions themselves. It is hardly surprising, however, that physicians who believed that partial-birth abortion was never medically necessary would not carry out such abortions. Many of those physicians, moreover, were maternal fetal experts who specialized in treating women with high-risk pregnancies (including women who had suffered complications from abortions)—and who were therefore perfectly capable of assessing the risks that would attend partial-birth abortions, even if they did not conduct that particular type of abortion themselves. Indeed, insofar as typical abortion providers, unlike physicians specializing in obstetrics and gynecology, do not provide long- term follow-up care to their patients, the testifying physicians were arguably better situated to assess long-term complications from abortions. And the very fact that practitioners in the field repeatedly indicated that partial-birth abortions were never medically necessary or justified, despite the contrary opinions of a few fellow practitioners, suggests that any differences in safety are debatable and sufficiently marginal that most practitioners (and certainly, therefore, Congress) can confidently rule out the need to resort to the procedure. On the other hand, only a few physicians perform partial-birth abortions, and many of those physicians are general practitioners, not specialists or academics. There is thus no basis for concluding that Congress's findings were not supported by substantial evidence simply because the district court may have disagreed with Congress and concluded that the physicians who testified against the Act were more credible.

d. Although the district courts in the other two cases challenging the Act ultimately agreed with the district court's conclusion in this case concerning the validity of Congress's findings, those district courts made various findings of their own, based on virtually identical records, suggesting that substantial evidence would support the proposition that partial-birth abortion is never medically necessary. In *National Abortion Federation v. Ashcroft*, the district court ultimately found that "a division of medical opinion exists about the necessity of D&X to preserve women's health." However, after comprehensively reviewing the testimony on the comparative safety of various abortion procedures, the court found that "the Government's expert witnesses reasonably and effectively refuted Plaintiffs' proffered bases for the opinion that D&X has safety advantages over other second-trimester abortion procedures." The court also found that "in no case could Plaintiffs point to a specific patient or actual circumstance in which D&X was necessary to protect a woman's health" and that "many of Plaintiffs' purported reasons for why D&X is medically necessary" are either "only theoretical" or "false."

Similarly, in *Planned Parenthood Federation of America, Inc. v. Ashcroft*, the district court ultimately found that "there continues to be a division of opinion among highly qualified experts regarding the necessity or safety of intact D&E." Like the district court in *National Abortion Federation*, however, the court found that "plaintiffs have not demonstrated the existence of any particular situation in which an intact D&E would be a doctor's only option to preserve the life or health of a woman."

Like the district court in this case, therefore, those courts would likely have upheld the statute if they had focused on the correct question: namely, whether substantial evidence supported Congress's ultimate finding that partial-birth abortion is never necessary to preserve the mother's health. Because substantial evidence did support that finding, the Act is not facially invalid because it lacks a health exception.

C. Even Assuming That Partial-Birth Abortion Has Marginal Health Advantages In Some Cases, A Statute That Prohibits Partial-Birth Abortion Does Not Impose An Undue Burden On A Woman's Access To An Abortion

Even if the Court refused to defer to Congress's considered findings, respondents' trial evidence at most suggested that partial-birth abortion is marginally safer than other abortion procedures in some circumstances. Absent a showing that it would "create significant health risks," however, a statute prohibiting partial-birth abortion does not impose an undue burden on a woman's access to an abortion.

Casey's undue-burden standard effectively replaced the strict-scrutiny standard from *Roe*. In adopting the undue-burden standard, the joint opinion in *Casey* emphasized that the government has a "profound interest in potential life," and reasoned that "the very notion that the government has a substantial interest in potential life leads to the conclusion that not all abortion regulations must be deemed unwarranted." Where the regulation at issue limits a specific method of abortion, the difference in safety must be significant enough that elimination of that method places a "substantial obstacle in the path of a woman seeking an abortion," in light of the continuing availability of other methods. A different rule would force courts to make difficult medical judgment calls and would devalue the vital government interests that *Casey* sought to bring back into the equation in reviewing abortion regulations.

The protection of innocent human life—in or out of the womb— is the most compelling interest the government can advance. The Act implicates not only the government's compelling interest in protecting human life, but also the government's specific (and no less compelling) interest in prohibiting a particular type of abortion procedure that closely resembles infanticide.

In passing the Act, Congress specifically found that partial-birth abortion "blurs the line between abortion and infanticide in the killing of a partially-born child just inches from birth"; that partial-birth abortion "also confuses the medical, legal, and ethical duties of physicians to preserve and promote life"; and that failing to prohibit the procedure would "promote a complete disregard for infant human life" and "further coarsen society to the humanity of not only newborns, but all vulnerable and innocent human life, making it increasingly difficult to protect such life." In light of the relative strength of the government's interest in prohibiting partial-birth abortion, and the relative weakness of a woman's interest in having access to a particular type of abortion procedure that has no health advantages (according to Congress), or at most marginal health advantages, when compared with other, unregulated types of procedures, the Act is constitutional under *Casey* because it does not impose an undue burden on a woman's access to an abortion.

Holding that the Act is valid only if it contains a health exception would substantially undermine the government's compelling interests in preventing partial-birth abortion. As proponents of the Act appreciated, a health exception, no matter how narrowly crafted, would potentially give a physician unfettered discretion in determining when a partial-birth abortion may be performed. Congress could thus have reasonably determined that a ban on partial-birth abortion that includes a health exception would amount to no ban at all.

D. To The Extent That The Court Believes That Stenberg Compels A Different Result, It Should Be Overruled

For the reasons explained above, the Act is constitutional under the principles adopted by the joint opinion in *Casey* and applied by this Court in *Stenberg*, notwithstanding the absence of a health exception. Although this Court reached a contrary result in *Stenberg* with respect to the state statute at issue there, *Stenberg* is distinguishable in a number of important respects from this case. Most notably, the statute at issue here is an Act of Congress accompanied by congressional findings—including the ultimate finding that partial-birth abortion is never medically indicated— that are amply supported by substantial evidence and therefore entitled to deference. In addition, the statute at issue carefully defines partial-birth abortion so that it does not reach the more common D&E procedure. Moreover, the trial record supporting the constitutionality of the Act is much more extensive than in *Stenberg*, where the trial lasted only one day (whereas the trial in this case lasted two weeks).

If this Court nevertheless concludes for any reason that its decision in *Stenberg* compels the conclusion that the Act is unconstitutional, however, *Stenberg* should be overruled. To be sure, values of stare decisis help ensure continuity in the law as developed by this Court. However, to the extent that the Court construes *Stenberg* to require invalidation of the statute at issue, continuing adherence to *Stenberg* could not further those values, because such a reading of *Stenberg* would be unfaithful to the Court's prior precedents, including *Casey*; and it would therefore only further unsettle this Court's abortion jurisprudence. Moreover, to the extent that *Stenberg* is read to require courts to disregard legislative findings and make fine-tuned judgments about the relative merits of particular medical techniques, it would place judges in an untenable position and would prove unworkable in practice. Indeed, the different analytical approaches reflected in the various lower-court opinions on the constitutionality of the

Act demonstrate that *Stenberg* has created confusion and proven unworkable already.

II. THE ACT IS NEITHER UNCONSTITUTIONALLY OVER BROAD NOR UNCONSTITUTIONALLY VAGUE

Before the lower courts, respondents also contended that the Act was facially invalid because (1) it reached not only D&X abortions, but also certain standard D&E abortions, and thus was unconstitutionally overbroad, and (2) it was unconstitutionally vague. The district court agreed with the first contention, but ultimately disagreed with the second. Although the court of appeals did not address either contention in light of its ruling on the lack of a health exception, it would be appropriate for respondents to invoke their alternative arguments against the statute and in support of the judgment, and appropriate for this Court to consider them. Each of those contentions lacks merit.

A. The Act Is Not Unconstitutionally Overbroad

1. In *Stenberg*, this Court held that the Nebraska statute at issue was invalid not only because it lacked a health exception, but also because it defined "partial birth abortion" in such a way as to reach standard D&E abortions as well as D&X abortions, and thereby imposed an undue burden on a woman's access to an abortion. That statute barred a physician from "deliberately and intention ally delivering into the vagina a living unborn child, or a substantial portion thereof, for the purpose of performing a procedure that the person performing such procedure knows will kill the unborn child." The Court noted that a standard D&E abortion "will often involve a physician pulling a 'substantial portion' of a still living fetus, say, an arm or leg, into the vagina prior to the death of the fetus." The Court thus reasoned that, "even if the statute's basic aim is to ban D&X, its language makes clear that it also covers a much broader category of procedures." The Court explained that the Nebraska statute did "not track the medical differences between D&E and D&X," nor did it "anywhere suggest that its application turns on whether a portion of the fetus' body is drawn into the vagina as part of a process to extract an intact

fetus after collapsing the head as opposed to a process that would dismember the fetus." "The plain language" of the statute, the Court concluded, "covers both procedures."

2. The Act contains a definition of "partial-birth abortion" that differs in two critical respects from the statutory definition at issue in *Stenberg*. First, the Act applies only where the person performing the abortion "deliberately and intentionally vaginally delivers a living fetus until, in the case of a head-first presentation, the entire fetal head is outside the body of the mother, or, in the case of breech presentation, any part of the fetal trunk past the navel is outside the body of the mother." By specifying so-called anatomical "landmarks," the Act excludes standard D&E abortions in which a smaller portion of the fetus, such as a foot or arm, is drawn through the cervix (or outside the mother's body altogether), and torn from the fetus, while the fetus is still living. Second, the Act applies only where the person performing the abortion also "performs an overt act, other than completion of delivery, that kills the partially delivered living fetus," and delivers the fetus with the purpose of performing that overt act. By requiring a discrete "overt act," the Act excludes standard D&E abortions in which the delivery of a portion of the fetus and the performance of the lethal act (i.e., the dismemberment of the fetus) are indistinguishable.

Not only is the Act's definition more precise than the definition at issue in *Stenberg*, but the fact that this case involves a federal statute gives the Court a much greater capacity to interpret the statute to avoid any constitutional difficulties than in a case, like *Stenberg*, involving a state statute. The Act's textual definition clearly reflects the intent to reach D&X abortions, but not standard D&E abortions. If there is any doubt on that score, however, the Court can interpret the statute to avoid any constitutional concerns. This is not a context in which the Court should hold Congress to impossible standards of draftsmanship.

3. The district court held that the Act still reached certain D&E abortions: namely, abortions in which a physician delivers the required portion of the fetus, but only then performs a discrete act that kills the fetus ("either by dividing it into two or more pieces or by reducing the skull and removing the fetus intact"). Where, however, a physician delivers a major portion of the fetus—i.e., the entire fetal head (in the case of a head-first delivery) or any part of the trunk past the navel (in the case of a feet-first delivery)—and then performs a discrete act that aborts the fetus, the procedure constitutes a "partial-birth abortion," in the literal sense of the phrase, rather than a standard D&E abortion, regardless whether the ultimate lethal act is (1) the dismemberment of the fetus, (2) the puncturing of its skull and vacuuming out of its brain, or (3) some other act (besides completion of delivery). Moreover, the Act would apply only where the physician had the specific intent to deliver the requisite portion of the fetus for the purpose of performing the ultimate lethal act at the outset of the procedure. The Act would therefore not cover situations in which a physician intended only to perform a standard D&E abortion, but ultimately had to perform a partial-birth abortion (for example, if the physician unintentionally delivered a major portion of the fetus, or if the physician at tempted to deliver the living but non-viable fetus intact but was unable to do so because the head became stuck). Because the Act reaches no standard D&E abortions, the district court erred by holding that it was overbroad.

B. The Act Is Not Unconstitutionally Vague

1. In order to survive a vagueness challenge, a statute "must give the person of ordinary intelligence a reasonable opportunity to know what is prohibited, so that he may act accordingly." The Constitution, however, does not impose "impossible standards of clarity." Instead, a statute is not vague if it is "clear what the statute as a whole prohibits." Moreover,

"speculation about possible vagueness in hypothetical situations not before the Court will not support a facial attack on a statute when it is surely valid in the vast majority of its intended applications."

2. The Act readily satisfies the relatively modest requirements of the void-for-vagueness doctrine. The Act prohibits only a particular type of abortion in which the physician "deliberately and intentionally vaginally delivers a living fetus" up to a specific anatomical point "outside the body of the mother"; does so "for the purpose of performing an overt act that the person knows will kill the partially delivered living fetus"; and then "performs the overt act, other than completion of delivery, that kills the partially delivered living fetus." In addition, the physician must "knowingly" perform that type of abortion. It is hard to imagine how the proscribed conduct could be defined any more precisely, at least without dramatically narrowing the scope of the statute.

3. Before the district court, respondents contended that various terms and phrases in the Act were unconstitutionally vague. Those contentions, however, lack merit. Although the Act prohibits "partial-birth abortion," any alleged vagueness in that phrase is irrelevant, because the Act proceeds to define the phrase with particularity. And none of the terms or phrases used within that definition is ambiguous. As the district court noted, the phrase "overt act" is a "standard statutory term of art," which appears in numerous other criminal statutes. And "overt act" is immediately qualified by the phrase "other than the completion of delivery," which serves to limit its scope. In addition, as the district court also noted, the term "living" in the phrase "living fetus" is a "commonplace word" of which "doctors have a practical understanding." "Living" refers to a fetus that is either potentially or actually viable: i.e., a fetus that "has a detectable heartbeat or pulsating umbilical cord." In short, because the Act contains no ambiguous terms and phrases, and because the Act as a whole plainly provides sufficient notice of the conduct that it prohibits, the district

court correctly held that the Act is not unconstitutionally vague.

III. BECAUSE THE ACT IS CONSTITUTIONAL, THE COURT NEED NOT FASHION ANY REMEDY

As explained above, the Act materially differs from the state statute at issue in *Stenberg* and is constitutional under a proper analysis. In the event, however, that this Court were to identify some aspect in which the Act is invalid, it may be possible to craft narrower injunctive relief along the lines suggested in *Ayotte v. Planned Parenthood of Northern New England.* Because the availability of narrower injunctive relief turns both on the nature of the statute's infirmity and on a statute-specific inquiry into legislative intent, the Court may wish to remand so that the lower courts can address that issue in the first instance. In any event, because the statute is, in fact, constitutional, further development of the remedial question implicated in *Ayotte* will need to wait for a different case. Here, Congress has identified a single, rarely used abortion procedure that it found to be medically unnecessary. Upholding that statute merely requires the Court to reaffirm the government's critical interests in regulating abortion procedures to protect life and prohibit procedures that blur the line between abortion and infanticide.

CONCLUSION

The judgment of the court of appeals should be reversed.[2]

Notes

References to citations, transcripts, footnotes, and some authorities omitted for sake of clarity.

1. *Elk Grove Unified School District, et al. v. Newdow*, No. 02-1624.
2. *Gonzales v. Carhart*, et al., No. 05-380.

APPENDIX

Model Briefs

Under the assumption that you can *never* read and study too many well-written legal arguments, the following are four briefs presented to the U.S. Supreme Court by attorneys for the federal government. They are offered here for their clarity of analysis and superb writing style.

Brief #1

The issue in this case is whether service on the U.S. Court of Military Commission Review disqualifies a judge from also serving on the Air Force Court of Criminal Appeals.

STATEMENT

The petitioners in these consolidated cases are military service members who were convicted of various offenses by military courts-martial. Their convictions and sentences were affirmed, in whole or in part, by the Army and Air Force Courts of Criminal Appeals (CCAs). Petitioners contend that they are entitled to new hearings before the CCAs because the panels that acted on their appeals included one or more military judges who were also appointed to the U.S. Court of Military Commission Review (CMCR) by the President, with the advice and consent of the Senate. Petitioners' challenges to the judges' simultaneous service on a CCA and the CMCR arise in the context of the Nation's specialized military justice system, which includes both courts-martial and military commissions.

A. The Court-Martial System

The Constitution empowers Congress to "make Rules for the Government and Regulation of the land and naval Forces." Since the Founding, Congress has exercised that authority by providing for the prosecution of offenses committed by military service members in courts-martial rather than in civilian Article III courts. Today, the court-martial system includes three levels of specialized tribunals.

1. The trial-level courts are courts-martial, which may be summary, special, or general. A general court-martial typically consists of a military judge and at least five members. A general court-martial has jurisdiction over all offenses under the Uniform Code of Military Justice (UCMJ), and may impose sentences up to confinement for life, or death. Summary and special courts-martial have more limited jurisdiction and impose lesser punishments. If a court-martial issues a conviction, its findings and sentence are reviewed by the officer who convened it, who may in some circumstances set aside a finding of guilt or reduce the sentence.

2. Before 1950, "military courts of appeals did not exist." Instead, "if a service member wanted to challenge a court-martial conviction, he pursued a collateral attack in an Article III court," typically by filing a petition for a writ of habeas corpus.

In 1950, Congress enacted the UCMJ, which established four intermediate appellate courts: the Army, Navy-Marine Corps, Air Force, and Coast Guard CCAs. The CCAs are composed of "appellate military judges," who may be "commissioned officers or civilians." Unless the defendant waives review, the relevant CCA is required to review all cases in which the sentence, as approved by the convening authority, includes death, confinement for more than one year, or a punitive discharge. The CCAs "may review *de novo* both factual and legal findings."

3. The highest court in the court-martial system is the CAAF. It consists of five civilian judges appointed to 15-year terms by the President with the advice and consent of the Senate. The CAAF must review the record in cases in which a CCA affirms a death sentence and cases in which a Judge Advocate General seeks further review. In all other cases, the CAAF has discretion to grant review upon a petition by the accused. When the CAAF grants discretionary review, it need only review the "issues specified in the grant of review." In all cases, its review is limited to issues of law.

Only a fraction of the cases decided by the CCAs are reviewed on the merits by the CAAF. In fiscal year 2016, for example, the CCAs reviewed a total of 1244 cases. The CAAF received nine mandatory filings and 719 petitions for discretionary review, of which it granted 66.

4. Until 1983, there was no avenue for direct review of the CAAF's decisions in this Court. Instead, this Court considered questions related to courts-martial only in habeas proceedings and other collateral challenges brought by the accused. That was "an unsatisfactory way to manage a system of judicial review," because it meant that there was no way for the United States to seek further review of adverse decisions by the CAAF—including decisions establishing important constitutional precedents or striking down military regulations.

In 1983, in response to a request by the Department of Defense (DOD), Congress redressed that asymmetry by enacting 28 U.S.C. 1259, which grants this Court jurisdiction to review certain CAAF decisions by writ of certiorari. Under Section 1259, this Court has jurisdiction to review the CAAF's decisions in cases on the CAAF's mandatory docket, cases in which the CAAF "granted a petition for discretionary review," and other cases in which the CAAF "granted relief." But Congress specified that this Court "may not review by a writ of certiorari any action of the CAAF in refusing to grant a petition for review."

B. The Military-Commission System and the Court of Military Commission Review

1. The other traditional form of military tribunal is the military commission, which has long been used to substitute for civilian courts in times of martial law or temporary military government, as well as to try members of enemy forces for violations of the laws of war. The Nation's current system of military commissions under the Military Commissions Act of 2009 (MCA), is "the product of an extended dialogue among the President, the Congress and this Court."

After Congress authorized the use of military force to respond to the terrorist attacks on September 11, 2001, the President issued an order providing for the use of military commissions to try noncitizen enemy combatants for certain offenses. In *Hamdan*, this Court held that those commissions exceeded existing statutory authority. Congress responded by enacting the Military Commissions Act of 2006, which it later replaced with the MCA.

The MCA "establishes procedures governing the use of military commissions to try alien unprivileged enemy belligerents for violations of the law of war and other offenses triable by military commission." An alien "unprivileged enemy belligerent" includes an alien who "was a part of al Qaeda at the time of the alleged offense." The procedures for military commissions are "based upon the procedures for trial by general courts-martial under the UCMJ," with some exceptions and modifications.

2. The CMCR is "an intermediate appellate tribunal for military commissions akin to each military branch's [CCA] for courts-martial." If the convening authority approves a military commission's finding of guilt, the case is referred to the CMCR for review. The CMCR applies the same standard of review as the CCAs: It "may affirm only such findings of guilty, and the sentence or such part or amount of the sentence, as it finds correct in law and fact and determines, on the basis of the entire record, should be approved." The CMCR's decisions are appealable to the D.C. Circuit.

3. The MCA provides that the Secretary of Defense may "assign persons who are appellate military judges to be judges on the

CMCR." A person so assigned must be "a commissioned officer of the armed forces." The MCA specifies that "no appellate military judge on the CMCR may be reassigned to other duties" unless the judge voluntarily requests re-assignment, retires or otherwise separates from the armed forces, is reassigned "based on military necessity," or is withdrawn from the CMCR "for good cause." The MCA further provides that the President may "appoint, by and with the advice and consent of the Senate, additional judges," who are not required to be military officers.

In practice, the large majority of the CMCR's judges have been military officers who were also serving as appellate military judges on a CCA. Because of the specialized nature of the CMCR's jurisdiction, there are times when "the Court's judges may have very little to do." "Consistent with that reality, the military judges who serve on the CMCR also continue to serve on the CCAs from which they are drawn."

C. The *al-Nashiri* Litigation

1. In November 2014, a military-commission defendant, Abd Al-Rahim Hussein Muhammed al-Nashiri, petitioned the D.C. Circuit for a writ of mandamus seeking disqualification of the military CMCR judges hearing an interlocutory appeal in his case. al-Nashiri contended that the judges were placed on the CMCR in violation of the Appointments Clause, which provides that the President "shall nominate, and by and with the Advice and Consent of the Senate, shall appoint" the "Officers of the United States," but that "Congress may by Law vest the Appointment of such inferior Officers, as they think proper, in the President alone, in the Courts of Law, or in the Heads of Departments." al-Nashiri argued that CMCR judges are principal officers rather than inferior officers, and that they therefore must be appointed to the CMCR by the President with the advice and consent of the Senate, rather than being assigned by the Secretary of Defense.

The D.C. Circuit denied the mandamus petition, holding that al-Nashiri had not established a "clear and indisputable" right to relief. The court did not decide whether CMCR judges are principal officers. It also did not decide whether, if they are, the Appointments Clause requires judges who have already been appointed as commissioned military officers by the President with the advice and consent of the Senate to be appointed a second time specifically to the CMCR. The court described those as "open questions." But the court suggested that "the President and the Senate could decide to put to rest any Appointments Clause questions" by nominating and confirming the military judges to the CMCR.

2. "The President chose to take that tack" as a prophylactic measure, without conceding it was constitutionally required. On March 14, 2016, the President submitted nominations to the Senate ratifying the Secretary of Defense's assignments of the appellate military judges serving on the CMCR. Those nominations clarified that, although the judges were being appointed by the President under Section 950f(b)(3), they would continue to be governed by the statutory provisions applicable to "appellate military judges" serving on the CMCR. The President nominated:

> The following named officers for appointment in the grades indicated in the United States Army or Air Force as appellate military judges on the CMCR under Title 10 U.S.C. In accordance with their continued status as appellate military judges pursuant to their assignment by the Secretary of Defense under 10 U.S.C. Section 950f(b)(2), while serving on the CMCR, all unlawful influence prohibitions remain under 10 U.S.C. Section 949b(b).

The nominated judges included Air Force Colonel Martin Mitchell, Army Colonels Larss Celtnieks and James Herring, and Army Lt. Colonel Paulette Burton. The Senate confirmed their nominations on April 28, 2016. On May 2, 2016, the judges took new oaths of office. And on May 25, 2016, the President appointed the judges to the CMCR by signing their commissions.

3. al-Nashiri responded to those developments by seeking to disqualify the military judges on his CMCR panel on a new ground. He invoked 10 U.S.C. 973(b)(2), which provides that, unless "otherwise authorized by law," a military officer may not hold certain "civil offices," including a "civil office" that "requires an appointment by the President by and with the advice and consent of the

Senate." al- Nashiri argued that Section 973(b) bars military officers from being appointed as CMCR judges.

The CMCR denied the motion on two independent grounds.
First, it held that military officers are "authorized by law" to serve
on the CMCR because 10 U.S.C. 950f(b)(2) specifically provides for
military officers to be judges on the court. Second, the CMCR held
that a CMCR judgeship is not a "civil office" for purposes of Section 973(b) because "disposition of violations of the law of war by
military commissions is a classic military function."

D. The Present Controversy

Petitioners are eight service members who were convicted of a
variety of offenses before courts-martial. The CCAs affirmed their
convictions and sentences in whole or in part. In each case, the
CCA panel included Judge Burton, Judge Celtnieks, Judge Herring,
or Judge Mitchell. All petitioners sought discretionary review by
the CAAF.

1. *Dalmazzi* and *Cox*

In *Dalmazzi*, the CAAF granted review to decide whether the President's appointment of Judge Mitchell to the CMCR had rendered
him ineligible to continue sitting on the CCA. During briefing, the
CAAF noted that the record did not disclose the date of Judge
Mitchell's appointment to the CMCR and ordered the parties to
submit the relevant documents. When those documents revealed
that Judge Mitchell was not appointed until after the CCA had
issued its decision, the CAAF ordered the parties to brief the question "whether the issues granted for review are moot."

After receiving the parties' briefs, the CAAF "vacated" its
order granting review and entered an order stating that the "petition for grant of review is denied." The CAAF explained that it had
granted review to decide "whether a military officer is statutorily
or constitutionally prohibited from simultaneously serving" on a
CCA and as a presidentially appointed judge on the CMCR. The
CAAF noted that a presidential appointment is not complete until
the President "performs some public act that evinces the appointment," usually by "sign[ing] a commission." And because Judge

Mitchell "had not yet been appointed" when the CCA acted, the CAAF stated that the case was "moot as to the simultaneous-service issues" on which it had granted review.

After denying review in *Dalmazzi*, the CAAF issued similar orders as to all six petitioners in *Cox*, whose CCA panels likewise had issued decisions before the judges were appointed to the CMCR. As in *Dalmazzi*, each order "vacated" the CAAF's prior order granting discretionary review and "denied" the petition for review.

2. Ortiz

In *Ortiz*, unlike the other cases, the CCA had issued its decision after the President appointed Judge Mitchell to the CMCR. The CAAF therefore decided the simultaneous-service issues on the merits, affirming the CCA's decision.

The CAAF first held that even if a CMCR judgeship were a "civil office" subject to Section 973(b), and even if military officers were not "authorized by law" to serve on the CMCR, any violation of Section 973(b) would not affect Judge Mitchell's service on the CCA. The CAAF observed that although Section 973(b) prohibits military officers from holding certain civil offices, it does not "operate to automatically effectuate the termination" of an officer who accepts a prohibited office. To the contrary, the CAAF noted that language mandating that result had been "repealed over thirty years ago," when Congress rewrote Section 973(b) in 1983. And the CAAF emphasized that its conclusion was confirmed by a savings clause Congress added when it repealed the automatic-termination language. That clause provides that "nothing in Section 973(b) shall be construed to invalidate any action undertaken by an officer in furtherance of assigned official duties."

The CAAF next held that an officer's simultaneous service on a CCA and the CMCR does not violate the Appointments Clause. The CAAF assumed without deciding that CMCR judges are principal officers. But the CAAF rejected the argument that it would violate the Appointments Clause for Judge Mitchell to serve as a principal officer on the CMCR while separately serving as a CCA judge, which is an inferior office. The court explained that the argument "presumed that Judge Mitchell's status as a principal officer on the CMCR somehow carries over to the CCA, and invests him with authority or status not held by ordinary CCA judges." The CAAF rejected that argument, explaining that "when Judge Mitchell sits as a CCA judge, he is no different from any other CCA judge."

Summary of Argument

I. The President's appointments of Judges Burton, Celtnieks, Herring, and Mitchell to the CMCR did not violate 10 U.S.C. 973(b). And even if they did, petitioners would not be entitled to relief from the CCA decisions affirming their convictions because Congress specifically provided that Section 973(b) does not invalidate the subsequent actions of a military officer who accepts a covered civil office.

A. Section 973(b) states that military officers may not hold certain "civil offices" unless they are "authorized by law" to do so. That statute does not bar the President from appointing military officers to the CMCR for two independent reasons.

First, a CMCR judgeship is not a "civil office." The CMCR is a military court modeled on the CCAs. Like the CCAs' review of courts-martial, the CMCR's review of military commissions is a military function that has long been performed by military officers. Accordingly, just as this Court has held that "the role of military judge on a CCA is 'germane' to that of military officer," the role of a military judge on the CMCR is likewise a military position, not a prohibited "civil office."

Second, military officers are authorized by law to serve on the CMCR because Congress provided that the Secretary of Defense may assign "commissioned officers" to be "judges on the CMCR." Petitioners deem that authorization insufficient because Section 950f(b)(3), which allows the President to appoint "additional judges to the CMCR," does not expressly mention military officers. But petitioners err in presuming that assigned and appointed judges hold two different "offices" for purposes of Section 973(b). By specifying that "judges on the CMCR shall be assigned *or* appointed," Congress made clear that both assigned and appointed judges hold the same office. Congress has thus authorized military officers to hold the single office it created in Section 950f.

B. Even if Section 973(b) prohibited the President from appointing military officers to the CMCR, there would be no basis for petitioners' remarkable assertion that the President's appointment of Judges Burton, Celtnieks, Herring, and Mitchell automatically terminated those judges from the military and voided the CCAs' decisions. Congress repealed language imposing an automatic-termination consequence in 1983 and replaced it with a broad savings clause directing that Section 973(b) may not be "construed to invalidate any action undertaken by an officer in furtherance of assigned official duties." Here, the judges decided petitioners' appeals "in furtherance of their assigned official duties" on the CCAs. The savings clause thus unambiguously forecloses petitioners' attempt to invoke Section 973(b) to "invalidate" the CCAs' decisions.

II. A military officer's simultaneous service on a CCA and the CMCR does not raise questions under the Appointments Clause or the Commander-in-Chief Clause. Petitioners identify nothing in the text or history of the Appointments Clause, or in this Court's decisions, to support their assertion that the Clause imposes an ill-defined "incompatibility" or "incongruity" limitation on the circumstances in which an individual may hold two separate federal offices. And even if such a limit existed, it would not be implicated here. A military judge's simultaneous service on a CCA and the CMCR is no more "incongruous" or "incompatible" than a district judge's service on the Foreign Intelligence Surveillance Court or a circuit judge's service on a three-judge district court. And petitioners' argument that the Commander-in-Chief Clause does not permit the restrictions on removal that petitioners assume are triggered by presidential appointment to the CMCR rests on the erroneous premise that Judges Burton, Celtnieks, Herring, and Mitchell are not subject to 10 U.S.C. 949b(b)(4), the statutory provision governing reassignment of military judges serving on the CMCR.

III. This Court lacks jurisdiction in *Dalmazzi* and *Cox*, but has jurisdiction in *Ortiz*.

A. Under 28 U.S.C. 1259(3), this Court's jurisdiction is limited to cases in which the CAAF "granted a petition for review." Section 1259(3) does not apply in *Dalmazzi* and *Cox* because the CAAF "vacated" its orders granting review and "denied" the petitions. That understanding is confirmed by 10 U.S.C. 867a(a), which expressly provides that this Court may not review "any action" by the CAAF "in refusing to grant a petition for review."

B. An amicus brief filed by Professor Bamzai argues that Section 1259 is an unconstitutional expansion of this Court's original jurisdiction and that the Court therefore lacks jurisdiction in all three cases. That is not correct. Congress has validly granted this Court appellate jurisdiction to review the decisions of the non-Article III courts Congress has created under its broad authority over federal territories and the District of Columbia. For the same reason, Section 1259 is a valid grant of appellate jurisdiction over the decisions of the CAAF—a court created pursuant to Congress's comparably broad authority to "make Rules for the Government and Regulation of the land and naval Forces."

IV. If the Court concludes that it has jurisdiction in *Dalmazzi* and *Cox*, it should not disturb the CAAF's discretionary denials of review. The CAAF did not abuse its discretion in vacating its grants of review and denying the petitions in those cases when it discovered that the questions it had agreed to decide were not squarely presented.

Argument

I. Petitioners Are not Entitled to Relief Under 10 U.S.C. 973(B)

Petitioners' principal claim rests on 10 U.S.C. 973(b), which provides that military officers may not hold certain "civil offices" unless they are "authorized by law" to do so. Petitioners assert that although Congress authorized military officers to be *assigned* to the CMCR by the Secretary of Defense, Section 973(b) bars the same military officers from being *appointed* to the CMCR by the President. Petitioners further assert that when the President appointed Judges Burton, Celtnieks, Herring, and Mitchell, Section

973(b) automatically terminated them from the military and rendered them ineligible to serve on the CCA panels that decided petitioners' appeals.

Both steps of petitioners' argument are unsound. Section 973(b) does not prohibit military officers from serving on the CMCR because a CMCR judgeship is not a "civil office" within meaning of Section 973(b), and because military officers are in any event "authorized by law" to serve on the court. And even if that were not so, nothing in Section 973(b) supports petitioners' assertion that officers who accept covered civil offices are automatically terminated from the military, voiding their subsequent actions. In seeking that startling result, petitioners ask this Court to reimpose a consequence that Congress deleted from the statute in 1983 and to ignore Congress's express directive that Section 973(b) may not "be construed to invalidate any action undertaken by an officer in furtherance of assigned official duties."

A. Section 973(b) Does Not Prohibit Military Officers from Serving on the CMCR

Congress created the CMCR as a military court, patterned after the CCAs, and it specifically authorized the Secretary of Defense to assign military officers to be CMCR judges. When the D.C. Circuit suggested that the officers' assignments to the CMCR raised questions under the Appointments Clause, the President and the Senate acted to eliminate those questions by nominating and confirming the officers to the same positions. The officers did not violate Section 973(b) by accepting the President's appointments.

1. A CMCR judgeship is not a "civil office" within the meaning of Section 973(b)

a. The bar to civil office-holding now codified at 10 U.S.C. 973(b) was first enacted in 1870. In its original form, it imposed a broader prohibition and carried the draconian consequence of automatic termination from the military upon acceptance of a civil office:

> It shall not be lawful for any officer of the army of the United States on the active list to hold any civil office, whether by election or appointment, and any such officer accepting or exercising the functions of a civil office shall at once cease

to be an officer of the army, and his commission shall be vacated thereby.

In enacting that provision, Congress sought to "assure civilian preeminence in government" by preventing "the military establishment from insinuating itself into the civil branch of government and thereby growing 'paramount' to it." For example, one Senator explained that "the theory of our Government is that the military should be separate from and subordinate to the civil authority." Another observed that "civil offices of the country" should not be "administered by the military authorities."

Congress carried forward the 1870 statute's basic prohibition, with minor amendments, for the next century. In 1968, the prohibition was codified as Section 973(b) and expanded to reach all military officers, not just those in the Army. Over the years, Congress also enacted a variety of statutes authorizing military officers to hold specific civil offices notwithstanding the general prohibition.

In 1983, the Office of Legal Counsel (OLC) concluded that Section 973(b) prohibited the "widespread" practice of appointing military lawyers to be Special Assistant U.S. Attorneys in the Department of Justice so that they could prosecute petty civil crimes on military reservations. OLC concluded that the lawyers were performing a "civil" function because they were prosecuting "offenses against the civil laws of the United States" and acting under the authority of "the Attorney General" rather than any "military source."

Congress responded to OLC's determination by "completely rewriting" Section 973(b). Section 973(b) now provides that "except as otherwise authorized by law," a military officer "may not hold, or exercise the functions of, a civil office in the Government of the United States" that is "an elective office," that "requires an appointment by the President by and with the advice and consent of the Senate," or that is in the Executive Schedule set forth in 5 U.S.C. 5312-5317. Section 973(b) also generally prohibits military officers from holding a "civil office" in a state or local government.

Because Section 973(b) does not define "civil office," that term must be construed "in accord with its ordinary or natural meaning." In this context, the natural meaning of "civil" is "non-military."

That natural meaning accords with Section 973(b)'s purpose of preserving the "separation of the military and civilian establishments." DOD has adopted the same understanding in exercising its authority to "prescribe regulations to implement" Under those regulations, a "civil office" is "a non-military office involving the exercise of the powers or authority of civil government."

b. A CMCR judgeship is not a "civil office" under Section 973(b) because review of military commissions, like review of courts-martial, is a military function. This Court has recognized that the use of military commissions to try enemy belligerents is "an important incident to the conduct of war" that "may constitutionally be performed by the *military arm* of the nation in time of war." "Following the analogy of courts-martial, military commissions in this country have invariably been composed of commissioned officers." And, like courts-martial, convictions before military commissions were traditionally subject to review by the convening officer. Accordingly, as the CMCR explained in *al-Nashiri*, "disposition of violations of the law of war by military commissions is a classic military function."

Consistent with that tradition, the MCA establishes a system of military commissions to try alien unprivileged enemy belligerents for law-of-war offenses committed in the context of hostilities against the United States. The MCA's procedures are "based upon" and largely consistent with the procedures governing general courts-martial under the UCMJ. 10 U.S.C. 948b(c). Like a general court-martial, a military commission is presided over by a "military judge," who must be "a commissioned officer of the armed forces." And like a general court-martial, a military commission is composed of between five and 12 "commissioned officers."

As particularly relevant here, the MCA's "review structure" is "virtually identical to the review system for courts-martial." "The 'scope of the CMCR's post-conviction review is a word-for-word copy' of the portion of the UCMJ that sets out the authority of each service's CCA, the military body that reviews court-martial convictions."

Like their counterparts on the CCAs, therefore, CMCR judges do not exercise "the powers or authority of civil government."

And for the same reason, the presence of military officers on the CMCR poses no threat to "civilian preeminence" in government.

c. This Court's decision in *Weiss* v. *United States* confirms that CMCR judges per form a military function. In *Weiss*, the Court noted that military judges on CCAs are selected by Judge Advocates General, a method that does not itself comply with the Appointments Clause. But the Court nonetheless held that the Clause was satisfied because the judges "were already commissioned officers when they were assigned" and thus "had already been appointed by the President with the advice and consent of the Senate" to their military offices.

In so holding, the Court assumed without deciding that the officers' prior appointments would satisfy the Appointments Clause for their new CCA positions only if the duties of a CCA judge were "germane" to their military offices. The Court had little difficulty concluding that any germaneness requirement was satisfied, because "all military officers, consistent with a long tradition, play a role in the operation of the military justice system." Among other things, officers convene, serve on, and review courts-martial.

The Court's reasoning in *Weiss* applies equally here. Like courts-martial, military commissions are part of the "military justice system" in which "all military officers, consistent with a long tradition, play a role." And just as "the role of military judge is 'germane' to that of military officer" when the judge serves on a CCA, it is also germane when the judge serves in a functionally equivalent role on the CMCR. That germaneness to an officer's military role confirms that a CMCR judgeship is not a "civil office" within the meaning of Section 973(b).

d. Petitioners provide no sound reason to question that conclusion.

First, petitioners assert that opinions by OLC, the Attorney General, and the Comptroller General have adopted a "very broad" interpretation of the term "civil office." But those opinions primarily addressed positions that were obviously non-military, and they thus described the breadth of the term "office"—not the meaning of "civil." The Olson Memorandum, for example, readily concluded that "the prosecution of offenses committed by persons not subject to the [UCMJ] seems clearly a 'civil' function," and devoted the bulk of its analysis to determining the meaning of "the statutory term '*office*.'" Petitioners thus err in reading the Olson Memorandum to conclude that a "civil office" includes any office that is "established by statute" and that "involve[s] the exercise of 'some portion of the sovereign power.'" That test identifies governmental "offices." But unless it is limited to *non-military* offices, it would sweep in many positions that are military rather than civil—including, for example, the Army Chief of Staff, Vice Chief of Staff, Deputy Chief of Staff, Assistant Chiefs of Staff, Chief of Engineers, and Judge Advocate General.

An 1893 Attorney General opinion confirms that Section 973(b) does not reach statutory offices performing military functions. The Attorney General was asked whether officers were terminated from the Army upon appointment to the California Debris Commission, a body under the "direction of the Secretary of War." In addition to concluding that the statute creating the Commission allowed the appointment of military officers, the Attorney General also determined that because the commissioners "acted under the direction of the Secretary of War" and "belonged to the War Department," "they did not, within the meaning of Section 973(b)'s predecessor, hold any civil office." The Attorney General thus concluded that the officers remained members of the Army, "merely detailed upon special duty, although the detail is to be effected by the President and the Senate." The same is true here.

Second, petitioners emphasize that "civilians can (and do) serve as CMCR judges." Petitioners assert that "even [an office] with military functions" is a "civil office" under Section 973(b) "so long as the office can be held *by* civilians." But that proves too much. It would mean, for example, that a CCA judgeship—a position this Court has deemed "germane" to the position of military officer—is a "civil office" because it can be held by "civilians." As it did with CCAs, Congress provided that civilians may serve on the CMCR. But it did not require the President to appoint any particular number of civilians, or any civilians at all, and the large majority of judges on the court have been military officers. The possibility that a civilian may hold an office with such military functions does not transform it into a prohibited "civil office."

Third, petitioners assert that the CMCR primarily focuses on "*domestic* law" rather than the law of war or other military matters. That is not correct. The CMCR was established to "review decisions of military commissions." The persons subject to trial by military commission are "alien unprivileged enemy belligerents." The MCA, by its terms, codifies "offenses that have traditionally been triable under the law of war or otherwise triable by military commission." Thus, like CCAs, the CMCR hears "matters as to which the expertise of military courts is singularly relevant."

Fourth, petitioners briefly suggest that the "novelty" of formal appellate review of military commissions means that such review cannot be a military function. The appellate review conducted by the CCAs was likewise a relative innovation, yet this Court did not hesitate to place it in the "long tradition" of military officers "playing a role in the operation of the military justice system." And although formal appellate oversight is new, military officers have long reviewed military-commission proceedings. During and immediately following the Civil War, for example, the Army Judge Advocate General's office reviewed the records of proceedings in 75,992 courts-martial, military commissions, and courts of inquiry and prepared 21,961 reports and opinions.

2. Military officers are "authorized by law" to serve as CMCR judges

Because a CMCR judgeship is not a "civil office," Section 973(b) would not disable military officers from serving on the court even if Congress had been silent about who is eligible to serve. But Congress was not silent. It specifically provided that "the Secretary of Defense may assign persons who are appellate military judges to be judges on the CMCR" and that "any judge so assigned shall be a commissioned officer of the armed forces." In light of that express authorization, Section 973(b) does not bar military officers from serving as judges on the CMCR for the additional reason that military officers are "authorized by law" to serve in that capacity.

a. Petitioners concede that Section 950f(b)(2) "expressly indicates" that military officers may serve as "judges" on the CMCR.

But they maintain that similar authorization is absent from Section 950f(b)(3), which allows the President to "appoint, by and with the advice and consent of the Senate, additional judges" to the CMCR. Petitioners' claim thus hinges on the proposition that an "additional judge" appointed under Section 950f(b)(3) and a "judge" assigned under Section 950f(b)(2) hold two different offices.

In fact, Section 950f establishes only one office: "judge on the CMCR." The Secretary of Defense may assign appellate military judges "to be judges on the CMCR," and the President may appoint "additional judges to the CMCR." But by specifying that "judges on the Court shall be assigned *or* appointed," Congress made clear that both assigned and appointed judges hold the same office—"judge on the Court."

The same was true in *Edmond* v. *United States*. There, this Court held that judges on the Coast Guard CCA could either be assigned by the Judge Advocate General or appointed by the Secretary of Transportation. Under the Appointments Clause, the Judge Advocate General's power to assign applied only to commissioned officers who had previously been appointed by the President with the advice and consent of the Senate, whereas the Secretary's power to appoint extended to civilians. *Ibid.* But despite those two modes of selection, the relevant statute creates only a single office—"appellate military judge" on the Coast Guard CCA.

b. Petitioners do not deny that *all* CMCR judges—assigned and appointed—are "'substantively identical' in terms of their duties." Petitioners nevertheless argue that assigned and appointed judges hold two different "offices" because they are selected and may be removed via different mechanisms. The mechanisms by which individuals are placed in and removed from an office are highly relevant under the Appointments Clause. But the question here is statutory, not constitutional: it is whether, under Section 973(b), Congress has "authorized by law" military officers to serve in the asserted "civil office." That question is resolved by Congress's decisions (1) to define a single statutory office, "judge on the CMCR," and (2) to authorize "commissioned officers of the armed forces" to fill that office. Petitioners speculate that "Congress may have had very good reasons" to permit military officers to be assigned to be CMCR judges without allowing them to be appointed to the same position. But the reasons petitioners hypothesize are far removed from the purpose of Section 973(b), which was to preserve the separation between civil and military functions and to "assure civilian preeminence in government." If those objectives are not threatened by a military officer's service as a CMCR judge pursuant to an assignment, they also are not threatened when the same officer holds the same office and performs the same functions pursuant to an appointment by the President.

c. Even if removal mechanisms were relevant under Section 973(b), petitioners' arguments would be misplaced here. Petitioners note that Congress specified that an "appellate military judge" serving on the CMCR may be reassigned to other duties under 10 U.S.C. 949b(b)(4). Petitioners also note (that, although the MCA does not expressly address the issue, the D.C. Circuit has recognized that a *civilian* appointed to the CMCR "may be removed by the President only for cause and not at will"—though the court did not have occasion to elaborate on what would constitute "cause" in this context. But petitioners err in assuming that, as a result of their presidential appointments, Judges Burton, Celtnieks, Herring, and Mitchell were made removable only under the standard applicable to civilians, and not under the procedures applicable to "appellate military judges" under Section 949b(b)(4). The President's nominations clarified that the judges would have "continued status as appellate military judges" and would remain subject to "Section 949b(b)." The judges' commissions likewise specify that they continue to be "Appellate Military Judges." Accordingly, notwithstanding their presidential appointments, the judges remained subject to reassignment under Section 949b(b).

* * *

When it enacted the MCA in 2009, Congress unambiguously intended for military officers to serve on the CMCR. After the D.C. Circuit concluded that the Secretary of Defense's assignment of military officers to the CMCR raised questions under the Appointments Clause, the President and the Senate heeded the D.C. Circuit's suggestion that they "put to rest any Appointments Clause questions" by "re-nominating and re-confirming the military judges to be *CMCR judges.*" This Court should reject petitioners' assertion that Section 973(b) barred that sensible course of action by the Political Branches.

B. Even if Section 973(b) Prohibited Military Officers from Serving on the CMCR, Congress Expressly Foreclosed the Relief Petitioners Seek

Section 973(b) provides that military officers "may not hold, or exercise the functions of," certain civil offices, but it does not itself prescribe a consequence if an officer accepts an appointment to a covered office. Petitioners nonetheless insist that the President's appointments of Judges Burton, Celtnieks, Herring, and Mitchell "resulted in their immediate termination from the military— thereby disqualifying them from continuing to serve on the CCAs" and rendering "all CCA decisions in which they participated" after the appointments "void." Congress has foreclosed that result.

1. As originally enacted in 1870, Section 973(b)'s predecessor provided that any officer who accepted a covered civil office would "at once cease to be an officer of the army." The precise language was amended over the next century, but until 1983 the statute continued to direct that "[t]he acceptance of such a civil office or the exercise of its functions by such officer terminates his employment."

When Congress amended the statute in 1983, it completely rewrote Section 973(b), "striking out subsection (b) and inserting in lieu thereof" new language. The amendment eliminated any provision for the automatic termination of officers who accept a covered civil office. Instead, Congress enacted an express savings clause directing that "nothing in Section 973(b) shall be construed to invalidate any action undertaken by an officer in furtherance of assigned official duties." Congress otherwise left the remedies for violations to the Secretary of Defense, who was authorized to "prescribe regulations to implement" Section 973.

The plain language of Section 973(b)(5)'s savings clause unambiguously forecloses the relief petitioners seek. Officers serving as military judges are "assigned to a CCA" by the relevant Judge Advocate General. Judges Burton, Celtnieks, Herring, and Mitchell thus decided petitioners' appeals as part of their "assigned official duties." And petitioners' claim that the asserted violation of Section 973(b) renders the CCAs' decisions "void" is undeniably an attempt to "invalidate" the judges' actions in furtherance of those duties. That should end the inquiry. "Where, as here, the statute's language is plain, 'the sole function of the courts is to enforce it according to its terms.'"

2. Petitioners do not appear to dispute that a natural reading of Section 973(b)(5) forecloses their claim. But they assert that Section 973(b)(5) "was only meant to have retroactive effect" and has no application to post-1983 events. Petitioners further assert that Section 973(b)(5) prohibits only the invalidation of actions taken in the covered civil office, not those taken in furtherance of an officer's military duties. Nothing in the text supports those limitations, and several features of the statute refute them.

Most obviously, Section 973(b)(5) is not, by its terms, retroactive. Instead, Congress specifically addressed pre-1983 events in a separate, uncodified provision that parallels, and is broader than, Section 973(b)(5):

Nothing in section, as in effect before the date of the enactment of this Act, shall be construed—

(1) to invalidate any action undertaken by an officer of an Armed Force in furtherance of assigned official duties; or

(2) to have terminated the military appointment of an officer of an Armed Force by reason of the acceptance of a civil office, or the exercise of its functions, by that officer in furtherance of assigned official duties.

That parallel uncodified provision specifically addressing pre-1983 events disproves petitioners' assertion that Section 973(b)(5) was intended to have retroactive effect—let alone *exclusively* retroactive effect. Indeed, in light of that provision, petitioners' retroactive-only reading of Section 973(b)(5) would render it superfluous.

There is likewise no merit to petitioners' assertion that Section 973(b)(5)'s protection for actions taken "in furtherance of assigned official duties" is limited to the officer's actions in the civil office. A military officer's "assigned official duties" plainly include his or her *military* duties—here, service on the CCAs. DOD's implementing regulations confirm that understanding, specifying that "no actions undertaken by a member in carrying out assigned military duties shall be invalidated solely by virtue of such member having held or exercised the functions of a civil office."

Finally, petitioners err in suggesting that if Section 973(b)(5) is interpreted to bar private parties from seeking judicial invalidation of actions taken by officers alleged to have violated Section 973(b), the statute would be deprived "of most of its teeth." In fact, Section 973(b) and its predecessors have been cited in only a handful of judicial decisions, and we are not aware of any case in which a court has relied on those provisions to provide relief to a private party. Instead, as the Olson Memorandum illustrates, Section 973(b) has been enforced administratively, in the same manner as countless other regulations of federal personnel that do not give rise to rights enforceable by members of the public.

3. Even if petitioners could clear the hurdle erected by Section 973(b)(5), they would still have to establish that Section 973(b) automatically terminated Judges Burton, Celtnieks, Herring, and Mitchell from the military upon their acceptance of appointments to the CMCR. In seeking to do so, petitioners acknowledge that "Congress deleted the automatic termination language from § 973(b)(2) when it amended that provision in 1983." Petitioners provide no valid reason to deny effect to Congress's action.

First, petitioners contend that the 1983 amendments should not be construed to depart from the "common-law doctrine of incompatibility," under which the holder of an office who accepted an incompatible or forbidden office was deemed to vacate the first office. But even assuming that the doctrine remains viable, the presumption that Congress intends to adhere to common-law rules does not apply "when a statutory purpose to the contrary is evident." Congress's repeal of the automatic-termination provision makes it quite "evident" that Congress intended to abandon that rule. Instead, Congress left it to DOD to determine the appropriate response to violations of Section 973(b). The administrative remedies may include "involuntary discharge or release from active duty." But in contrast to the pre-1983 regime, those remedies are now imposed as a result of administrative action by DOD rather than automatically upon acceptance of a covered office.

Second, petitioners note that at the same time it amended Section 973(b), Congress enacted a provision specifying that a military officer could accept a position on the Red River Commission. In the portion of that provision on which petitioners rely, Congress further specified that, "notwithstanding the provisions of section 973(b)," the officer's acceptance of that position "shall not terminate or otherwise affect such officer's appointment as a military officer." Petitioners state that "there would have been no need" for that language if Congress had eliminated the automatic-termination rule. But there would have been no need for that language even *with* an automatic-termination rule. The statute expressly provided that "the President may appoint a regular officer" to the Red River Commission. *Ibid.* Because a military officer is "authorized by law" to hold that position, the appointment would not violate Section 973(b) in the first place. Third, petitioners argue that the legislative history of the 1983 amendments does not discuss abolition of the automatic-termination rule. But "it is not the law that a statute can have no effects which are not explicitly mentioned in its legislative history."

Fourth, petitioners state that "the government's regulations reinforce the conclusion that immediate separation from the military" remains the automatic consequence of a violation of Section 973(b). In fact, those regulations say the opposite. They provide that service members "affected by the prohibitions against exercising the functions of a civil office *may request* retirement (if eligible), discharge, or release from active duty," and that the relevant Secretary "*may* approve these requests, consistent with the needs of the Service." Termination thus is not automatic upon the acceptance of the prohibited office; it is expressly made discretionary.

And the regulation further specifies that a Secretary may not grant a request for retirement or discharge in several circumstances, such as when the service member is "obligated to fulfill an active duty service commitment."

II. Simultaneous Service on a CCA and the CMCR Does not Raise Constitutional Questions

Petitioners sought this Court's review of the question whether "simultaneous service on both the CMCR and a CCA violates the Appointments Clause." Petitioners' merits brief all but abandons the Appointments Clause as a freestanding claim, instead arguing that the asserted need to avoid constitutional questions under the Appointments on which petitioners rely was not expressing OLC's view; it was quoting an email from DOD. And while that email stated that Section 973 would "prohibit continuation of military status" after acceptance of a civil office, it did not suggest that Section 973(b) itself would automatically terminate that status. The same is true of the 2002 DOD advisory memo (which in any event discussed a now-superseded version of Directive 1344.10).

A. Judges Burton, Celtnieks, Herring, and Mitchell were placed in two distinct offices: CCA judge and CMCR judge. As petitioners do not and could not dispute, they were placed in each of those offices in a manner consistent with the Appointments Clause.

CCA judges are "inferior Officers." Because military judges are "already commissioned officers" appointed by the President with the advice and consent of the Senate, the Appointments Clause allows them to be assigned to the CCAs without a "second appointment." And even assuming that CMCR judges are principal officers, the judges have now been appointed to the CMCR by the President with the advice and consent of the Senate. Those appointments "put to rest any Appointments Clause questions." Petitioners nonetheless contend that it somehow violates the Appointments Clause for a single individual to serve simultaneously as a CCA judge (an inferior office) and as a CMCR judge (a principal office, in petitioners' view). Petitioners assert that simultaneous service on the CMCR and a CCA "might be functionally incompatible" or "incongruous." But petitioners identify nothing in the text or history of the Appointments Clause, or in this Court's decisions, to support their assertion that the Clause imposes such ill-defined "incompatibility" or "incongruity" limits.

Even if the Appointments Clause constitutionalized some "incompatibility" or "incongruity" limitation on simultaneous service, it would not be implicated here. The CCAs and the CMCR do not have overlapping jurisdiction, and they do not review each other's decisions. Placing CCA judges on the CMCR, with its narrower jurisdiction and lighter docket, is analogous to placing Article III judges on specialized Article III courts like the Foreign Intelligence Surveillance Court and the Foreign Intelligence Surveillance Court of Review. Simultaneous service on the CCA and the CMCR thus would not violate even the common-law incompatibility principle, which applies only if two offices "have the right to interfere, one with the other," or where one of the offices is "subordinate" to the other.

Petitioners appear to contend that the problem with simultaneous service is that other judges on the CCAs might be "unduly influenced by" the status of Judges Burton, Celtnieks, Herring, and Mitchell as (assumed) principal officers on the CMCR. But as the CAAF explained, that argument erroneously "presumes that a judge's status as a principal officer on the CMCR somehow carries over to the CCA, and invests him with authority or status not held by ordinary CCA judges." "That is not the case." "When such a judge sits as a CCA judge, he is no different from any other CCA judge."

Nor is there any general principle that a multi-member adjudicative body may not be composed of members who have differing status in other contexts. CCA panels can be composed of judges who hold different military ranks. The original Circuit Courts consisted of Justices of this Court sitting with district judges. Today, three-judge district courts include both district and circuit judges. And both district judges and retired Justices of this Court sit by designation on panels of the courts of appeals.

B. Petitioners also briefly suggest that it could raise questions under the Commander-in-Chief Clause if military officers could be appointed to the CMCR, where, in petitioners' view, they could be removed only for inefficiency, neglect of duty, or malfeasance. As previously explained, however, that argument rests on a mistaken premise: Judges Burton, Celtnieks, Herring, and Mitchell remained subject to the reassignment provisions in 10 U.S.C. 949b(b) even after their appointments. Petitioners do not contend that the restrictions on reassignment in Section 949b(b) impinge on the President's authority as Commander in Chief.

III. This Court Lacks Jurisdiction in *Dalmazzi* and *Cox*, but Has Jurisdiction in *Ortiz*

A. This Court Lacks Jurisdiction in *Dalmazzi* and *Cox* Because Section 1259(3) Does Not Authorize Review of the CAAF's Denial of Discretionary Review

In granting certiorari, this Court directed the parties to brief the question whether it has jurisdiction in *Dalmazzi* and *Cox*. The Court lacks jurisdiction in those cases because the CAAF ultimately denied the petitions for discretionary review.

1. The CAAF granted review in *Dalmazzi* and *Cox* to decide constitutional and statutory questions arising from a military officer's simultaneous service on a CCA and as a presidentially appointed judge on the CMCR. When it became clear that Judges Burton, Celtnieks, Herring, and Mitchell had not actually been appointed to the CMCR until after the CCAs issued their decisions, the CAAF vacated its grants of review and denied the petitions because the cases were "moot as to the simultaneous-service issues" on which it had granted review.

Petitioners seek this Court's review of those orders under Section 1259(3), which confers jurisdiction in "cases in which the CAAF granted a petition for review." But the CAAF "vacate[d]" its orders granting review and then "denied" the petitions. As a result, *Dalmazzi* and *Cox* are no longer cases in which the CAAF "granted a petition for review" within the meaning of Section 1259(3). That understanding is confirmed by a related provision, which precludes this Court's review of "any action" by the CAAF "in refusing to grant a petition for review":

Decisions of the United States Court of Appeals for the Armed Forces are subject to review by the Supreme Court by writ of certiorari as provided in U.S.C. 1259. The Supreme Court may not review by a writ of certiorari under this section *any action* of the CAAF in refusing to grant a petition for review. By its plain terms, Section 867a(a)'s preclusion of review applies here because the CAAF ultimately denied— *i.e.*, "refused to grant"—the petitions.

2. Although we highlighted Section 867a(a) at the certiorari stage, petitioners do not cite it—let alone attempt to reconcile their position with its plain text. The arguments petitioners do advance are unpersuasive.

First, petitioners argue that these cases fall within Section 1259(3)'s literal terms because the CAAF initially "granted a petition for review." But petitioners do not appear to deny that the CAAF had authority to reconsider its orders granting review. That authority flows from the principle that a court "ordinarily has the power to modify or rescind its orders at any point prior to final judgment." And once the CAAF exercised that authority and vacated its orders granting review, these cases ceased to be "cases in which the CAAF granted a petition for review."

Courts of appeals have reached the same conclusion under 28 U.S.C. 1292(b), which confers jurisdiction over an interlocutory appeal if the district court enters an order certifying that the statutory standard is met. When a district court initially enters the required order but then withdraws it before the court of appeals takes jurisdiction, the withdrawal "destroys the court of appeals' jurisdiction." The same principle applies here.

Second, petitioners contend that the context and legislative history of Section 1259(3) support their interpretation. In fact, the opposite is true. When DOD proposed what is now Section 1259, it explained that the statute would "preclude direct Supreme Court review in cases where the CAAF declined to exercise its discretionary jurisdiction." The Chief Judge of the CAAF thus recognized that, if the proposal were enacted, the CAAF "would hold the key allowing access to the Supreme Court." The Senate Report echoed the same point, noting that "the number of cases which reach the Supreme Court" would be "dependent on the frequency with which the CAAF grants an accused's petition for review."

Petitioners could not contend that this Court would have jurisdiction if the CAAF had noted the date of the judges' appointments *before* it granted the petitions and then issued exactly the same written decision denying review at the outset. Petitioners identify no sound reason why this Court's jurisdiction should turn on the fortuity of whether the CAAF notes such a defect before or after it grants a petition for review. To the contrary, just as this Court would have no ready criteria by which to review the CAAF's initial denials of discretionary review, it is equally unclear what standards it would apply to the CAAF's discretionary decision to deny review in a case in which it initially granted a petition.

Third, petitioners contend that the government's position here is inconsistent with its position in *United States* v. *Denedo*. That is not so. *Denedo* involved Section 1259(4), which gives this Court jurisdiction over cases "in which the CAAF granted relief." The government argued, and this opinions resolving the merits. But petitioners do not and could not contend that there was any such evasion here. The CAAF denied the petitions in *Dalmazzi* and *Cox*, but it promptly resolved the relevant questions in *Ortiz*, the first case in which they were squarely presented. And petitioners err in impugning the CAAF's practice in other cases of denying or dismissing petitions for review when, "after granting review, it concludes that it lacks jurisdiction." Like any court, the CAAF is powerless to act on the merits of a case if it lacks jurisdiction.

B. This Court Has Jurisdiction in *Ortiz* Because 28 U.S.C. 1259 Is a Valid Grant of Appellate Jurisdiction

An amicus brief filed by Professor Bamzai argues that Section 1259 is an unconstitutional expansion of the Court's original jurisdiction—which would mean that this Court lacks jurisdiction in *Ortiz* as well, and that it likewise lacked jurisdiction in each of the nine cases it has previously reviewed under Section 1259.15. That is not correct. Section 1259 is a valid grant of appellate jurisdiction, and this Court therefore has jurisdiction in *Ortiz*.

1. Article III grants this Court original jurisdiction "[i]n all Cases affecting Ambassadors, other public Ministers and Consuls, and those in which a State shall be a party," and provides that "in all other cases" the Court "shall have appellate Jurisdiction, both as to Law and Fact, with such Exceptions, and under such Regulations as the Congress shall make." It has been settled since *Marbury* v. *Madison*, that Congress may not expand the original jurisdiction conferred by Article III. In that case, the Court famously held that to issue a writ of mandamus requiring an Executive Branch officer to deliver a commission would be "to sustain an original action for that paper, and therefore seems not to belong to appellate, but to original jurisdiction." The Court explained that "the essential criterion of appellate jurisdiction" is "that it revises and corrects the proceedings in a cause already instituted, and does not create that cause."

2. Judged by that criterion, this Court's review of the CAAF's decisions under Section 1259 is appellate, not original. A writ of certiorari to the CAAF "revises and corrects the proceedings in a cause already instituted"—specifically, a criminal proceeding in a specialized system of military courts that have been recognized since the Founding as competent to try and punish offenses by service members.

The court-martial "is older than the Constitution." Indeed, the *Federalist Papers* discuss "trials by courts-martial" under the Articles of Confederation. The Constitution authorized Congress to carry forward the court-martial system by empowering it to "make Rules for the Government and Regulation of the land and naval Forces." And by exempting "cases arising in the land or naval forces," the Fifth Amendment's Grand Jury Clause contains a "recognition and sanction of an existing military jurisdiction."

This Court has long recognized that those constitutional provisions "show that Congress has the power to provide for the trial and punishment of military and naval offenses in the manner then and now practiced by civilized nations," and that its power to do so is "entirely independent" of Article III. The Court has thus held that the judgments of a properly constituted court-martial, acting within its jurisdiction, "rest on the same basis, and are surrounded by the same considerations which give conclusiveness to the judgments of other legal tribunals." The valid, final judgments of military courts, like those of any court of competent jurisdiction have res judicata effect." They are likewise given effect under the Double Jeopardy Clause.

The Constitution's broad grant of authority to Congress to "make rules for the government of the military" does not "freeze court-martial usage at a particular time." "Congress has gradually changed the system of military justice so that it has come to more closely resemble the civilian system." In so doing, it has established "an integrated system of military courts and review procedures." That system has broad jurisdiction over offenses committed by service members, including offenses unconnected with military service. As a result, courts-martial exercise jurisdiction that overlaps with the criminal jurisdiction of federal and state courts. And the decisions of courts-martial are reviewed by the CCAs and by the CAAF, a court composed of civilian judges appointed for fixed terms and removable only for specified causes.

3. Professor Bamzai argues that because the CAAF is an Article I tribunal located "within the Executive Branch," any review of the CAAF's decisions is original rather than appellate. But as Professor Bamzai acknowledges, this Court's appellate jurisdiction is not limited to reviewing the proceedings of Article III courts. The Court also exercises appellate jurisdiction over state courts, and the non-Article III courts Congress has established for federal territories and the District of Columbia.

This Court upheld the exercise of appellate jurisdiction over non-Article III territorial courts in *United States* v. *Coe*. The Court explained that Congress's plenary authority to "make all needful Rules and Regulations respecting the Territory or other Property belonging to the United States," authorizes it to establish non-Article III "legislative courts" for the territories. And the Court concluded that "the judicial action of all inferior courts established by Congress may, in accordance with the Constitution, be subjected to the appellate jurisdiction of the supreme judicial tribunal of the government."

This Court has likewise held that Congress's power "to exercise exclusive legislation in all cases whatsoever" over the District of Columbia authorizes it to establish non-Article III courts for the District. The Court explained that "the requirements of Article III must in proper circumstances give way to accommodate plenary grants of power to Congress to legislate with respect to specialized areas having particularized needs and warranting distinctive treatment."

The system of courts-martial Congress has established under Article I, § 8, Cl. 14, stands on similar footing. "It too involves a constitutional grant of power that has been historically understood as giving the political Branches of Government extraordinary control over the precise subject matter at issue." Indeed, the Court in *Palmore* identified the court-martial system as one of the "specialized areas having particularized needs" where Congress has permissibly created non-Article III courts.

Accordingly, just as the decisions of the territorial courts "may, in accordance with the Constitution, be subjected to the appellate jurisdiction" of this Court, Congress may grant this Court appellate jurisdiction to review the CAAF's decisions. And because courts-martial, like territorial courts, "are unique historical exceptions" to Article III grounded in "other provisions of the Constitution," this Court can uphold Section 1259 without deciding whether Congress could confer jurisdiction on the Court to review directly the decisions of other non-Article III tribunals, such as those that adjudicate matters of "public rights."

4. Professor Bamzai observes that in a line of cases beginning with *Ex parte Vallandigham*, this Court has held or stated that it lacks jurisdiction to review the decisions of military commissions. But those cases, including *Vallandigham*, noted the absence of *statutory* jurisdiction. Accordingly, just a few years before Congress enacted Section 1259, this Court cited *Vallandigham* and several of the other decisions on which Professor Bamzai relies as standing for the proposition that Congress has "never deemed it appropriate to confer on this Court 'appellate jurisdiction to supervise the administration of criminal justice in the military'"—not the far more sweeping proposition that Congress *could not* confer such jurisdiction.

To be sure, the Court's opinion in *Vallandigham* also indicated that review in that case would have been inconsistent with Article III. But the military commission at issue there was not a court established by Congress; it was, instead, created on the authority of a commanding general, who conducted the only review of its findings and sentence. As a result, the writ of certiorari sought was to be directed to the Army Judge Advocate General, not to any tribunal. And in concluding that the military commission was not of a "judicial character," the Court relied in part on *United States* v. *Ferreira*, which held that a district judge was not acting in a judicial capacity when he rendered decisions subject to review by the Secretary of the Treasury. The CAAF, in contrast, is a court established by Act of Congress in the system of military justice recognized by the Constitution, and its decisions are of the same judicial character as those of the territorial courts and the District of Columbia Court of Appeals.

IV. Even If This Court Has Jurisdiction in *Dalmazzi* and *Cox*, It Should Not Disturb the CAAF's Discretionary Denials of Review

Even if this Court concludes that it has jurisdiction in *Dalmazzi* and *Cox*, it should not disturb the CAAF's denial of review in those cases. As petitioners do not dispute, the CAAF had discretion to grant or deny the petitions for review. At most, therefore, this Court could review the CAAF's action for "abuse of discretion." The CAAF did not abuse its discretion in denying review in *Dalmazzi* and *Cox* after it discovered that the questions it had agreed to decide were not presented. This Court, too, has dismissed writs of certiorari as improvidently granted when it becomes apparent that the question on which it granted review is not cleanly presented.

Petitioners contend that the CAAF erred in describing its denial of review in *Dalmazzi* as a matter of "mootness." But as the context makes clear—and as petitioners acknowledge—the CAAF's statement that the case was "moot as to the issues" on which it had granted review was not meant to convey that the case was moot in the Article III sense. Instead, it reflected the CAAF's conclusion that the case did not actually present the relevant issues.

The CAAF's use of colloquial language in expressing that conclusion furnishes no basis for review.

Petitioners also contend that the petitioners in *Dalmazzi* and *Cox* have valid claims under Section 973(b) even though Judges Burton, Celtnieks, Herring, and Mitchell were not appointed to the CMCR until after they acted on the appeals in those cases. Petitioners observe that Section 973(b) provides that an officer may not "hold, or exercise the functions of," a prohibited civil office, and they argue that the judges "exercised the functions" of a CMCR judge even before their appointments.

Even if that argument were correct, it would not establish an abuse of discretion. The CAAF was presented with the same argument. But it did not address that argument, and did not otherwise resolve the merits of the statutory and constitutional challenges in *Dalmazzi* and *Cox*. Instead, it denied discretionary review—perhaps because it concluded that the applicability of Section 973(b) during the four weeks between the judges' confirmation and their appointments lacked sufficient continuing importance to warrant an exercise of its discretionary jurisdiction. In taking that step, the CAAF acted well within its discretion.

Conclusion

In *Dalmazzi* and *Cox*, the writs of certiorari should be dismissed for lack of jurisdiction. In *Ortiz*, the judgment of the CAAF should be affirmed.[1]

Brief #2

The issue in this case is whether the fact that a driver in lawful possession or control of a rental car is not listed on the rental agreement will defeat the otherwise reasonable expectation of privacy protected by the Fourth Amendment.

Statement

Following a conditional guilty plea in the U.S. District Court for the Middle District of Pennsylvania, petitioner was convicted of possession of heroin with the intent to distribute it, in violation of 21 U.S.C. 841(a)(1), and possession of body armor by a prohibited person, in violation of 18 U.S.C. 931(a)(1). He was sentenced to 120 months of imprisonment, to be followed by three years of supervised release. The court of appeals affirmed.

On September 17, 2014, petitioner accompanied Latasha Reed to the Willow Brook Mall in Wayne, New Jersey, so that she could rent a Ford Fusion from Budget Rent A Car System, Inc., a subsidiary of Avis Budget Group, Inc. (Avis). The "exact nature" of petitioner's relationship with Reed is "disputed." Petitioner and Reed arranged for Reed to rent the car by herself, without identifying any other potential drivers, and then for petitioner to use the car that she had acquired. Avis rents its cars only to drivers who satisfy certain criteria. At the rental counter, Avis requires a prospective renter to present a driver's license and certify that the license is "currently valid."

A prospective renter must also certify certain facts about his or her driving history and criminal background—namely, that he or she has "never been convicted of obtaining a vehicle unlawfully, possessing a stolen vehicle, or using a vehicle in a crime or in connection with an unlawful act"; that "within the past 36 months," he or she "ha[s] not had 3 or more accidents" or "been convicted of DWI/DUI/DWAI," "leaving the scene of an accident," "failure to report an accident," or "reckless driving"; and that "within the past 24 months," he or she "has not had 3 or more convictions for moving violations." Avis informs the prospective renter that those certifications are "material" to its "decision to rent or permit him or her to drive its vehicle." Petitioner has prior convictions for conduct that includes riding in a stolen van and striking a law-enforcement officer with a vehicle.

Like other rental-car companies, Avis prohibits renters from allowing anyone to drive a rented car who is not specifically authorized to do so under the rental agreement. The rental agreement provides that, other than the renter, the only authorized drivers are (1) the renter's spouse, (2) the renter's co-employee acting on company business, and (3) another person who appears at the time of the rental and signs an authorized driver form.

While still at the rental counter, prospective renters are asked whether "anyone else will be driving the vehicle." Such "other drivers," who may be added for a fee, "must also be at least 25 years old and validly licensed." The rental agreement, which lists the renter and additional authorized drivers, "must stay in the vehicle at all times," If a renter were to permit an unauthorized person to drive the car, Avis would deem the rental agreement "void," and it "would recover the vehicle."

In this case, petitioner "just sat in his own car," in "front of the building," while Reed entered the Avis office alone, made the necessary certifications about her own eligibility as a renter, signed the rental agreement, and paid for the rental. The agreement informed her that if she "provided false or misleading information, her use of the vehicle is prohibited and unauthorized."

The agreement also expressly provided, in capital letters, that "PERMITTING AN UNAUTHORIZED DRIVER TO OPERATE THE VEHICLE IS A VIOLATION OF THE RENTAL AGREEMENT." In addition to signing the agreement itself, Reed separately signed a notice within the agreement that included the statement "no additional drivers allowed without prior written consent." Reed also initialed a statement that "the only ones permitted to drive the vehicle other than the renter are the renter's spouse, the renter's co-employee (with the renter's permission, while on company business), or a person who appears at the time of the rental and signs an Additional Driver Form." The agreement contained a space for an "Additional Driver" to sign, which was left blank.

After completing her transaction, Reed rejoined petitioner. The two then exchanged cars in the shopping-mall parking lot, with petitioner taking sole possession of the rental car, even though the rental agreement did not permit him to drive it. Later that day, petitioner began driving the rental car by himself to Pittsburgh, Pennsylvania, which is six or seven hours away from Wayne.

During that trip, petitioner was stopped by the Pennsylvania state police on Interstate 81 outside of Harrisburg. A police officer had begun to trail him after perceiving him to be driving a rental car in a suspicious manner. The officer pulled the car over, with the intention of issuing a warning, after observing him violating a Pennsylvania statute prohibiting lane misuse. When the officer approached the car, he noticed that petitioner was extremely nervous. He asked petitioner for his driver's license and the rental agreement. Explaining that he had "washed" his driver's license, petitioner produced an interim New York driver's license that lacked a photograph. Petitioner also produced the rental agreement and acknowledged that he himself was not the renter. He stated that, instead, "a friend" had rented the car.

The officer began processing the information petitioner had provided, with a brief interruption while he and petitioner moved the cars to a safer location a short distance down the highway. When the officer checked petitioner's identification, the computer returned a name different from the one on petitioner's interim license. Around the same time, a second officer arrived. While the officers were attempting to sort out the identification issue, petitioner explained that he was traveling to Pittsburgh to visit a woman pregnant with his child. He reiterated that the car had been rented by a "friend."

The officers subsequently observed that petitioner was "not on the renter agreement." They eventually determined that the name returned by the computer was an alias; that petitioner had a lengthy criminal history that included drug and weapons charges; and that petitioner had an outstanding non-extradition arrest warrant in New Jersey for a probation violation. The officers asked petitioner to get out of the rental car, and patted him down.

After issuing petitioner a warning for the traffic violation, and apologizing for the delay, the officers asked him whether he had anything illegal in the car. Petitioner said that he did not. The officers asked for his consent to search the car. At that point, petitioner stated that he had a "blunt" (which the officers understood to be a reference to a marijuana cigarette) in the car, and he offered to retrieve it. The officers declined to let him do so, but continued to seek consent for a search.

They later testified that the circumstances gave them probable cause to justify a search of the car even without consent, but that it was their practice to seek consent in all cases. They told petitioner, however, that they did not actually need his consent to search the car because he was not an authorized driver under the rental agreement. According to the officers, petitioner consented to the search. As the search began, petitioner admitted to recently using cocaine.

The officers opened the trunk and found body armor, which people with certain prior convictions are prohibited from possessing. In light of that discovery, petitioner's continued nervous behavior, and his criminal history, the officers decided to detain, but not arrest, petitioner. After petitioner was informed that he would be placed in handcuffs for purposes of such detention, petitioner attempted to flee on foot. The officers (who had been joined by a third off-duty officer) caught up with him and arrested him. After resuming the search, the officers found 49 bricks of heroin in the trunk. The rental car was towed to Harrisburg.

A federal grand jury in the U.S. District Court for the Middle District of Pennsylvania returned an indictment charging petitioner with one count of possession of heroin with the intent to distribute it, in violation of 21 U.S.C. 841(a)(1), and one count of possession of body armor by a prohibited person, in violation of Petitioner moved to suppress the evidence obtained from the rental car on Fourth Amendment grounds. After conducting an evidentiary hearing, which included testimony from an Avis representative, the district court denied the motion.

The court determined, as an initial matter, that the evidence was not the fruit of an unlawful seizure, because the stop had been based on the observation of a traffic violation and had not been unreasonably prolonged. The court additionally determined that petitioner had "no expectation of privacy in the car" that would permit him to challenge the officers' search of it. The court observed that petitioner "was not a party to the rental agreement" and "did not pay for the rental."

Petitioner entered a conditional guilty plea to the charges, reserving his right to appeal the denial of his suppression motion. The Probation Office's presentence report described Reed as

petitioner's "former girlfriend" and recounted petitioner's statement that "he had been romantically involved" with a different
woman, who lives in Pennsylvania, "intermittently for five years."
The district court imposed a ten-year prison sentence. The court
of appeals affirmed.

The court upheld the district court's determination that the
stop was lawful, and rejected petitioner's challenge to the search.
The court of appeals explained that "the sole occupant of a rental
vehicle" has no "Fourth Amendment expectation of privacy when
that occupant is not named in the rental agreement," and may not
"challenge a search of that vehicle." The court cited circuit precedent holding that "society generally does not share or recognize
an expectation of privacy for those who have gained possession
and control over a rental vehicle they have borrowed without the
permission of the rental company."

Summary of Argument

The court of appeals correctly recognized that petitioner did not
have "a legitimate expectation of privacy," in a rental car that he
had no legitimate basis to drive. Reed could not authorize him to
drive Avis's car, and taking it without authorization did not make
it his own "effect" for purposes of the Fourth Amendment.

Petitioner's argument rests on the untenable premise that he
is entitled to Fourth Amendment rights for doing something that
he was not allowed to do. This Court's precedent makes clear that
had he been a passenger in a car that someone else had rented,
he would have had no right to challenge the search of its trunk.

Taking the wheel without permission and leaving behind the
actual renter did not give him additional constitutional protection.
Someone who is not "'legitimately on premises,'" such as someone
who is driving "a stolen automobile," cannot challenge a search of
those premises. Petitioner cannot claim to have been "legitimately
on premises" here, where Reed's transfer of Avis's car violated an
express written directive from the rightful owner.

Even if petitioner could satisfy the threshold requirement of
legitimate presence, he cannot carry his further burden to show a
legitimate expectation of privacy. He cannot establish any enforceable property rights in Avis's car, given that Reed could not

legitimately allow him to take it. Indeed, traditional common-law principles suggest the transfer here was affirmatively unlawful. And although it is possible to have a reasonable expectation of privacy in the absence of property rights, petitioner cannot establish that society would recognize non-property-based privacy rights in his appropriation of someone else's car. Reed's handover of the car was at the very least a breach of contract, in derogation of Avis's own right to decide whom it will entrust to drive its cars. It is common knowledge that car rental is a personal transaction that does not make the car available for general enjoyment, and strawman car rentals disserve society by frustrating law-enforcement efforts to prevent smuggling and other crimes. Petitioner errs in contending that he acquired a constitutionally protected interest in Avis's car simply by asserting "possession and control" over it.

If that alone were the test, then even Reed's putative permission would be irrelevant; indeed, even a car thief would have Fourth Amendment rights. In any event, petitioner's position insupportably suggests that he could himself bequeath Fourth Amendment rights in the car to subsequent transferees and that those rights would remain with the car no matter how long the rightful owner was divested of its property. His approach would also create an anomalous regime in which someone has more Fourth Amendment rights when the actual renter is not present than when she is, and in which those rights can appear and disappear on a moment's notice. And his further suggestion that he has special Fourth Amendment rights by virtue of his relationship with Reed, the nature of which is disputed, is neither properly presented nor legally sustainable.

Argument

Petitioner Had No Fourth Amendment Interest in a Rental Car that He Was Prohibited from Driving

The Fourth Amendment protects "the right of the people to be secure in their persons, houses, papers, and effects, against unreasonable searches." It does not, however, allow people to challenge searches of "effects" that are not "theirs," and petitioner's unauthorized possession of Avis's rental car did not in any sense make that car his or give him a reasonable expectation of privacy in it. Petitioner did not own the car, had not rented it, and was not allowed to drive it. He cannot assert Fourth Amendment rights to object to its search.

A. Petitioner's Illegitimate Presence in Avis's Car Cannot Support a Fourth Amendment Claim

Petitioner's only ground for asserting a Fourth Amendment interest in the search of Avis's car is the fact that he was driving it, in violation of the rental agreement. This Court has never recognized a Fourth Amendment claim premised on prohibited activity. It should not do so here.

As the constitutional text makes clear, "Fourth Amendment rights are personal rights which, like some other constitutional rights, may not be vicariously asserted."

It has therefore "long been the rule that a defendant can urge the suppression of evidence obtained in violation of the Fourth Amendment only if that defendant demonstrates that *his* Fourth Amendment rights were violated by the challenged search."

Absent the existence of recognized property rights capable of invasion through "physical intrusion," the touchstone of such a demonstration is an affirmative showing that the defendant had a "legitimate expectation of privacy in the invaded place." For a "subjective expectation of privacy" to be "legitimate," it must be "one that society is prepared to recognize as reasonable." That is, it must be "one that has 'a source outside of the Fourth Amendment, either by reference to concepts of real or personal property law or to understandings that are recognized and permitted by society.'"

Applying that framework, this Court held in *Rakas* v. *Illinois*, "that automobile passengers could not assert the protection of the Fourth Amendment against the seizure of incriminating evidence from a vehicle where they owned neither the vehicle nor the evidence."

Although the passengers were "'legitimately on the premises' in the sense that they were in the car with the permission of its owner," they "neither owned nor leased" the car, and "asserted neither a property nor a possessory interest in the automobile, nor an interest in the property seized." They had thus "made no showing that they had any legitimate expectation of privacy in the glove compartment or area under the seat of the car," from which the incriminating evidence had been gathered. "Like the trunk of an automobile," the Court explained, "these are areas in which a passenger *qua* passenger simply would not normally have a legitimate expectation of privacy."

The analysis in *Rakas* forecloses petitioner from establishing a legitimate expectation of privacy in the trunk of a rental car he neither owns nor leases simply by taking control of the rental car illegitimately—that is, without the owner's authorization and contrary to the rental contract.

A primary argument of the passengers in *Rakas* rested on the Court's statement in *Jones* v. *United States*, that "anyone legitimately on premises where a search occurs may challenge its legality." The Court in *Rakas* rejected the defendants' reliance on *Jones*, in which the Court had allowed Jones to challenge "the search of an apartment owned by a friend" who "had given Jones permission to use it" for purposes including storage of possessions and an overnight stay. The Court in *Rakas* explained that, outside the specific context of *Jones*, "the phrase 'legitimately on premises' creates too broad a gauge for measurement of Fourth Amendment rights." Legitimate presence, *Rakas* makes clear, is a necessary, but not a sufficient, foundation for asserting Fourth Amendment rights.

The Court in *Rakas* emphasized its prior recognition in *Jones* that "one wrongfully on the premises could not move to suppress evidence obtained as a result of searching them." "The Court in *Jones*," *Rakas* explained, "was quite careful to note that 'wrongful' presence at the scene of the search would not enable a defendant to object to the legality of the search." That is because "by virtue of his wrongful presence," the defendant "cannot invoke the privacy of the premises searched." The Court additionally explained that, in light of its previous "clear statement" of that principle, it would be "inexplicable" to think that "a person present in a stolen automobile at the time of a search may object to the lawfulness of the search of the automobile."

Petitioner's solo excursion in Avis's car does not satisfy the legitimate-presence prerequisite for a Fourth Amendment claim. Petitioner has never identified any legitimate basis for him to take the car to Pittsburgh. He knew that the car was a rental and that he was not the renter; he waited outside the Avis office while Reed went inside by herself to rent the car. It is also uncontested that he was "not listed as an authorized driver on the rental agreement," in renting the car, Reed did not add him as an additional driver. When they switched cars in the parking lot and petitioner began to "operate the vehicle," that was a clear "violation" of the express terms "of the rental agreement." Had they not hidden their swap of the vehicles from Avis, their subterfuge would have led Avis to consider the rental agreement "void" and to "recover the vehicle."

Petitioner contends that the "fact that he was not authorized by the contract to *drive* the car is beside the point" because he could have "possessed, stored possessions in, or excluded others from the vehicle" whether he was the driver or not. That contention cannot be squared with *Rakas*. Under *Rakas*, even an authorized passenger, when he is neither the owner nor the renter of a car, has no Fourth Amendment interest in its trunk (where the contraband in this case was found). Petitioner's claim to rights greater than those of an authorized passenger thus necessarily hinges on the assertion of some more significant connection to the car. But any such connection would have to be based on his presence as the driver—the very thing the rental agreement rendered illegitimate and unauthorized.

Petitioner would disregard the express prohibitions of the rental agreement on the theory that rental-car companies "know and expect" some unauthorized drivers to operate their rental cars. But Avis's recognition that some renters will breach the rental agreement in that manner, and its specification of the insurance-coverage consequences of such a breach, does not negate the agreement's explicit designation of "the only ones permitted to drive the vehicle other than the renter" or its plain and emphatic instruction that "PERMITTING AN UNAUTHORIZED DRIVER TO OPERATE THE VEHICLE IS A VIOLATION OF THE RENTAL AGREEMENT."

Rather, those consequences enforce Avis's prohibition of unauthorized drivers. And the steps that Avis takes to authenticate the renter and identify additional drivers, and to "recover the vehicle" when unauthorized operation renders the rental agreement "void," refute any notion that it is indifferent to who drives its cars.

To the extent that petitioner suggests that a defendant satisfies the legitimate-presence requirement so long as his actions do not amount to criminal activity, that suggestion is misguided. Petitioner knew that the car belonged to Avis, that Reed alone had rented it, and that he had done nothing to gain Avis's permission to operate it. He thus had no legal basis for driving it. Whether or not his actions carried legal consequences precisely identical to theft, petitioner's operation of the car by himself in contravention of the rental agreement cannot be considered legitimate. Nor could or did the officers make it so by asking him to move the car for safety purposes during the course of the stop—apparently before discovering that he was not an authorized driver. At a minimum, petitioner's unauthorized assertion of control over the car should not give him a greater Fourth Amendment interest in it than a legitimately present passenger would have.

Petitioner objects to considering the terms of a "private agreement" in this context, but his reluctance is at odds with the text, history, and judicial interpretation of the Fourth Amendment. As a textual matter, many interests in "effects" (or "houses) are created and defined by underlying private agreements, such as a bill of sale, lease agreement, or oral arrangement. As a historical matter, the "significance of property rights in the search-and-seizure analysis" likewise counsels respect for the limitations that the rightful owner of property places on the persons who may be present there. And as a jurisprudential matter, this Court's consideration of whether a defendant was "legitimately on the premises" has relied on private agreements governing the defendant's access to the premises in question. *Jones*, for example, turned on Jones's friend's (presumably oral) "consent to Jones's presence" in, and use for certain purposes of, his apartment.

Indeed, petitioner's own argument that he was legitimately present in the car rests on private agreements—namely, the written agreement in which Avis consented to rent the car to Reed and the (oral or implicit) agreement in which Reed gave her own permission for petitioner to drive it. Petitioner acknowledges that if his actions technically amounted to theft, he would have no legitimate expectation of privacy in Avis's car.

His only basis for distinguishing his actions from theft is that Reed rented the car and then purported to allow him to drive it away. But Reed's own rights in the car are based solely on the rental agreement, which forbade her from doing that. Petitioner would thus rely on the rental agreement to make his actions legitimate while ignoring the express terms of the agreement making those actions illegitimate. He cannot have it both ways.

Petitioner's objection to determining legitimacy by reference to the terms of a written agreement is particularly misplaced because the existence of such an agreement makes the determination relatively easy. Although petitioner suggests that looking to such agreements is "highly impractical," this Court has previously analyzed oral agreements, and the inquiry will often be even more straightforward when the terms of the agreement are reduced to writing.

The relative clarity of a written agreement will aid not only courts reviewing suppression motions, but also (to the extent it might be necessary) facilitate interactions between the police and motorists in the field. The rental agreement here, for example, had to "stay in the vehicle at all times," and it explicitly stated who was permitted to drive the car. The officers here had no apparent difficulty determining that petitioner was driving a car without authorization, and could have contacted the rental-car company with any questions.

Petitioner errs in suggesting that disallowing his Fourth Amendment claim here would require disallowing the claims of legitimate renters who may have committed minor breaches of the rental agreement. Petitioner, who had no basis for taking the wheel and treating Avis's car as his own, is differently situated from a legitimate renter to whom Avis has in fact entrusted its car.

The complete absence of a legitimate justification to drive a car is different in kind from restrictions on a legitimate driver's activities. Contractual prohibitions on, for example, hand-held cellphone use, driving without a seat belt, or using the incorrect fuel are not inherently directed at the driver's possessory interest. The violation of such a provision does not have direct bearing on *who* may operate the car, and it does not call into question the renter's initial authority to do so—authority petitioner never at any point acquired. Petitioner's examples involving breaches of the terms of residential leases are even further afield.

This Court has "on numerous occasions pointed out that cars are not to be treated identically with houses or apartments for Fourth Amendment purposes." And even in the context of dwellings, this Court's Fourth Amendment precedents support a distinction between legitimate occupants who violate the terms of occupancy and those who are not legitimately present to begin with.

That distinction is even clearer in the context of a car. A car's "function is transportation and it seldom serves as one's residence or as the repository of personal effects." Someone present in a car is either a driver, who requires legitimate authorization, or a passenger, who would not have Fourth Amendment rights in the car's trunk.

When he drove off alone, petitioner was not a legitimately present person who was merely engaging in an unpermitted activity. He was someone whose very presence in the car, impermissibly asserting sole dominion over its core function, was illegitimate.

B. Neither Property Rights Nor Societal Expectations Support Petitioner's Assertion of a Fourth Amendment Interest in Avis's Car

Even assuming it were not foreclosed by the legitimate presence rule, petitioner's claim to a legitimate expectation of privacy in Avis's car lacks foundation. Petitioner cannot show that any expectation of privacy had "a source outside of the Fourth Amendment," either in "concepts of personal property law" or in "understandings that are recognized and permitted by society." Petitioner had no relevant property rights in the car and his unauthorized use of it was in no way "permitted."

1. Petitioner had no enforceable property rights in a car he was not allowed to drive

This Court's examination of property rights in the context of the Fourth Amendment has focused on the law of trespass or the defendant's "right to exclude" others from the property that was searched. Those sources of law do not support petitioner's assertion of a Fourth Amendment interest in Avis's car.

A rental agreement is a bailment in which the rental-car company is the bailor and the renter is the bailee. The bailment is one for mutual benefit, in which the rental-car company gives the renter temporary custody of its property (the rental car) and the renter pays a fee and agrees to return the property at a specified time.

The rental agreement in this case is also a particular type of bailment, one that is "personal to the bailee." In "permitting Reed to drive its vehicle," Avis (the bailor) placed its "confidence" in Reed (the bailee) "personally." Avis decided to let Reed rent a car only after reviewing her driver's license, and seeking information about her driving history and criminal background, to ensure that she was an appropriate driver. Someone like petitioner, with a history of criminal offenses involving vehicles, would have to make false statements in order to rent one of Avis's cars. "As a general rule, a bailee has no right to delegate the right to use the property to another person, unless there is some understanding or agreement to that effect."

That limitation is inherent in bailments that are personal to the bailee. And as this case exemplifies, rental-car companies typically cement that limitation by making it explicit in the agreement through a provision that expressly prohibits the renter from delegating the right to drive the car to any person without authorization.

The rental agreement in this case admonished the renter in three separate places—one in all capital letters—not to permit any unauthorized drivers to operate the car.

b. As a bailee, a legitimate renter acquires certain property rights in the car, including the right to sue for a trespass to chattels, for the term of the bailment. An illegitimate driver like petitioner, however, would have no such rights. Indeed, under traditional common-law principles, an unauthorized rental-car driver could *himself* be considered a trespasser.

Petitioner attempts to provide a property-law basis for his Fourth Amendment claim by asserting that Reed's permission to take the car "created a subsidiary bailment, sometimes called a 'subbailment,'" that made him a subbailee with a "possessory property interest" in Avis's car. But Reed's lack of authority to give—and binding obligation *not* to give—that permission divests it of any such legal effect. "The transaction by which one person receives possession of the chattel of another is ineffectual if"—as is the case here—"the person delivering the chattel is without authority from the owner to transfer the property interest in the goods, and has no other power so to transfer them."

The cases petitioner cites do not show otherwise. In three of them, the authority of the bailee to transfer the property to a third person was not questioned. In the fourth case, the court addressed only the property rights of the bailee (not the putative subbailee), concluding that she maintained "constructive possession" of the property, notwithstanding the creation of any subbailment. Far from creating legal rights in the putative subbailee, the unauthorized transfer of a rental car may amount to a tort—or, potentially, even a crime.

The treatise on which petitioner himself relies for his subbailment argument explains that "a bailee who, wrongfully and without authority, sub-bails the goods to an independent third party commits a conversion." It defines a subbailment as a transfer of goods by the bailee "with or without the authority of the bailor" only for the purpose of "assessing the *responsibilities*"—not the *rights*—of the transferee.

It instead explains that "the lack of authority to sub-bail may, if known to the sub-bailee, make his reception of the goods," like the bailee's transfer of them, "a conversion."

Although the rule is not universal, other authorities agree that "any attempt on the part of the bailee to part with the title or possession of the subject matter of the bailment in violation of the contract of bailment constitutes a conversion." And in some jurisdictions and circumstances, the unauthorized driver of a rental car could be prosecuted for a crime, such as theft or unauthorized use of a motor vehicle.

Additional common-law remedies available against the unauthorized driver of a rental car reinforce petitioner's lack of any cognizable property right in Avis's car.

Where, as here, "the bailment is personal to the bailee by virtue of confidence reposed in him personally," any attempt by the bailee "to transfer his interest to a third person" would "give the bailor the right to put an end to the bailment"—and may be deemed to end it automatically. Consistent with that principle, Avis considers a rental agreement to be "void" if an unauthorized driver takes the wheel.

Upon termination of the bailment, the right of immediate possession reverts to the bailor. Thus, under the common law, petitioner's possession and use of Avis's car was possible only insofar as he was able (illegitimately) to conceal his actions from Avis. In driving the car, he faced the constant threat of discovery and dispossession of the vehicle by law enforcement.

Even in the absence of a prior police report by Avis, a lawful traffic stop could lead Avis to ask, as rental-car companies often do, that steps be taken to preclude the unauthorized driver from occupying the car and to return the car to its rightful owner.

2. No societal understanding provided petitioner with a reasonable expectation of privacy in his unauthorized operation of Avis's car

Although a defendant can sometimes establish a legitimate expectation of privacy without showing "a common-law interest in real or personal property," petitioner has not done so here. The "personal and societal values protected by the Fourth Amendment" do not support petitioner's assertion of constitutional rights in Avis's car. Operation of a rental car in the circumstances here does not serve any "functions recognized as valuable by society," but is instead detrimental to property rights, commerce, and public safety. Any expectation of privacy petitioner may have had was therefore not "one that society is prepared to recognize as reasonable."

As a threshold matter, to the extent that the unauthorized transfer or use of a rental car constitutes a tort or a crime, society has decided not to countenance it. Tort law and criminal law define the rules through which society regulates primary conduct. It makes no sense for the law to impose civil or criminal liability for an act and yet recognize it as one that creates a "legitimate expectation of privacy."

At a minimum, petitioner's appropriation of Avis's car was a breach of contract lacking any justification that could outweigh the important interests that the breached contractual provisions seek to preserve. Like any property owner, rental-car companies have an interest in ensuring that their property is used responsibly. Without the ability to ensure that their cars are being driven by those qualified to do so, rental-car companies face increased risks—not only of accident and injury, but also "of theft, of the car not being returned, of the car being taken to an unauthorized location, and of the car being used for unauthorized purposes."

The rental agreement here accordingly restricted operation of the car to the renter and a limited set of persons—a spouse or a co-employee on company business—who would have a marriage or business based legal connection to the renter, and for whom the renter could vouch and act as the point person. When petitioner took over Reed's rental car in breach of the rental agreement, without any foundation for believing that the rental-car company had consented to the transfer, he could not claim any expectation of privacy in the car that society would regard as objectively reasonable. Commercial rental cars are typically easy for potential drivers to identify. Petitioner certainly knew that he was driving a rental car, given that he acquired it from Reed in the parking lot outside the rental office and acknowledged to the police that a "friend" had rented it. It is, in addition, common knowledge that commercial rental companies like Avis do not offer up their vehicles for general enjoyment, but instead allow the use of their cars based on specific transactions with specific customers. Restrictions on who may drive a rental car are ubiquitous in the industry. The record in this case establishes that Avis both discusses the issue with prospective renters and requires them to confirm their understanding in writing, and petitioner offers no reason to believe that Avis's practice in that regard is atypical.

A non-renter like petitioner is a stranger to the rental agreement who cannot reasonably expect the same privacy protections as someone who is covered by it. Even where a defendant has transacted face-to-face with someone authorized to grant a property right, this Court has viewed a limited "connection" between the parties as a factor that cuts against a reasonable expectation of privacy in the use of that property.

Here, no connection of any kind existed between petitioner and Avis, the only entity that could authorize him to drive the car. To the extent that the rental agreement contemplated him at all, it was solely to exclude him as a driver. Petitioner's only connection was to Reed, a person who had no authority to let him take Avis's car.

No societal interest countenances petitioner's acceptance of a car offered in direct violation of the rightful owner's instructions. An *authorized* driver's expectation of privacy would, of course, generally be reasonable.

And it might well remain so even in the absence of specific property rights—say, in the case of a good-faith renter who is slightly late in returning a car and has thus allowed the rental agreement to expire for a brief period of time. But whatever leeway society might give to an authorized driver who exceeds the terms of his authorization, it would not extend to someone like petitioner, whose actions were never legitimate.

The unauthorized driving of rental cars also frustrates enforcement of the criminal laws. A criminal like a drug trafficker may well prefer to use a rental car, rather than his own car, to avoid the risk of forfeiture if his illicit actions are discovered. And driving a car rented by someone else, thereby obfuscating the identity of the driver, is a common way to provide further protection to a criminal enterprise.

Petitioner suggests that denying constitutional protection to his conduct would invite a dragnet sweep of rental cars on the roadways. But "the reality hardly suggests abuse." Petitioner points to no actual evidence of the practices he fears in the jurisdictions where it has been the law for decades that an unauthorized driver lacks a legitimate expectation of privacy in a rental car. That is presumably because powerful legal and practical obstacles discourage such a practice.

First, the police cannot stop a car simply because it is a rental; they must have "reasonable suspicion to believe that criminal activity may be afoot." Anyone in the car—including a passenger or unauthorized driver—may (as petitioner did below) challenge a stop as a seizure of his or her person for which such suspicion was lacking, regardless of whether he or she has rights with respect to a subsequent search of the car. Second, an unauthorized driver like petitioner could also potentially challenge the search directly, to the extent that it infringed on a reasonable expectation of privacy with respect to particular effects within the car. Third, petitioner's proposal would be an ineffective law-enforcement tactic. Because not every breach of the rental agreement is equivalent to relinquishing the car to an unpermitted driver, a search would go unchallenged only if the car's occupant turns out to be an unauthorized driver like petitioner. But officers are unlikely to know before stopping the car whether a particular driver is authorized.

C. Petitioner's "Possession And Control" Test Is Unsound

Petitioner contends that his Fourth Amendment rights in Avis's car should depend not on whether he was an authorized driver under the rental agreement, but instead on whether he had "possession of and control over a closed space."

That approach is unsupported by precedent and inherently flawed.

Nothing in this Court's precedents supports petitioner's proposed "possession and control" test. His assertion that "all that mattered" in *Jones* "was that the visitor had some measure of 'dominion and control,'" disregards that the visitor also "had permission to use the apartment," from someone with actual (or at least unquestioned) authority to grant it. The same was true of the overnight guest whose Fourth Amendment rights were recognized in *Minnesota* v. *Olson*. And it was also true of the defendants in the other cases on which petitioner's proposal relies.

Even petitioner recognizes that the Fourth Amendment rights of a rental-car driver cannot turn on "possession and control" alone. He acknowledges, for example, that under this Court's decision in *Rakas*, a person who has "stolen" a rental car cannot object to its search, notwithstanding that he both possesses and controls it. He also appears to acknowledge that a person who has possession and control of a rental car would nevertheless lack a reasonable expectation of privacy in the car if the person lacked "the renter's permission to drive" it. Petitioner does not attempt to articulate any principle underlying those apparent exceptions to his proposed rule. But by accepting them, petitioner implicitly acknowledges that the possession and control must be "legitimate." This Court explained in *Rakas*, for example, that "one who owns or *lawfully* possesses or controls property will in all likelihood have a legitimate expectation of privacy by virtue of the right to exclude."

And *Rakas* viewed the absence of a "possessory interest in the automobile"—*i.e.*, the absence of a "*right* to control" and "exclude others,"—as significant. Petitioner's position thus rests not on whether he had "possession and control" of Avis's car, but on whether his assumption of possession and control—in contravention of the express terms of the rental agreement—was an act that "the law recognizes as 'legitimate.'" For the reasons explained above, it was not.

Petitioner's position that Reed's unauthorized say-so was sufficient to give him a legitimate interest in Avis's car has no logical stopping point and would produce anomalous results. First, his view implies that someone who received the car from *him* would also have a legitimate expectation of privacy while driving it.

Although petitioner undoubtedly lacks authority to transfer the car to someone else, that does not distinguish him from Reed, whose own transfer was likewise unauthorized. Petitioner would presumably acknowledge that a legitimate expectation of privacy ceases to exist at some point in a chain of unauthorized automobile transfers. The only sensible point is the initial impermissible handover—in this case, Reed's.

Second, petitioner's view suggests no temporal restrictions. One would think that after some number of days and weeks beyond the term of Reed's rental, the rental car would be considered "stolen," if it had still not been returned. But given that petitioner does not believe that the conditions of Reed's rental have any bearing on his Fourth Amendment rights, petitioner has no basis for identifying when that temporal endpoint would be.

Third, petitioner's approach would have reasonable expectations of privacy blink in and out of existence, moment by moment, in insupportable ways. Petitioner suggests that sole occupancy of a vehicle in itself is constitutionally significant, asserting that a passenger acquires a Fourth Amendment interest in a car if the driver leaves him in it while visiting a store. But the understanding that the trunk, glove compartment, and other areas of the car do not belong to the passenger, does not change simply because the driver ducks out to buy a soda, even if the driver trusts the passenger with the keys for purposes of "listening to the radio" during the driver's brief absence. On petitioner's rationale, the Court's holding in *Minnesota* v. *Carter*—that the defendants could not "claim the protection of the Fourth Amendment in the home of another" based on a short-term commercial venture there—would have come out the other way had the police happened to arrive while the defendants were inside, but the leaseholder was out running a brief errand.

To the extent that petitioner suggests that a "close familial connection to the renter" entitles him to special Fourth Amendment rights that others in his circumstances would not have, that argument is neither properly presented nor doctrinally sound. Petitioner's briefs in the court of appeals did not press the point he now raises, and the court did not address it. Petitioner's opening brief referred to Reed as his "girlfriend" (not his fiancée). It noted that they had children together, but it did not otherwise discuss the nature of their relationship or urge it as a separate ground for finding that he had Fourth Amendment rights in the car she had rented. He did not, for example, suggest that the relationship fit within the "extraordinary circumstances" exception that the court below had recognized to the general rule precluding Fourth Amendment claims by unauthorized rental-car drivers.

It is well-established that "where issues are neither raised before nor considered by the Court of Appeals, this Court will not ordinarily consider them." Consideration of petitioner's new argument would be particularly unwarranted here, where the petition for a writ of certiorari likewise referred to Reed as petitioner's "girlfriend," and did not identify the quasi-marriage relationship he now asserts as a point of distinction from decisions he alleged to conflict with the decision below.

The factual dispute is particularly pertinent because the record does not clearly support the proposition that petitioner, "by his conduct, has exhibited an actual (subjective) expectation of privacy," based on his relationship with Reed. He told the officers during the stop that the car had been rented by a "friend."

Although he testified at the suppression hearing that he and Reed had been engaged when she rented the car, he later told the Probation Office that he had been "romantically involved" with another woman, in another State, "intermittently for five years." The Probation Office report described Reed as petitioner's "former girlfriend" and did not view her as "an appropriate verification source" for "his personal history information."

And petitioner did not testify that he believed he was (or claim that he actually was) authorized to drive Avis's car on the ground that he was Reed's "spouse."

In any event, petitioner's asserted close relationship with Reed provides no basis for extending Fourth Amendment rights to encompass his claim in the car she rented. To the extent that society expects families to share rental cars, that expectation is reflected in rental agreements' express exemption of spouses from the general prohibition on unauthorized drivers, and by state laws that deem spouses to be authorized drivers for at least certain purposes.

Here, petitioner has made no showing of any special relationship or exceptional circumstances that should allow him to clothe himself in whatever rights Reed acquired as a renter. His assertion of her rights in this circumstance is thus akin to the sort of "vicarious Fourth Amendment claims" that this Court has long rejected, partly in recognition that they "exact a substantial social cost" because "relevant and reliable evidence is kept from the trier of fact and the search for truth at trial is deflected."

Petitioner, on this record, gives all appearances of having used Reed as a straw renter to allow him to take sole control of a rental car that he would not have been able to rent himself. He did so either knowingly or in unreasonable unawareness of his lack of legitimate rights in the car. Petitioner retained reasonable expectations of privacy and security in his "person," but he had no reasonable expectation of privacy or security in the trunk of the rental car—an "effect" he had no legitimate authority to possess or control.

Conclusion

The judgment of the court of appeals should be affirmed.[2]

Brief #3

The issue in this case is the extraterritorial application of the Fourth Amendment's prohibition on unjustified deadly force, as concerned a cross-border shooting of an unarmed Mexican citizen in an area controlled by the United States.

Statement

In *Bivens v. Six Unknown Named Agents of Federal Bureau of Narcotics*, this Court created a common-law cause of action for damages against federal officials who allegedly violated a U.S. citizen's Fourth Amendment rights by conducting a warrantless search in the United States. In this case, petitioners seek to invoke *Bivens* to recover damages from a U.S. Border Patrol agent for the death of their son, a Mexican national, as the result of a shooting across the international border separating the United States and Mexico. Petitioners allege that the shooting violated standards for the use of force found in the Fourth and Fifth Amendments, and they contend that those constitutional provisions and the judicially created *Bivens* remedy should be extended to aliens injured outside this country

1. According to the allegations in petitioners' complaint, on June 7, 2010, petitioners' son, Sergio Adrian Hernández Guereca (Hernández), a 15-year-old Mexican national, was with friends in the cement culvert that separates El Paso, Texas, from Ciudad Juarez, Mexico. The international border runs down the middle of the culvert, and there is a fence at the top of the embankment on the U.S. side. Petitioners allege that Hernández and his friends were playing a game in which they crossed the border into the United States, ran up the embankment to touch the fence, and then ran back into Mexico.

Petitioners allege that respondent Jesus Mesa, Jr., a U.S. Border Patrol agent, arrived on the scene, detained one of Hernández's friends in the culvert on the U.S. side of the border, and then, while standing in U.S. territory, fatally shot Hernández, who was in Mexico at the time and who "had no interest in entering the United States." Petitioners further allege that Hernández was "unarmed and unthreatening" at the time.

After a "comprehensive" investigation of the incident, the Department of Justice (DOJ) declined to bring criminal charges against Agent Mesa. DOJ explained that the shooting "occurred while smugglers attempting an illegal border crossing hurled rocks from close range at Agent Mesa, who was attempting to detain a suspect." DOJ added that its investigation indicated that Agent Mesa "did not act inconsistently with U.S. Border Patrol policy or training regarding use of force." DOJ's statement expressed the United States' regret about Hernandez's death, and it reiterated the United States' commitment to investigating and prosecuting allegations of excessive force and "working with the Mexican government to prevent future incidents."

2. Petitioners sued the United States, several federal agencies, and unknown U.S. Border Patrol agents, asserting claims under the Federal Tort Claims Act (FTCA); the Alien Tort Statute (ATS); and *Bivens*. Petitioners later named Agent Mesa as one of the individual defendants, alleging that he violated Hernández's Fourth and Fifth Amendment rights while attempting to apprehend him on suspicion of illegal entry into the United States.

a. The district court dismissed petitioners' FTCA and ATS claims. Under the Federal Employees Liability Reform and Tort Compensation Act of 1988, an FTCA claim against the United States is generally the exclusive remedy for torts committed by federal employees within the scope of their employment. In this case, DOJ certified that Agent Mesa and the other individual defendants were acting within the scope of their employment. Petitioners did not challenge that certification and did not oppose the substitution of the United States as the sole defendant for their FTCA and ATS claims.

The FTCA generally makes the United States liable for torts committed by federal employees within the scope of their employment, but excludes "any claim arising in a foreign country." That exclusion "bars all claims based on any injury suffered in a foreign country, regardless of where the tortious act or omission occurred." Here, the district court dismissed petitioners' FTCA claims because Hernández was in Mexico when he was shot.

The ATS grants district courts jurisdiction over certain suits by aliens "for a tort committed in violation of the law of nations or a treaty of the United States." The district court dismissed petitioners' ATS claims because no provision of law waives the United States' sovereign immunity for such claims.

b. The district court also dismissed petitioners' *Bivens* claims against Agent Mesa. Those claims were not barred by the Westfall Act, which exempts suits "brought for a violation of the Constitution." But the court concluded that petitioners' Fourth Amendment claim was foreclosed by *United States* v. *Verdugo-Urquidez*, which held that the Fourth Amendment had no application to the search and seizure of a Mexican citizen's property in Mexico. And the court concluded that petitioners' Fifth Amendment claim was barred by *Graham* v. *Connor*, which held that a claim that a law enforcement officer used excessive force in making a seizure can arise only under the Fourth Amendment, not the more general rubric of substantive due process.

3. Initially, a three-judge panel of the court of appeals affirmed in part, reversed in part, and remanded.

a. The panel held unanimously (albeit based on somewhat different rationales) that the Fourth Amendment did not apply to Agent Mesa's alleged actions because Hernández was in Mexico when he was shot.

b. The panel majority concluded, however, that Agent Mesa's alleged actions violated the Fifth Amendment, which the majority found applicable even though Hernández was in Mexico when he was shot. The majority relied on *Boumediene* v. *Bush*, which held that the Suspension Clause of the Constitution applies to certain aliens detained at the U.S. Naval Station at Guantanamo Bay, Cuba, where the United States lacks "*de jure* sovereignty" but exercises "*de facto* sovereignty" because of "its complete jurisdiction and control over the base." The majority reasoned that *Boumediene* supported the extraterritorial application of the Fifth Amendment here because Hernández was "a civilian killed outside an occupied zone or theater of war," and because he was in an area of Mexico near the border where the majority believed the United State exercises a degree of control sufficiently comparable to that which it exercises at Guantanamo Bay.

The panel majority further held that, although this Court has "consistently refused to extend *Bivens* liability to any new context," petitioners' claim on behalf of an alien injured abroad could be brought under *Bivens*. The majority also held that Agent Mesa was not entitled to qualified immunity on petitioners' Fifth Amendment claim.

c. Judge DeMoss dissented in part, concluding that "the Fifth Amendment does not protect a non-citizen with no connections to the United States who suffered an injury in Mexico where the United States has no formal control or *de facto* sovereignty."

4. The court of appeals granted petitions for rehearing *en banc* filed by the United States and by Agent Mesa. The 15-member *en banc* court then affirmed the dismissal of petitioners' claims against Agent Mesa without dissent.

a. The court first held that petitioners had failed to allege a violation of the Fourth Amendment because Hernández was "a Mexican citizen who had no 'significant voluntary connection' to the United States" and "was on Mexican soil at the time he was shot." Only two judges declined to join that reasoning. As at the panel stage, Judge Dennis concurred in the result. He concluded that *Boumediene* requires a more pragmatic inquiry than the one he believed this Court applied in *Verdugo-Urquidez*, but he nonetheless determined that the Fourth Amendment is inapplicable here because "judicial entanglement with extraterritorial Fourth Amendment excessive-force claims" would be "impracticable and anomalous." Judge Graves did not dissent from the court's Fourth Amendment holding, but his partial concurrence stated that the court "should carefully adjudicate" that claim.

b. The court was "somewhat divided on the question of whether Agent Mesa's conduct violated the Fifth Amendment," but it was "unanimous" in holding that he is entitled to qualified immunity because "any properly asserted right was not clearly established." The court stated that "reasonable minds can differ on whether *Boumediene* may some-day be explicitly extended" to provide extraterritorial application of the Fifth Amendment to aliens, but it held that "nothing in *Boumediene* presages, with the directness that the 'clearly established' standard requires, whether this Court would extend the territorial reach of a different constitutional provision and would do so where the injury occurs not on land controlled by the United States, but on soil that is indisputably foreign and beyond the United States' territorial sovereignty."

c. Several judges filed concurring opinions. Judge Jones, joined by three of her colleagues, agreed with the district court that petitioners' excessive-force claim could arise, if at all, only under the

Fourth Amendment, not the Fifth. In any event, she would have held that the Fifth Amendment does not apply to aliens abroad.

Judge Prado disagreed with Judge Jones about the merits of petitioners' Fifth Amendment claim, but agreed that Agent Mesa is entitled to qualified immunity because the Fifth Amendment's applicability to these circumstances is not clearly established.

Judge Haynes, joined by two other judges, wrote separately to address petitioners' ATS claim, which is not at issue here. She also observed, however, that petitioners' "concern that people in Mesa's situation can commit wrongful acts with impunity is not accurate." She noted, for example, that petitioners could have sought "federal-court review of the Attorney General's scope-of-employment certification," which could have permitted them to pursue ATS claims against Agent Mesa, as well as tort claims under state or Mexican law. She also stated that redress may be available "through Mexican diplomatic channels."

d. Because it rejected petitioners' Fourth and Fifth Amendment claims on other grounds, the *en banc* court did not consider whether *Bivens* should be extended to this novel context.

Summary of Argument

I. In granting certiorari, this Court directed the parties to address the question whether petitioners' claims may be asserted under *Bivens* v. *Six Unknown Named Agents of Federal Bureau of Narcotics*. That antecedent question resolves this case: The judicially created *Bivens* remedy should not be extended to aliens injured abroad.

In *Bivens*, this Court recognized an implied private right of action for damages against federal officers alleged to have violated a citizen's Fourth Amendment rights. But because the Court's subsequent decisions have clarified that "implied causes of action are disfavored," the Court has long "been reluctant to extend *Bivens* liability 'to any new context or new category of defendants.'" And the Court has admonished that *Bivens* should not be extended to any new context where special factors suggest that Congress is the appropriate body to provide any damages remedy.

Petitioners seek to extend *Bivens* to injuries suffered by aliens abroad—a significant and unprecedented expansion. That expansion is inappropriate because Congress, not the Judiciary, should decide whether and under what circumstances to provide monetary remedies for aliens outside our borders who are injured by the government's actions. An injury inflicted by the United States on a foreign citizen in another country's sovereign territory is, by definition, an incident with international implications. This case illustrates that point: Both the problem of border violence in general and the specific incident at issue here have prompted exchanges between the United States and Mexico, and Mexico's amicus brief confirms its sovereign interest in those issues.

The need for caution before inserting the courts into such sensitive matters of international diplomacy is reinforced by the fact that, in a variety of related contexts—including the statutory remedy for persons deprived of constitutional rights by *state* officials—Congress has taken care not to provide aliens injured abroad with the sort of judicial damages remedy petitioners seek. Instead, where Congress has addressed injuries inflicted by the government on aliens abroad, it has relied on voluntary payments or administrative claims mechanisms. And the general presumption against extraterritoriality further confirms that *Bivens* should not apply here: It would be anomalous to extend a judicially inferred remedy to a case where the Court would not extend an express statutory cause of action absent a clear indication that Congress intended to reach injuries outside our Nation's borders.

II. The *en banc* court of appeals held that the Fourth Amendment did not apply to Agent Mesa's alleged conduct because Hernández was an alien located in Mexico who had no connection to the United States. That conclusion was compelled by *United States* v. *Verdugo-Urquidez*, which held that the Fourth Amendment had "no application" to the search and seizure of an alien's property in Mexico. This Court reached that conclusion after a careful analysis of the Fourth Amendment's text, purpose, and history, as well as the "significant and deleterious consequences for the United States" that would follow from extending the Fourth Amendment to aliens abroad.

Petitioners do not deny that *Verdugo-Urquidez* forecloses their claim. Instead, they assert that *Verdugo-Urquidez* is no longer good law because it employed an approach to extraterritoriality that purportedly conflicts with Justice Kennedy's concurring opinion in that case and with this Court's subsequent decision in *Boumediene* v. *Bush*. But Justice Kennedy "joined" the Court's opinion in *Verdugo-Urquidez* and agreed with the "persuasive justifications stated by the Court." And nothing in *Boumediene*—which addressed the application of the right to habeas corpus in an area where the United States maintains *de facto* sovereignty—undermines either *Verdugo-Urquidez*'s analysis or its holding that the Fourth Amendment generally does not apply to aliens abroad.

In contrast, petitioners' *ad hoc*, totality-of-the-circumstances approach to the extraterritorial application of the Fourth Amendment finds no support in *Boumediene* or in any other decision of this Court. Petitioners' all-factors-considered test is unworkable; it would upend an understanding on which Congress and the Executive Branch have relied; and it could "significantly disrupt the ability of the political branches to respond to foreign situations involving our national interest."

III. Agent Mesa is entitled to qualified immunity on petitioners' substantive-due-process claim because his alleged actions did not violate any clearly established Fifth Amendment right. To overcome a motion to dismiss based on qualified immunity, a *Bivens* plaintiff must plead facts establishing that "every reasonable official" in the defendant's position would have known that his actions violated the asserted constitutional right. The dispositive question here is thus whether "every reasonable official" in Agent Mesa's position "would have understood that what he is doing violates the Fifth Amendment."

Petitioners do not dispute the court of appeals' unanimous conclusion that it was not clearly established that an alien in Hernández's position had Fifth Amendment rights. Instead, petitioners maintain that the court should have conducted the qualified-immunity analysis as if Hernández were a U.S. citizen because Agent Mesa did not know with certainty that he was an alien. Petitioners are correct that the qualified-immunity analysis focuses on facts known to the defendant at the time of the challenged conduct. But it does not follow that the analysis in this case should assume, counterfactually, that Agent Mesa knew Hernández was a U.S. citizen. Instead, the question is whether every reasonable officer in Agent Mesa's position would have known that his alleged actions violated the Fifth Amendment, where the officer did not know Hernández's nationality with certainty but had no reason to believe that he was a U.S. citizen. The answer to that question is no—both because no case law addresses the application of the Fifth Amendment to uses of force against persons of unknown nationality outside the United States, and because it is not clearly established that the Fifth Amendment (rather than the Fourth Amendment) has any application to such uses of force, regardless of the nationality of the affected individual.

Argument

I. The Judicially Created *Bivens* Remedy Should not Be Extended to Aliens Injured Abroad

In granting certiorari, this Court directed the parties to address the question whether the claim in this case may be asserted under *Bivens* v. *Six Unknown Named Agents of Federal Bureau of Narcotics*. The availability of a *Bivens* remedy is "antecedent" to the questions on which petitioners sought this Court's review. That antecedent question resolves this case. Even if petitioners were correct that the Fourth and Fifth Amendments protected Hernández in Mexico, and even if those rights were clearly established at the time of the incident, petitioners' claims were properly dismissed because *Bivens* should not be extended to aliens injured abroad.

A. This Court Has Consistently Declined to Extend *Bivens* to Contexts Where Congress Is the More Appropriate Body to Craft any Damages Remedy

1. In *Bivens*, this Court "recognized for the first time an implied private action for damages against federal officers alleged to have violated a citizen's constitutional rights." The Court held that, despite the absence of such a remedy in the Fourth Amendment itself or in any statute, federal officers could be sued for damages

for conducting a warrantless search in the United States. In creating that common-law cause of action, however, the Court emphasized that the context of the case presented "no special factors counselling hesitation in the absence of affirmative action by Congress."

Since deciding *Bivens* in 1971, this Court has "extended its holding only twice." In *Davis* v. *Passman*, the Court allowed a congressional employee to sue for sex discrimination in violation of the Fifth Amendment. And in *Carlson* v. *Green*, the Court allowed a federal prisoner to sue prison officials for Eighth Amendment violations. In each case, the Court reiterated that it found "no special factors counselling hesitation in the absence of affirmative action by Congress."

In the more than 35 years since *Carlson*, this Court "ha[s] consistently refused to extend *Bivens* liability to any new context or new category of defendants." Eight decisions of this Court squarely rejected efforts to expand *Bivens*.

On three other occasions, the Court *sua sponte* questioned the existence of a *Bivens* remedy even though the parties had not raised the issue.

This Court's steadfast refusal to extend *Bivens* reflects its changed understanding of the scope of judicial authority to create private rights of action. *Bivens* "relied largely on earlier decisions implying private damages actions into federal statutes." But in the decades since *Bivens*, the Court has made clear that the creation of damages remedies is a legislative function, and it has "retreated from its previous willingness to imply a cause of action where Congress has not provided one." The Court has "repeatedly said that a decision to create a private right of action is one better left to legislative judgment in the great majority of cases." And it has "declined to 'revert' to 'the understanding of private causes of action that held sway'" when *Bivens* was decided. The Court has thus explained that its "reluctance to extend *Bivens*" rests on its more recent decisions clarifying that "implied causes of action are disfavored."

2. This Court's decisions establish two hurdles for a party seeking to extend *Bivens*. First, the presence of "any alternative, existing process for protecting the relevant interest" may be "a convincing

reason for the Judicial Branch to refrain from providing a new and freestanding remedy in damages." Second, "even in the absence of such an alternative," inferring a damages remedy under *Bivens* is still disfavored, and a court must determine whether judicially created relief is warranted, "paying particular heed to any special factors counselling hesitation before authorizing a new kind of federal litigation."

The "special factors" that may foreclose the extension of *Bivens* are not limited to factors showing that a damages remedy would be inappropriate in a particular setting. They also include factors suggesting that Congress, not the judiciary, is the appropriate entity to make that legislative judgment—or that Congress's failure to provide a remedy "has not been inadvertent," The special factors referenced in *Bivens* itself, for example, "related to the question of who should decide whether a damages remedy should be provided," not "the merits of the particular remedy that was sought." Consistent with that focus on congressional intent and institutional competence, this Court has asked "whether there are reasons for allowing Congress to prescribe the scope of relief that is made available." And the Court has "declined to create a new substantive legal liability without legislative aid" if "Congress is in a better position to decide whether or not the public interest would be served by creating it."

B. Congress, not the Judiciary, Is the Appropriate Body to Decide Whether to Provide a Damages Remedy for Aliens Injured Abroad by U.S. Officials

In asking this Court to create a *Bivens* remedy for an alien injured outside the United States, petitioners "seek a significant extension of *Bivens*." An injury inflicted by the U.S. government on a foreign citizen in another country's sovereign territory is, by definition, an incident with international implications. Claims based on such injuries thus affect the Nation's foreign affairs—and the nature of the government's activities abroad means that those claims will often implicate national security as well. Those special factors indicate that Congress, not the Judiciary, is the appropriate body to decide whether and under what circumstances to provide monetary remedies. The need for caution is reinforced by the fact that, in a variety of statutes, Congress has long taken care *not* to provide aliens injured abroad with the sort of judicial damages remedy petitioners seek. And the general presumption against extraterritoriality further confirms that *Bivens* should not be extended to this novel context.

1. Claims by aliens injured abroad implicate foreign affairs and national security

a. "The conduct of the foreign relations of our Government is committed by the Constitution to the Executive and Legislative— 'the political'—Departments." Foreign affairs is thus "a domain in which the controlling role of the political branches is both necessary and proper." In recognition of the political branches' special competence and responsibility, this Court has long held that "matters intimately related to foreign policy and national security are rarely proper subjects for judicial intervention."

This Court's decisions make clear that *Bivens* should not be expanded to an area that the Constitution commits to the political branches. In *Chappell*, the Court declined to extend *Bivens* to claims by military personnel against superior officers because "Congress, the constitutionally authorized source of authority over the military system of justice," had not provided such a remedy. The Court explained that "any action to provide a judicial response by way of such a remedy would be plainly inconsistent with Congress' authority in this field." And in *Stanley*, the Court relied on *Chappell* to hold that *Bivens* does not extend to any claim incident to military service, again emphasizing that "congressionally uninvited intrusion into military affairs by the judiciary is inappropriate."

The same logic precludes the extension of *Bivens* to aliens injured abroad by U.S. government officials. The United States is answerable to other sovereigns for injuries inflicted on their citizens within their territory, and such injuries thus inevitably have implications for foreign affairs. Judicial examination of the government's treatment of aliens outside the United States would inject the courts into sensitive matters of international diplomacy and risk "what this Court has called in another context 'embarrassment of our government abroad' through 'multifarious pronouncements by various departments on one question.'" More generally, "damage remedies against military and foreign policy officials for allegedly unconstitutional treatment of foreign subjects causing injury abroad" could carry other "foreign affairs implications" that "cannot be ignored"—including "the danger of foreign citizens' using the courts to obstruct the foreign policy of our government."

This case illustrates the inevitable foreign-affairs implications of *Bivens* suits by aliens injured abroad. The Government of Mexico has filed an amicus brief explaining that it has an interest in this case because, "as a sovereign and independent state, Mexico has a responsibility to maintain control over its territory and to look after the well-being of its nationals." Issues of border violence, including cross-border shootings, have been of great concern to the United States' bilateral relationship with Mexico for several years. In 2014, the two governments established a joint Border Violence Prevention Council to provide a standing forum in which to address issues of border violence. Mexico and the United States have also addressed cross-border shootings in other forums, including the annual U.S.–Mexico Bilateral Human Rights Dialogue. And the incident at issue here has prompted bilateral exchanges, including Mexico's request that Agent Mesa be extradited to face criminal charges. The United States declined to extradite Agent Mesa, but it has reiterated its commitment to "work with the Mexican government within existing mechanisms and agreements to prevent future incidents."

Petitioners' suit seeks to insert the Judiciary into this sensitive diplomatic arena, and to have the courts adopt a view of the underlying incident that differs from the one taken by the Executive Branch. Judicial involvement in such matters should come, if at all, only at Congress's invitation and under circumstances prescribed by the legislature.

b. Petitioners assert that there should be no concern about interfering with U.S. foreign policy because the Government of Mexico supports the availability of a damages remedy in this case.

But that only illustrates the problem. Petitioners ask this Court to make a judgment about whether the provision of a damages remedy to an alien injured abroad would be consistent with U.S. foreign policy. The Judiciary is ill-suited to make such determinations—and attempting to make them on a case-by-case basis would itself intrude on foreign affairs. "Congress is in a far better position than a court" to make the delicate judgments involved in providing remedies to aliens abroad who are injured by the government's actions, and to "tailor any remedy" as appropriate.

c. Opening the courthouse doors to *Bivens* suits by aliens injured abroad would also have implications for national security. Such suits might, for example, be brought based on military or intelligence activities. National security is also implicated where, as here, the security of the border is at issue. The Department of Homeland Security (DHS) and its components, including the U.S. Border Patrol, have been charged by Congress with preventing terrorist attacks within the United States and securing the border. "This country's border-control policies are of crucial importance to the national security and foreign policy of the United States." Many *Bivens* suits based on injuries to aliens abroad would thus add national-security considerations to the direct implications for foreign affairs inherent in *all* such litigation.

2. Congress's consistent decisions not to provide a judicial damages remedy to aliens injured abroad confirm that a *Bivens* remedy is inappropriate

A variety of statutes indicate that Congress's failure to provide the judicial remedy petitioners seek "has not been inadvertent." Those related congressional policy judgments warrant "appropriate judicial deference."

a. Traditionally, injuries suffered by aliens abroad were addressed through diplomatic negotiations or by voluntary *ex gratia* payments to the injured parties. The United States continues to rely on such measures in many contexts.

In certain recurring circumstances, however, Congress has determined that the United States' interests would be better served by establishing administrative claims procedures. In 1942, during

World War II, Congress enacted the Foreign Claims Act (FCA) "to promote and maintain friendly relations" with the increasing number of foreign countries in which U.S. military personnel were stationed. The FCA allows the military to establish administrative claims commissions to pay certain claims for personal injuries, death, or property damage suffered by "any inhabitant of a foreign country" as a result of the noncombat activities of U.S. military forces.

A companion statute, the International Agreement Claims Act, allows the military to make payments under "an international agreement which provides for the settlement or adjudication and cost sharing of claims against the United States arising out of the acts or omissions of a member or civilian employee of an armed force of the United States." Such cost-sharing provisions are included in a number of status-of-forces agreements applicable to U.S. forces stationed abroad.

More recently, Congress has enacted limited exceptions to the FTCA's foreign-country exclusion to allow payments for torts arising from the overseas operations of the Department of State, and the Drug Enforcement Administration (DEA). In those statutes, as under the FCA, Congress provided an administrative remedy it did not permit the injured parties to bring FTCA suits in court. And in establishing and shaping those limited remedies, Congress made considered decisions about which injuries to make compensable and under what conditions they should be compensated.

Congress has not adopted a similar claims procedure for aliens injured abroad by the actions of U.S. Border Patrol agents. Instead, Congress has left such injuries to be addressed through diplomatic or other means. But these statutes provide further reason not to infer a *Bivens* remedy because they indicate that Congress has made deliberate choices about the circumstances under which to provide monetary remedies for aliens injured abroad— and because they show that where Congress *has* provided such remedies, it has done so through administrative mechanisms, not by authorizing suits in federal court.

b. Where Congress has provided judicial damages remedies, moreover, it has taken care not to extend those remedies to injuries of the sort petitioners assert here. The statutory remedy for individuals whose constitutional rights are violated by *state* officials is limited to "citizens of the United States or other persons within the jurisdiction thereof." Accordingly, if Agent Mesa were a state official, petitioners would have no remedy under Section 1983. Petitioners identify no reason why *Bivens*—the "more limited federal analog" to Section 1983 should sweep more broadly.

Similarly, in enacting the FTCA, the most comprehensive statute providing remedies for injuries inflicted by federal employees, Congress specifically excluded "any claim arising in a foreign country." That is a strong indication that Congress did not intend a damages remedy for injuries occurring abroad. Petitioners correctly observe that the foreign-country exception was motivated in part by Congress's "unwillingness to subject the United States to liabilities depending upon the laws of a foreign power," which would have governed FTCA claims arising abroad. But petitioners are wrong to suggest that avoiding the application of foreign law was Congress's only goal. Even before DOJ raised concerns about foreign law, the bill that became the FTCA excluded "all claims 'arising in a foreign country *in behalf of an alien.*'" That history demonstrates that Congress's decision not to provide an FTCA remedy to *aliens* injured abroad reflected adherence to the traditional practice of addressing such injuries through nonjudicial means.

More recently, in the Torture Victim Protection Act of 1991 (TVPA), Congress created a cause of action for damages against "an individual who, under actual or apparent authority, or color of law, of any foreign nation," subjects another individual to "torture" or "extrajudicial killing." "But the statute exempts U.S. officials, a point that President George H.W. Bush stressed when signing the legislation." "In confining the coverage of statutes such as the FTCA and the TVPA, Congress has deliberately decided not to fashion a cause of action" for aliens injured abroad by government officials. *Ibid.* Congress's repeated decisions not to provide such a remedy counsel strongly against providing one under *Bivens*.

3. The presumption against extraterritoriality reinforces the inappropriateness of extending *Bivens* to aliens injured abroad

The presumption against extraterritoriality further confirms that *Bivens* should not be extended to aliens injured abroad. It is a basic principle of our legal system that, in general, "U.S. law governs domestically but does not rule the world." In statutory interpretation, that presumption is reflected in the canon that "when a statute gives no clear indication of an extra- territorial application, it has none." That canon "helps ensure that the Judiciary does not erroneously adopt an interpretation of U.S. law that carries foreign policy consequences not clearly intended by the political branches."

Petitioners assert that the presumption against extraterritoriality is relevant only to "interpreting *statutes,*" not to defining the scope of a common-law remedy like *Bivens.* But this Court has held otherwise. In *Kiobel,* the Court held that although the presumption "typically" applies to statutory interpretation, "the principles underlying the canon of interpretation similarly constrain courts" recognizing common-law causes of action.

Kiobel involved the ATS, a jurisdictional statute that "does not expressly provide any causes of action," but that this Court had previously held is "best read as having been enacted on the understanding that the common law would provide a cause of action for a modest number of international law violations." Although the international law rules asserted by the plaintiffs applied abroad, this Court held that courts recognizing causes of action under the ATS must be guided by the presumption against extraterritoriality. In fact, the Court admonished that "the danger of unwarranted judicial interference in the conduct of foreign policy is *magnified* in the context of the ATS, because the question is not what Congress has done, but instead what courts may do." That danger is still greater in the *Bivens* context, where courts are asked to create a common-law cause of action without even the minimal congressional guidance found in the ATS.

The presumption against extraterritoriality should thus "constrain courts exercising their power" under *Bivens.* And as this

Court recently explained, the presumption counsels against extending a private damages remedy to injuries suffered abroad even if the underlying substantive rule has extraterritorial reach. In *RJR Nabisco, Inc.* v. *European Community*, the Court held that some provisions in the Racketeer Influenced and Corrupt Organizations Act (RICO), govern foreign conduct. But "despite its conclusion that the presumption had been overcome with respect to RICO's substantive provisions," the Court "separately applied the presumption against extraterritoriality to RICO's cause of action." The Court held that the private right of action did not reach injuries suffered abroad—even injuries caused by domestic conduct—because "nothing in RICO provides a clear indication that Congress intended to create a private right of action for injuries suffered outside of the United States."

Accordingly, even if Congress had enacted a statute expressly providing a damages remedy for individuals whose constitutional rights are violated by federal officers—and even if petitioners were correct that the Fourth and Fifth Amendments apply in this extraterritorial context—this Court would not extend that statutory remedy to this case absent "clear indication" that Congress intended to reach "injuries suffered outside of the United States." Given this Court's longstanding reluctance to extend *Bivens*, it would be "grossly anomalous to apply *Bivens* extraterritorially when courts would not apply an identical statutory cause of action for constitutional torts extraterritorially."

C. Petitioners Identify No Sound Reason to Extend *Bivens* to the Novel Context Presented Here

Petitioners provide no sound reason to extend *Bivens* for the first time in more than 35 years.

1. Petitioners principally contend that they lack an adequate alternative remedy. But this Court has made clear that while the *presence* of an alternative remedy may preclude the extension of *Bivens*, the "absence of statutory relief for a constitutional violation does not by any means necessarily imply that courts should award money damages against the officers responsible for the violation." "Even in the absence of an alternative," a *Bivens* remedy

is inappropriate if there are "any special factors counselling hesitation." And the Court has instructed that "it is irrelevant to a 'special factors' analysis whether the laws currently on the books afford the plaintiff an 'adequate' federal remedy for his injuries." The Court has therefore declined to extend *Bivens* even where that result left no "prospect of relief for injuries that must now go unredressed."

Moreover, petitioners err in asserting that the denial of a *Bivens* remedy "creates a legal no-man's land in which federal agents can kill innocent civilians with impunity." DOJ investigates and prosecutes allegations of excessive force by federal law-enforcement officers, including U.S. Border Patrol agents. It is currently prosecuting an agent for murder based on a cross-border shooting. The possibility of such prosecutions provides a strong deterrent against the sort of shootings petitioners posit, and a successful prosecution would also result in an order providing restitution for the victim's family.

In addition, the United States is answerable to Mexico for any uses of force across the international border, and the two nations continue to work to reduce such incidents. In conjunction with those bilateral efforts, U.S. Customs and Border Protection (CBP) has revised its training requirements, use-of-force policies, and investigative practices in the six years since the shooting at issue in this case. U.S. Border Patrol agents are subject to internal review and discipline under regulations promulgated pursuant to a specific congressional directive.

In 2014, the CBP revised its use-of-force policy to incorporate recommendations made by DHS's Inspector General and an independent review body. At the same time, CBP undertook "a comprehensive review and redesign of its basic training curriculum." And as of February 2015, CBP has instituted a new procedure in which specially trained teams including representatives from the DOJ's Civil Rights Division review every incident in which death or serious injury results from the use of force by a CBP officer.

Furthermore, the Westfall Act protects Agent Mesa from state-law tort suits only because DOJ certified that he was acting within the scope of his employment. Such "scope-of-employment certifications are reviewable in court." And although petitioners did not exercise their right to seek judicial review here, tort remedies are available in instances where federal agents act outside the scope of their employment.

2. Petitioners also assert that the arguments against extending *Bivens* to aliens injured abroad impermissibly "double count" the considerations militating against extending the underlying constitutional provisions. In their view, if the Fourth and Fifth Amendments apply to aliens abroad, *Bivens* should too. But the whole premise of the special-factors inquiry is that a judicially created damages remedy is *not* appropriate for every constitutional violation—indeed, "in most instances this Court has found a *Bivens* remedy is unjustified." The question in every new context is whether Congress, rather than the Judiciary, is the appropriate body to "prescribe the scope of relief that is made available." Here, a powerful combination of factors shows that the scope of any damages remedy for aliens injured abroad by U.S. officials is "better left to legislative judgment." Those injuries implicate sensitive questions of diplomacy and national security; Congress has consistently withheld the sort of judicial remedy plaintiffs seek; and the presumption against extraterritoriality confirms that it would be inappropriate to extend a damages remedy beyond our Nation's borders absent legislative guidance.

II. The Fourth Amendment Does not Apply to Aliens in Hernández's Position

The *en banc* court of appeals held, without dissent, that the Fourth Amendment did not apply to Agent Mesa's alleged conduct because Hernández was an alien in Mexico who had no connection to the United States. That conclusion was compelled by this Court's decision in *United States* v. *Verdugo-Urquidez*, which held that the Fourth Amendment had "no application" to the search and seizure of a nonresident alien's property in Mexico. Petitioners do not deny that *Verdugo-Urquidez* forecloses their claim. And *Verdugo-Urquidez* is entirely consistent with this Court's subsequent decision in *Boumediene* v. *Bush*, which addressed the application of the right to habeas corpus in an area where the United

States maintained "*de facto* sovereignty." The Court should therefore decline petitioners' invitation to abandon *Verdugo-Urquidez* in favor of an ill-defined and unworkable totality-of-the-circumstances test for the extraterritorial application of the Fourth Amendment.

A. *Verdugo-Urquidez* Held That The Fourth Amendment Generally Does Not Apply To Aliens Abroad

1. In *Verdugo-Urquidez*, this Court addressed the applicability of the Fourth Amendment to the search and seizure of property located in Mexico and owned by a Mexican citizen. Verdugo-Urquidez, a suspected leader of a drug cartel, had been apprehended by Mexican authorities and transported to the United States, where he was held pending trial. A DEA agent stationed in the United States "arranged for searches of Verdugo-Urquidez's Mexican residences," one of which was in the border city of Mexicali. Those searches, which were carried out by DEA agents working with Mexican authorities, resulted in the seizure of evidence implicating Verdugo-Urquidez in the distribution of illegal drugs.

The Court framed the question presented as "whether the Fourth Amendment applies to the search and seizure by United States agents of property that is owned by a nonresident alien and located in a foreign country." Although the searches were "arranged" from the United States after Verdugo-Urquidez had been brought to this country, the Court observed that any Fourth Amendment violation "occurred solely in Mexico," the location of the properties subject to the challenged searches and seizures.

In holding that the Fourth Amendment had "no application" to such searches and seizures, *Verdugo-Urquidez*, the Court conducted a comprehensive analysis using a variety of interpretative methods. It began by noting that the text of the Fourth Amendment codifies a right held by "the people." Although the Court viewed the text as "by no means conclusive," it stated that the Framers' use of that term, in contrast with the broader language found in the Fifth and Sixth Amendments, suggests that the Fourth Amendment protects "a class of persons who are part of a national community or who have otherwise developed sufficient connection with this country to be considered part of that community."

The Court placed greater weight on "the history of the drafting of the Fourth Amendment," which shows that "its purpose was to restrict searches and seizures which might be conducted by the United States in domestic matters." After reviewing that history, the Court concluded that "it was never suggested that the provision was intended to restrain the actions of the Federal Government against aliens outside of the United States."

The Court also found "no indication that the Fourth Amendment was understood by contemporaries of the Framers to apply to activities of the United States directed against aliens in foreign territory or in international waters." The Court noted, for example, that in 1798 Congress authorized privateers to seize French vessels, "but it was never suggested that the Fourth Amendment restrained the authority of Congress or of United States agents to conduct operations such as this."

The Court then surveyed more than a century of case law and observed that aliens had been afforded constitutional protections only when "they had come within the territory of the United States and developed substantial connections with this country." The Court concluded that although Verdugo-Urquidez was being held in the United States at the time of the challenged searches, he could not claim Fourth Amendment protection under the logic of those decisions because he was "an alien who has had no previous significant voluntary connection with the United States."

Finally, the Court emphasized that extending the Fourth Amendment to aliens abroad "would have significant and deleterious consequences for the United States." The Court noted that "the United States frequently employs Armed Forces outside this country for the protection of American citizens or national security." And it warned that the application of the Fourth Amendment to such uses of force "could significantly disrupt the ability of the political branches to respond to foreign situations involving our national interest."

The Court described the obvious harms that would follow if "aliens with no attachment to this country" could "bring actions for damages to remedy claimed violations of the Fourth Amendment in foreign countries or in international waters." But the Court also cautioned that even if *Bivens* were "deemed wholly inapplicable in cases of foreign activity," extraterritorial application of the Fourth Amendment to aliens would still "plunge the political branches into a sea of uncertainty as to what might be reasonable in the way of searches and seizures conducted abroad." The Court concluded that any restrictions on such searches and seizures "must be imposed by the political branches through diplomatic understanding, treaty, or legislation."

2. For more than a quarter century, this Court and others have understood *Verdugo-Urquidez* to establish that the Fourth Amendment generally does not apply to searches and seizures of aliens outside the United States.

That rule forecloses petitioners' Fourth Amendment claim. Petitioners' complaint alleges that Hernández "was a citizen of the Republic of Mexico" and that, at the time of the shooting, he was "on his native soil of Mexico" and "had no interest in entering the United States." Hernández thus lacked even the connection to this country held by Verdugo-Urquidez, who was lawfully present in the United States when the challenged searches occurred. Accordingly, petitioners "cannot assert a claim under the Fourth Amendment" as interpreted in *Verdugo-Urquidez*.

B. Neither Justice Kennedy's Concurring Opinion Nor This Court's Subsequent Decision In Boumediene Undermines *Verdugo-Urquidez*'s Holding

Petitioners do not dispute that the rule announced by this Court in *Verdugo-Urquidez* forecloses their Fourth Amendment claim. They also do not attempt to make the showing that this Court demands before overruling one of its precedents. Instead, petitioners assert that *Verdugo-Urquidez* is no longer good law because its purportedly "formalist" approach is inconsistent with the approach to extraterritoriality they contend is reflected in Justice Kennedy's concurrence in that case and the Court's subsequent decision in *Boumediene*. Petitioners are mistaken. Justice Kennedy "joined" "the opinion of the Court" in *Verdugo-Urquidez*, including its holding that the Fourth Amendment generally does not apply to aliens abroad. Justice Kennedy also made clear that his views did not "depart in fundamental respects" from the opinion he joined.

Justice Kennedy's only expressed disagreement with the Court concerned its reliance "on the reference to 'the people' in the Fourth Amendment." In all other respects, Justice Kennedy agreed with the Court's analysis, which looked to precisely the sort of "general principles of interpretation" he regarded as controlling—including the history and purpose of the Fourth Amendment; the contemporary understanding of the Framers; and the "deleterious consequences" that would follow from the extraterritorial application of restrictions on searches and seizures developed to constrain domestic law enforcement. Justice Kennedy endorsed these "other persuasive justifications stated by the Court." And he also agreed with the Court that "the Constitution does not create, nor do general principles of law create, any juridical relation between our country and some undefined, limitless class of noncitizens who are beyond our territory."

2. Petitioners likewise err in asserting that *Boumediene* implicitly overruled *Verdugo-Urquidez*. *Boumediene* held that the Suspension Clause applies to certain aliens detained by the United States at the Guantanamo Bay Naval Station, where the Court concluded that the United States exercises "complete jurisdiction and control" equivalent to "*de facto* sovereignty." The Court rejected the government's argument that the United States' lack of *de jure* sovereignty established that the Suspension Clause had no application at Guantanamo Bay, stating that "questions of extraterritoriality turn on objective factors and practical concerns, not formalism."

Based on the history of the Suspension Clause and this Court's prior decisions, *Boumediene* concluded that the reach of the Clause should be determined based on three factors specifically keyed to that provision's protection of the right to use habeas corpus to test the legality of executive detentions: "(1) the citizenship and status of the detainee and the adequacy of the process through which that status determination was made; (2) the nature of the sites where apprehension and then detention took place; and (3) the practical obstacles inherent in resolving the prisoner's entitlement to the writ."

In applying that framework to hold that the petitioners in *Boumediene* were protected by the Suspension Clause notwithstanding their alienage and location outside the *de jure* sovereignty of the United States, the Court repeatedly relied on the fact that "in every practical sense Guantanamo is not abroad" because "it is within the constant jurisdiction of the United States." The Court also emphasized the historic function of the Suspension Clause as a judicially enforceable limit on executive detention. As the Court explained, the Suspension Clause "was one of the few safeguards of liberty specified in a Constitution that, at the outset, had no Bill of Rights," and the Clause serves as "an essential mechanism in the separation-of-powers scheme."

3. *Boumediene* thus rested crucially on two factors: the United States' *de facto* sovereignty over Guantanamo Bay and the tradition and function of habeas corpus as a judicial check on executive detention. This Court's decision did not determine the reach of the Suspension Clause in areas over which the United States does not maintain *de facto* sovereignty. It also did not define the extraterritorial application of other constitutional provisions—much less overrule *Verdugo-Urquidez*'s specific holding on the extraterritorial reach of the Fourth Amendment.

Verdugo-Urquidez's analysis and holding are, moreover, entirely consistent with *Boumediene*'s approach to the question of extraterritoriality presented in that case. And like *Boumediene*, it carefully considered the practical consequences of extra-territoriality. Petitioners' assertion that *Verdugo-Urquidez* reflects "formalism" or relied solely on the Fourth Amendment's textual reference to "the people" ignores these "other persuasive justifications stated by the Court."

Boumediene thus casts no doubt on the conclusion that, in accordance with *Verdugo-Urquidez*, the Fourth Amendment has no application in this case. Unlike Guantanamo Bay, Northern Mexico, including the area near the border where Hernández was shot, is not under the sovereignty of the United States, *de facto* or otherwise. That area is sovereign Mexican territory that U.S. personnel generally may not even enter absent permission from the Mexican government. *Boumediene* involved a site where "no law other than the laws of the United States" applied, and where under the Guantanamo Bay lease agreement Cuba "effectively had no rights as a sovereign." Here, in contrast, the United States is answerable to Mexico for any cross-border uses of force. And whereas the writ of habeas corpus was intended to serve as a *post hoc* judicial check on executive detentions, the Fourth Amendment is a substantive individual right that was codified to restrain the conduct of domestic law enforcement, that was not understood by the Framers to apply to aliens abroad, and that could significantly interfere with vital American military and intelligence activities if given such extraterritorial application.

C. This Court Should Reject Petitioners' *Ad Hoc* Approach to the Extraterritorial Application of the Fourth Amendment

1. Although petitioners purport to advocate a test for Fourth Amendment extraterritoriality derived from *Boumediene*'s three-factor test for the Suspension Clause, they actually propose an open-ended judicial inquiry into the wisdom of applying the Fourth Amendment based on the totality of the circumstances presented in each case. On petitioners' view, the application of the Fourth Amendment to aliens abroad depends on the intrusiveness of the search or seizure at issue, including whether it resulted in a loss of life; the particular characteristics of the alien—here, that Hernández was "an unarmed civilian teenager"; whether the injury occurred in an area that is part of a "shared border community" that is "heavily patrolled"; whether the U.S. officer was in the United States and subject to compulsory process in foreign courts; the alien's distance from the U.S. border; whether the alien was in an area in which U.S. officers have previously used force; and whether the officer's alleged conduct is inconsistent with U.S. statutes and regulations.

Petitioners' open-ended list of factors appears to have been tailor-made to fit the particular circumstances of this case. It has no basis in *Boumediene* or the decisions on which *Boumediene* relied. Although those decisions considered "objective factors and practical concerns," they did so to reach categorical conclusions about extraterritoriality like the one adopted in *Verdugo-Urquidez*—not to impose open-ended, case-by-case tests like the one petitioners urge here. In *Boumediene*, for example, the Court held that the Suspension Clause "has full effect at Guantanamo Bay"—it did not parse the individual circumstances of particular detainees. Similarly, the Insular Cases adopted categorical rules about the applicability of constitutional provisions in particular territories. Petitioners do not cite any decision adopting the sort of *ad hoc* approach they advocate—much less one imposing such a test to extend constitutional protections to an ill-defined and uncertain class of aliens outside the *de jure* and *de facto* sovereignty of the United States.

2. Petitioners' indeterminate approach would, moreover, "plunge the political branches into a sea of uncertainty" about the application of the Fourth Amendment to military and intelligence activities abroad. Such uncertainty would itself be "impracticable and anomalous"—particularly in the Fourth Amendment context, where this Court has repeatedly expressed its "general preference to provide clear guidance to law enforcement through categorical rules."

The need for clarity especially acute abroad, where restrictions on searches and seizures have potential implications not only for law enforcement, but also for military and intelligence activities. As *Verdugo-Urquidez* observed—and as the Nation's experience in the intervening decades has only reinforced—"the protection of American citizens or national security" sometimes requires the use of armed force abroad. Similarly, the United States routinely collects intelligence abroad to gather information that is "essential to the national security of the United States."

Both Congress and the Executive Branch have relied on *Verdugo-Urquidez*'s holding that the Fourth Amendment generally does not protect aliens abroad. The Foreign Intelligence Surveillance Act of 1978 (FISA), Executive Order 12,333, and other laws and regulations governing intelligence activities are structured around that understanding. The government also conducts other classified intelligence-gathering activities abroad. Petitioners' proposed test would cast a cloud of uncertainty over those vital activities.

To be sure, although the amorphous nature of petitioners' approach makes it difficult to be certain, the government would have arguments that military and intelligence activities should not be subject to Fourth Amendment scrutiny even under their approach. And the government would have strong arguments that such activities would in any event satisfy any Fourth Amendment reasonableness standard that might apply. But as this Court explained, uncertainty about the Fourth Amendment's extraterritorial reach—and the prospect of case-by-case judicial adjudications—could itself "significantly disrupt the ability of the political branches to respond to foreign situations involving our national interest."

3. Petitioners seek to avoid the disruptive implications of their position by asserting that this case involves only the immediate border area, not "extraterritoriality of the Fourth Amendment more broadly." But even if petitioners' test were so cabined, it would still be unworkable. Under their view, courts would have to decide, among other things, whether it would make a difference if (1) the alien is wounded, rather than killed, (2) the alien is an armed adult, rather than an unarmed minor; (3) the alien is searched, rather than seized; (4) the injury occurred in an isolated area of the border, not a cross-border community; (5) the injury occurred in an area that is not frequently patrolled, rather than one that is; (6) the U.S. official or the alien was a considerable distance from the border, rather than a few feet from it; or (7) the U.S. official was on the Mexican side of the border, working with Mexican authorities. Be- cause petitioners' test is free-floating, rather than grounded in the history or function of the Fourth Amendment, it offers courts no basis for determining whether any of those differences matter.

That uncertainty could raise questions about the government's vital efforts to secure the Nation's borders. For example, the U.S. Border Patrol relies on "sophisticated systems of surveillance," including "'thermal imaging systems,'" and those systems "do not look strictly inward." Petitioners' test would also raise questions about any joint U.S.–Mexican law-enforcement activities on the Mexican side of the border zone—including one of the searches at issue in *Verdugo-Urquidez* itself, which occurred in the border city of Mexicali. As Judge DeMoss observed, petitioners' approach to extraterritoriality around the border "devolves into a line drawing game" without principled lines—and that game "is entirely unnecessary because there is a border between the United States and Mexico."

Another fundamental problem with petitioners' approach is that it is not actually limited to the border area. Petitioners carefully avoid conceding that the Fourth Amendment is inapplicable outside some ill-defined border zone, and they offer no principled basis for drawing such a distinction. To the contrary, the test they urge this Court to adopt calls for an *ad hoc* totality-of-the-circumstances inquiry for *all* questions about the application of the Fourth Amendment to aliens abroad. And many of the factors they identify could have broader application.

To take one example, petitioners assert that that it is significant that this case involves the loss of life. But situations that "require an American response with armed force"—and thus risk the loss of life—"may arise half-way around the globe." Petitioners also contend that it is important to the result here that the United States exercises a degree of control across the border because U.S. Border Patrol have the ability to use force against individuals in Mexico. But the same could be said about areas near hundreds of military bases and other U.S. installations abroad; about any area patrolled by the U.S. military; or about any location within the reach of U.S. military weapons.

Petitioners also emphasize that Agent Mesa was in the United States when he fired his weapon. But U.S. military personnel can trigger the use of deadly force abroad from within the United States. An even broader set of searches and seizures abroad are traceable to decisions made within our borders. *Verdugo-Urquidez*, for example, involved searches that occurred in Mexico, but were planned in a DEA office in California. Indeed, as this Court observed in a related context, virtually any claim of injury allegedly caused by a U.S. officer in a foreign country can be "repackaged" as a claim based on actions in the United States.

Petitioners thus ask this Court to adopt an ill-defined and uncertain test for the extraterritorial reach of the Fourth Amendment.

In *Verdugo-Urquidez*, this Court declined to adopt a rule that could have "significantly disrupted the ability of the political branches to respond to foreign situations involving our national interest" even though the particular facts of that case involved DEA-led searches of two houses in Mexico. The Court's concerns remain equally weighty today, and they counsel decisively against petitioners' proposed departure from *Verdugo-Urquidez*'s holding.

III. Agent Mesa Is Entitled to Qualified Immunity on Petitioners' Fifth Amendment Claim Because His Alleged Actions Did not Violate any Clearly Established Fifth Amendment Right

All 15 members of the *en banc* court of appeals agreed that Agent Mesa was entitled to qualified immunity on petitioners' substantive-due-process claim because his alleged actions did not violate any clearly established Fifth Amendment right. That unanimous holding was correct.

A. Petitioners' Claim Is Barred by Qualified Immunity Unless Every Reasonable Officer in Agent Mesa's Position Would Have Known that His Alleged Actions Violated the Fifth Amendment

"The doctrine of qualified immunity shields officials from civil liability so long as their conduct 'does not violate clearly established constitutional rights of which a reasonable person would have known.'" The doctrine is designed to ensure "that fear of liability will not 'unduly inhibit officials in the discharge of their duties,'" and that capable individuals are not deterred from public service or distracted from the performance of their responsibilities. Qualified immunity promotes those objectives by affording "both a defense to liability and a limited 'entitlement not to stand trial or face the other burdens of litigation.'"

To survive a motion to dismiss based on qualified immunity, a *Bivens* plaintiff must "plead facts showing (1) that the official violated a constitutional right, and (2) that the right was clearly established at the time of the challenged conduct." "A clearly established right is one that is 'sufficiently clear that every reasonable official would have understood that what he is doing violates that right.'" That standard requires either "controlling authority" or "a robust 'consensus of cases of persuasive authority'" establishing that the official's conduct was unconstitutional. The authority need not be "directly on point," but it must be sufficiently similar to place the constitutional question "beyond debate."

As these decisions make clear, the qualified-immunity inquiry is not about the reasonableness or wrongfulness of an official's conduct in the abstract. Instead, qualified immunity applies unless the defendant's actions clearly violated the specific right that provides the basis for the plaintiff's claim. A right is clearly established for qualified-immunity purposes only if "every reasonable official would have understood that what he is doing violates *that right*." Accordingly, the "clearly established right" violated by the officer's conduct must "be the federal right on which the claim for relief is based." Here, petitioners allege that Agent Mesa violated an asserted substantive-due-process right to be free from excessive force. The dispositive question is thus whether "every reasonable official" in Agent Mesa's position "would have understood that what he is doing violates the Fifth Amendment."

B. It Would Not Have Been Clear to Every Reasonable Officer in Agent Mesa's Position that His Alleged Actions Violated the Fifth Amendment

The *en banc* court of appeals unanimously held that, at the time of the incident at issue here, it was not clearly established that the Fifth Amendment applied to an alleged use of excessive force by a U.S. official against an alien located in Mexico. Petitioners do not disagree with that characterization of the law, and could not plausibly do so in light of this Court's past recognition that "it is well established that certain constitutional protections," including the Fifth Amendment, "are unavailable to aliens outside of our geographic borders." Instead, petitioners maintain that the court of appeals should have conducted the qualified-immunity analysis as if Hernández were a U.S. citizen because Agent Mesa did not know with certainty that Hernández was an alien at the time of the incident.

Petitioners are correct that the qualified-immunity analysis focuses on facts known to the defendant at the time of the challenged conduct. But that means that the question in this case is whether every reasonable officer in Agent Mesa's position would have known that the Fifth Amendment applies to the use of force against an individual of unknown nationality located outside the United States, where the officer has no reason to believe that the individual is a U.S. citizen. And for two independent reasons, the answer to that question is no.

1. Petitioners are correct that qualified-immunity focuses on facts known to the officer at the time of the challenged conduct. This Court has explained that the "dispositive inquiry" is "whether it would be clear to a reasonable officer that his conduct was unlawful *in the situation he confronted*," and the Court has therefore focused on the facts that the officer "reasonably understood" when he acted. That approach follows from qualified immunity's goal of ensuring that officials are held liable in damages only if they violated "clearly established statutory or constitutional rights of which a reasonable person would have known." That standard is not satisfied if the application of a right was not clear based on the facts known to the officer.

2. Petitioners assert that the court of appeals departed from the proper approach to qualified immunity by relying on Hernández's status as an alien, a fact that petitioners contend was unknown to Agent Mesa at the time of the incident. As the government explained in its brief in opposition, the court did not expressly address the after-acquired facts issue on which petitioners now focus. Had it done so, it might have framed the qualified-immunity question more precisely, to account for Agent Mesa's asserted lack of certainty about Hernández's nationality. But that framing would not have altered the court's ultimate conclusion, because no precedent clearly establishes how the Fifth Amendment applies where, as here, an officer confronts a person of unknown nationality outside the United States who the officer has no reason to believe is a U.S. citizen.

Petitioners observe that, as a general matter, it is clearly established that a law enforcement officer "may not seize an unarmed, nondangerous suspect by shooting him dead." But the decisions petitioners cite to support that proposition involved individuals in the United States. The "situation Agent Mesa confronted," was different. Petitioners' complaint alleges that Hernández was in Mexico at the time of the incident, and petitioners do not allege any facts suggesting that Agent Mesa had any reason to believe that Hernández was a U.S. citizen. To the contrary, the complaint indicates that Agent Mesa believed (correctly) that Hernández was *not* a U.S. citizen because it alleges that Agent Mesa was "attempting to apprehend him on suspicion of illegal entry into the United States."

Petitioners cite no decision addressing the application of the Fifth Amendment to an officer's use of force against a person who is outside our Nation's territory and who the officer has no reason to believe is a U.S. citizen. Petitioners instead contend that Agent Mesa is not entitled to qualified immunity because petitioners allege that he engaged in conduct that, if proved, would violate U.S. Border Patrol regulations governing the use of force, federal and state murder statutes, and international law. But those other sources of law have no bearing on the qualified-immunity inquiry. "Officials sued for constitutional violations do not lose their qualified immunity merely because their conduct violates some statutory or administrative provision," even if the relevant statute or regulation "advance[s] important interests or was designed to protect constitutional rights."

Instead, the question is whether the contours of the specific constitutional right on which petitioners rely—the Fifth Amendment—were "sufficiently clear that every reasonable official" in Agent Mesa's situation "would have understood that what he is doing violates *that right*." And because petitioners identify no authority addressing the application of the Fifth Amendment to the novel circumstances presented here, the answer to that question is no.

3. Agent Mesa is also entitled to qualified immunity for an independent reason unrelated to Hernández's citizenship or to any issue about after-acquired facts: It is not clearly established that an excessive- force claim like this one can ever be asserted under the Fifth Amendment, or whether such claims must arise, if at all, only under the Fourth Amendment.

"Because the Fourth Amendment provides an explicit textual source of constitutional protection" against seizures, this Court has held that "*all* claims that law enforcement officers have used excessive force—deadly or not—in the course of an arrest, investigatory stop, or other 'seizure' of a free citizen," as distinct from a person in custody, "should be analyzed under the Fourth Amendment rather than under a 'substantive due process' approach." That principle precludes reliance on the Fifth Amendment "if a plaintiff's claim is 'covered by' the Fourth Amendment."

Here, petitioners' claim is "covered by" the Fourth Amendment in the sense that it involves a "seizure." Petitioners allege that Agent Mesa shot Hernández "while attempting to apprehend him," and "there can be no question that apprehension by the use of deadly force is a seizure," Accordingly, the district court and four members of the court of appeals concluded that petitioners' Fifth Amendment claim fails on the merits because "if petitioners have any claim at all, it arises from the Fourth, not the Fifth Amendment."

Judge Prado disagreed, concluding that because the Fourth Amendment does not apply extraterritorially, it does not "cover" the excessive-force claim at issue here and thus does not preclude resort to substantive due process. But Judge Prado did not suggest that the applicability of the Fifth Amendment to facts like these was clearly established. To the contrary, it appears that no appellate decision has addressed that question. The disagreement among the members of the court of appeals on that question of first impression reinforces the absence of clearly established law. "If judges disagree on a constitutional question, it is unfair to subject public employees to money damages for picking the losing side of the controversy."

And the fact that the threshold applicability of the Fifth Amendment was not clearly established provides an independently sufficient basis for holding that Agent Mesa is entitled to qualified immunity.

Conclusion

The judgment of the court of appeals should be affirmed.

Respectfully submitted.[3]

Brief #4

The issue in this case is whether the double jeopardy clause bars the government from retrying defendants after a jury has returned irreconcilably inconsistent verdicts of conviction and acquittal and the convictions are later vacated for legal error unrelated to the inconsistency.

Statement

Following a jury trial in the U.S. District Court for the District of Puerto Rico, petitioners were convicted of, *inter alia*, federal program bribery, in violation of 18 U.S.C. 666. Petitioners were sentenced to 48 months of imprisonment, to be followed by three years of supervised release. As relevant here, the court of appeals vacated petitioners' bribery convictions on grounds of instructional error and remanded for further proceedings. On remand, before retrial, the district court denied petitioners' motions for acquittals on the bribery charges under the Double Jeopardy Clause. The court of appeals affirmed.

1. From January 2005 until early 2011, petitioner Hector Martínez-Maldonado was a senator for the Commonwealth of Puerto Rico. Petitioner Juan Bravo-Fernandez was the president of Ranger American, a private security firm in Puerto Rico that provided services such as armored car transportation and security guard staffing. During the time relevant to this case, Martínez-Maldonado was chairman of the Senate's Public Safety Committee, which had

jurisdiction over bills related to the security industry in Puerto Rico.

In early 2005, Bravo-Fernandez began advocating for legislation that, if enacted, would "provide substantial financial benefits" to him. On February 23, 2005, he presented a proposed bill, which became Senate Project 410 (SP 410) to Martínez-Maldonado. In early March 2005, Bravo-Fernandez provided a proposed bill that became Senate Project 471 (SP 471) to Martínez-Maldonado. Bravo-Fernandez and Martínez-Maldonado were not friends and had no relationship before Bravo-Fernandez's advocacy for the two bills.

In his role as chairman of the Senate's Public Safety Committee, Martínez-Maldonado "was in a position to exercise a measure of control over the introduction and progression of the bills through the Committee and the Senate." Another senator, Jorge de Castro Font, was chairman of the Senate's Rules and Calendars Committee, which exercised control over which bills were brought to a vote and when.

On March 2, 2005, Bravo-Fernandez purchased several tickets for $1,000 each to attend a professional boxing match between the popular Puerto Rican boxer Félix "Tito" Trinidad and Ronald Lamont "Winky" Wright, which was scheduled to occur in Las Vegas in May 2005. Bravo-Fernandez's telephone records from that day reflect that he made multiple calls to de Castro Font and Martínez-Maldonado shortly after he purchased the tickets to the boxing match.

Later in March 2005, Bravo-Fernandez met with Martínez-Maldonado and an aide to discuss the status of SP 471. The aide testified that Bravo-Fernandez and Martínez-Maldonado also discussed the trip to Las Vegas to watch the boxing match. After Bravo-Fernandez left the office, the aide testified that he told Martínez-Maldonado that it would be improper to accept the trip because Bravo-Fernandez was asking Martínez-Maldonado to pass legislation.

On April 20, 2005, Martínez-Maldonado presided over a Public Safety Committee hearing on SP 471, at which Bravo-Fernandez testified. The next day, Bravo-Fernandez reserved a hotel room at the Mandalay Bay Hotel in Las Vegas. Bravo-Fernandez also arranged first-class airline tickets for himself, Martínez-Maldonado, and de Castro Font from Puerto Rico to Las Vegas. On May 11, 2005, Martínez-Maldonado issued a Committee report in support of SP 471.

On May 13, 2005, Bravo-Fernandez, Martínez- Maldonado, and de Castro Font flew to Las Vegas and checked into the Mandalay Bay Hotel, where they stayed for two nights in separate rooms. Bravo-Fernandez paid for Martínez-Maldonado's room the first night. The three men went out to dinner the first night, with Bravo-Fernandez paying the $495 bill. The second night, they attended the boxing match, sitting in the $1,000 seats purchased by Bravo-Fernandez.

On May 15, 2005, the three men flew from Las Vegas to Miami, where they stayed at the Marriott South Beach in individual rooms that Bravo-Fernandez paid for, at a total cost of $954.75. On May 16, 2005, they returned to Puerto Rico. On May 17, 2005, de Castro Font scheduled an immediate Senate floor vote on SP 471. Martínez-Maldonado and de Castro Font both voted in favor of the bill. The next day, Martínez-Maldonado issued a Committee report supporting SP 410. On May 23, 2005, de Castro Font scheduled an immediate floor vote on SP 410. Again, Martínez-Maldonado and de Castro Font voted in favor of the bill.

On June 22, 2010, a federal grand jury in the District of Puerto Rico returned an indictment charging petitioners with federal program bribery, in violation of 18 U.S.C. 666; conspiracy, in violation of 18 U.S.C. 371; and interstate travel in aid of racketeering, in violation of 18 U.S.C. 1952(a)(3)(A) (Travel Act). Martínez-Maldonado was additionally charged with obstruction of justice, in violation of 18 U.S.C. 1512.

Following a jury trial, petitioners were convicted of federal program bribery, in violation of 18 U.S.C. 666. The jury acquitted petitioners of conspiring to violate Section 666 and of violating the Travel Act in furtherance of violating Section 666.

The district court sentenced each petitioner to 48 months of imprisonment.

The court of appeals vacated petitioners' federal program bribery convictions, holding that the jury instructions had erroneously permitted the jury to find petitioners "guilty of offering and receiving a gratuity, rather than a bribe." As a matter of first impression, and "unlike most circuits to have addressed the issue," the court held that Section 666 criminalizes only quid pro quo bribes, and not gratuities.

The court of appeals recognized that "significant portions" of the jury instructions and the government's closing argument "were consistent with a bribery theory under Section 666," including Jury Instruction 22, titled "Bribery," which stated that "bribery requires that the government prove beyond a reasonable doubt the existence of a *quid pro quo* or, in plain English, an agreement that the thing of value that is given to the public official is in exchange for that public official promising to perform official acts for the giver." But the court observed that other language in the jury instructions involving Section 666 stated that the government did not need to prove that an agreement to offer or accept a thing of value was made before the recipient took official action, and thus permitted a finding of guilt based on a reward for a completed act.

The court of appeals noted that the evidence at trial supported a finding of guilt on both an exchange theory and a gratuity theory. Because the court could not say with certainty that the jury did not rely on a gratuity theory, it vacated petitioners' Section 666 convictions and remanded for further proceedings.

2. The case returned to the district court for a possible retrial of petitioners on the federal program bribery charges.

Before retrial, petitioners moved for judgments of acquittal on the Section 666 offenses under the Double Jeopardy Clause. Petitioners argued that collateral estoppel precluded retrial on those charges because, in petitioners' view, the jury had necessarily found that they were not guilty of violating Section 666 when it acquitted them of conspiring and traveling with the intent to violate Section 666.

The district court denied the motions. The court rejected petitioners' argument that the jury's verdict on the conspiracy and Travel Act charges demonstrated that the jurors had necessarily decided that petitioners did not commit bribery, given that the jury had also convicted petitioners of a standalone bribery offense, and thus "necessarily found all elements of section 666 federal program bribery to be proven beyond a reasonable doubt." Although those convictions had been vacated for instructional error, the court concluded that they remained a relevant part of the record when "determining what the jury necessarily decided" for purposes of applying collateral estoppel.

Considering the convictions and acquittals together, the district court was "not persuaded that it could glean the underlying facts and theory" that led to the acquittals on the conspiracy and Travel Act counts. The court explained that "the fact that the jury unanimously found that all elements of the substantive section 666 charge were met when they convicted" on the bribery counts "would seem to suggest that at least one other element of" the conspiracy and Travel Act charges "was not satisfied." Petitioners' argument "that a rational jury *could not* have found the absence of an agreement, an overt act, or interstate travel" demonstrated only "that the jury acted irrationally and the verdict simply was inconsistent." Petitioners, the court concluded, therefore could not meet their burden of showing that the "jury necessarily decided the issue of bribery in their favor."

3. The court of appeals affirmed, holding that the collateral estoppel component of the Double Jeopardy Clause did not bar the government from retrying petitioners on the Section 666 counts. Under this Court's decision in *Ashe* v. *Swenson*, the court of appeals observed, a defendant who can show that the jury necessarily decided an issue in his favor in a prior prosecution that ended in an acquittal may preclude relitigation of that issue in a subsequent prosecution. To determine whether a defendant has carried that burden, *Ashe* directed that courts must examine all relevant record material and assess whether "a 'rational jury,' as a practical matter, decided adversely to the government an issue to be relitigated in the new prosecution."

The court of appeals recognized that this Court adopted "an important limitation" on preclusion principles in *United States* v. *Powell*, which held that collateral estoppel is inapplicable when

344 A LITIGATOR'S GUIDE TO BUILDING YOUR BEST ARGUMENT

the jury acts irrationally by returning inconsistent verdicts. In that situation, "*Powell* concluded that there is no way to know without speculating which of the inconsistent verdicts—the acquittal or the conviction—the jury really meant," and so collateral estoppel principles "are impossible to apply." The court of appeals noted that, "in light of *Powell*," petitioners did "not deny that a true inconsistency in what the jury has done in acquitting on one offense while convicting on another can make unanswerable *Ashe*'s question about what the jury necessarily decided in rendering the acquittal."

Applying *Ashe* and *Powell*, the court of appeals concluded that collateral estoppel did not apply because the jury verdicts in petitioners' trial were truly inconsistent. The court observed that "the jury was offered the same theories of Section 666 liability as to every count involving Section 666, whether as a predicate offense or a standalone crime." Because the jury had found petitioners guilty of violating Section 666 but not guilty of conspiracy and traveling with the intent to violate Section 666, the court could not "reconcile the verdicts." That inconsistency, the court held, made it impossible to determine that the jury had necessarily decided that petitioners did not commit bribery in violation of Section 666.

The court of appeals rejected petitioners' argument that the Section 666 convictions could not be considered in determining what the jury decided because those convictions had been vacated for legal error. *Ashe*, the court observed, "instructed that, for purposes of determining the collateral estoppel effect of acquittals, courts must undertake a 'practical' analysis based on the 'record' of the prior proceeding, and with 'an eye to all the circumstances of the proceedings.'" The court reasoned that "like the acquittals on which petitioners rely, the convictions in this case are part of what the jury decided at trial." "Thus, for purposes of deciding whether the jury necessarily decided that the government failed to prove that petitioners violated Section 666," the court observed, "the fact that the jury also convicted petitioners of violating Section 666 would seem to be of quite obvious relevance, even though the convictions were later vacated."

The court of appeals also rejected petitioners' effort to analogize vacated convictions to counts on which a jury has hung, which are not a relevant part of the record for purposes of applying collateral estoppel under *Yeager* v. *United States*. Hung counts cannot "create a 'truly inconsistent' verdict," the court observed, because, as *Yeager* emphasized, they do not constitute jury decisions at all. Under that "line of reasoning in *Yeager*," the court of appeals concluded that "vacated counts should be treated differently from hung counts" because "vacated convictions, unlike hung counts, *are* jury decisions, through which the jury *has* spoken." *Ibid.* When such a conviction creates a true inconsistency, the court explained, "*Powell's* 'prudent acknowledgment' that inconsistent verdicts make it impossible to determine what a jury necessarily decided is not undermined by the mere fact" that the conviction has been vacated.). The court therefore "concluded that vacated convictions, unlike hung counts, are relevant to the *Ashe* inquiry into what a jury necessarily decided when acquitting on counts related to the vacated convictions."

Summary of Argument

The collateral estoppel component of the Double Jeopardy Clause does not bar a retrial of petitioners on the Section 666 offenses. The jury in the first trial returned irreconcilably inconsistent verdicts, convicting petitioners of violating Section 666 but acquitting them of conspiring and traveling with the intent to violate Section 666. In light of that inconsistency, petitioners have not carried their burden of showing that the jury necessarily decided that they were not guilty of violating Section 666.

A. A defendant seeking to preclude relitigation of an issue under the Double Jeopardy Clause bears the burden of demonstrating, based on a practical and realistic review of the entire record, that the jury in the prior trial necessarily decided the issue in his favor when it acquitted him. In *United States* v. *Powell*, this Court held that a defendant cannot satisfy that burden when the jury returns inconsistent verdicts. In that situation, a defendant cannot show that the acquittal reflects the jury's conclusion that the government had not proved its case. *Powell* accordingly held, in accordance with general preclusion principles, that collateral estoppel does not apply.

In this case, the jury returned irreconcilably inconsistent verdicts by convicting petitioners of violating Section 666 but acquitting them of offenses involving Section 666 as a predicate. Because the district court instructed on the same theories of liability for all counts involving Section 666, no rational jury could have reached those contradictory results. The inconsistent verdicts make it impossible to know what the jury necessarily decided in its acquittals. Petitioners therefore have not met their burden of showing the most essential prerequisite for applying collateral estoppel: that the jury actually resolved facts in their favor.

B. Petitioners cannot avoid that conclusion by noting that their convictions for violating Section 666 were subsequently vacated for instructional error. That error—which applied equally to all of the Section 666 offenses—does not resolve the inconsistency in the verdicts and so cannot provide a basis for viewing the acquittals as reflecting the jury's factual conclusion that petitioners were not guilty of violating Section 666.

1. Petitioners err in relying on *Yeager* v. *United States*. That case did not hold, as petitioners assert, "that an acquittal retains its preclusive effect despite any inconsistency with a hung count." Rather, *Yeager* held that a hung count *cannot* be inconsistent with an acquittal because it does not represent a jury determination at all. *Yeager* emphasized that "a jury speaks only through its verdict" because those are the only decisions that represent the unanimous agreement and collective judgment of all 12 members of the venire. A hung count, in contrast, cannot be "evidence of the jury's irrationality" because the jury as a whole has failed to agree. Thus, as *Yeager* itself emphasized, a mix of acquittals and hung counts presents "an entirely different context" than "inconsistent *verdicts*." *Yeager* accordingly has no application here, where the jury as a whole acted irrationally by returning irreconcilably inconsistent verdicts.

Petitioners further misread *Yeager* in suggesting that it adopted a rule that events that do not terminate jeopardy must be disregarded when conducting a collateral estoppel inquiry. Logically, many events at trial may fail to terminate jeopardy, yet will inform an inquiry into what the jury necessarily decided for purposes of applying collateral estoppel. By treating those two separate double jeopardy questions as intrinsically linked, petitioners urge a line of reasoning that *Yeager* itself expressly rejected.

2. Principles of finality and respect for the jury's verdict do not support petitioners' suggestion that courts must disregard a jury's inconsistency when applying collateral estoppel. Petitioners base that suggestion on *Powell*, but misunderstand its whole point. *Powell* refused to set aside a conviction that was inconsistent with an acquittal—and so preserved the finality of both verdicts—precisely because in that situation it is impossible to know that the jury necessarily resolved the facts in the defendant's favor, and it is thus unreasonable to treat the acquittal as the verdict the jury "really meant." That rationale does not lose its force when a conviction is vacated for legal error because vacatur does not erase the jury's inconsistency, alter what the jury necessarily decided, or excuse a defendant's inability to answer that question. If a defendant cannot satisfy his burden of showing that the jury decided facts in his favor at the conclusion of the initial trial, as *Powell* held, then he remains unable to show that the jury decided facts in his favor for purposes of applying collateral estoppel in a second trial.

3. Petitioners are also wrong to suggest that this Court has approved a categorical rule that vacated convictions may not be used against a defendant for any purpose. To the contrary, this Court has recognized in a different case involving the Double Jeopardy Clause that an invalid conviction may—despite its unconstitutionality for other purposes—be relied upon to determine what the jury that returned that conviction necessarily decided. Lower courts, too, have held in a variety of contexts that vacated convictions may reveal what the jury necessarily determined in its other verdicts or provide other relevant and admissible evidence in subsequent proceedings. Contrary to petitioners' suggestion, the court of appeals' decision below fits comfortably with precedent.

C. Policy arguments do not support petitioners' contention that courts should ignore a jury's inconsistency when applying collateral estoppel. Petitioners maintain that without the availability of collateral estoppel in this context prosecutors would be encouraged to overcharge cases and press unreasonable interpretations of criminal statutes. But petitioners offer no evidence that prosecutors strategically overcharge and adopt indefensible interpretations of statutes in hopes of obtaining an inconsistent verdict so as to defeat the application of collateral estoppel in any ensuing retrial. And such speculative policy arguments—which rest on a highly attenuated causal chain—cannot excuse petitioners' inability to show that the jury necessarily found facts in their favor.

Petitioners' policy arguments also ignore the significant interests in permitting retrial when a conviction is vacated for legal error. Those interests deserve respect here, where the evidence supported a bribery conviction on a proper theory, the jury was instructed on that theory, the jury returned a conviction for bribery, and petitioners have not shown that the jury necessarily found that they did not commit bribery.

ARGUMENT

Collateral Estoppel Does not Apply Because the Inconsistent Verdicts Prevent Petitioners from Satisfying their Burden of Showing that the Jury Necessarily Decided that They Were not Guilty of Violating Section 666

Petitioners cannot carry their burden of showing that the jury in their first trial necessarily determined that they were not guilty of bribery in violation of Section 666. The jury returned inconsistent verdicts, making it impossible to determine that the jury resolved that issue in petitioners' favor. Nor does it matter that the convictions were subsequently vacated for unrelated legal error. Vacatur of the convictions does not erase the historical fact of the jury's inconsistency and does nothing to establish that the jury that convicted petitioners of violating Section 666 necessarily found that they were not guilty of that offense. The court of appeals thus correctly held that collateral estoppel does not apply.

A. The Inconsistent Verdicts in Petitioners' First Trial Prevent Them from Showing that the Jury Necessarily Decided that They Did not Commit Bribery

1. The Double Jeopardy Clause provides that no person shall "be subject for the same offence to be twice put in jeopardy of life or limb." In *Ashe* v. *Swenson*, this Court interpreted the Clause to incorporate the principle of collateral estoppel, which "means simply that when an issue of ultimate fact has once been determined by a valid and final judgment, that issue cannot again be litigated between the same parties in any future lawsuit."

To establish that the collateral estoppel component of the Double Jeopardy Clause applies, "the burden is 'on the defendant to demonstrate that the issue whose relitigation he seeks to foreclose was actually decided in the first proceeding.'" If multiple "possible explanations for the jury's acquittal verdict at the first trial" exist, a defendant cannot satisfy that burden because he cannot show that any particular issue "was determined in [his] favor."

To determine what a jury in a prior trial has necessarily decided, this Court's "cases require an examination of the entire record, taking into account the pleadings, evidence, charge, and other relevant matter." The Court has explained that "the inquiry 'must be set in a practical frame and viewed with an eye to all the circumstances of the proceedings.'"

The Court has further clarified that "to identify what a jury necessarily determined at trial, courts should scrutinize a jury's decisions, not its failures to decide." Thus, *Yeager* held that "a hung count is not a 'relevant' part of the 'record of the prior proceeding.'" "Because a jury speaks only through its verdict," the Court reasoned, "its failure to reach a verdict cannot—by negative implication—yield a piece of information that helps put together the trial puzzle."

In contrast, courts have held that convictions from the same jury are relevant under *Ashe* because they may reveal that the jury either did or did not resolve a particular issue in the defendant's favor when acquitting on a related count. In *Schiro*, for example, this Court considered whether the defendant's conviction for felony murder reflected a jury finding that he did not have an intent to kill, and ultimately concluded that the verdict "did not necessarily depend on a finding" of lack of intent.

2. a. As the court below recognized, this Court's precedents establish "an important limitation on the application of the rule of collateral estoppel" when a jury has reached inconsistent verdicts in the prior proceeding. When an acquittal is inconsistent with a conviction on a related count—such as when a jury acquits on a predicate offense but convicts on a compound offense—the Court has observed that it is impossible to determine what the jury necessarily decided in acquitting, making "principles of collateral estoppel no longer useful."

As *Powell* explained, "inconsistent verdicts present a situation where 'error,' in the sense that the jury has not followed the court's instructions, most certainly has occurred, but it is unclear whose ox has been gored." A defendant cannot establish that "the acquittal on the predicate offense was proper—the one the jury 'really meant,'" because "it is equally possible that the jury, convinced of guilt, properly reached its conclusion on the compound offense, and then through mistake, compromise, or lenity, arrived at an inconsistent conclusion on the lesser offense." The Court has accordingly declined to treat the acquittal as "showing that jurors were not convinced of the defendant's guilt.'" The "inconsistency is reason, in itself, for not giving preclusive effect to the acquittal" in a subsequent prosecution.

Indeed, to the extent that any meaning can be attributed to an acquittal that is inconsistent with a conviction, this Court has recognized that the most likely explanation is that the jury believed the defendant was guilty of both counts but should only be punished for one crime.

The Court accordingly "interprets the acquittal as no more than the jurors' assumption of a power which they had no right to exercise, but to which they were disposed through lenity." The possibility that the jury "acquitted out of compassion" fortifies the conclusion that the inconsistent verdicts did not necessarily resolve facts in the defendant's favor.

b. This Court's recognition that inconsistent verdicts cannot trigger collateral estoppel accords with general preclusion principles. "The estoppel doctrine is premised upon an underlying confidence that the result achieved in the initial litigation was substantially correct." "Where a determination relied on as preclusive is itself inconsistent with some other adjudication of the same issue, that confidence is generally unwarranted." And particularly where the same jury returns inconsistent verdicts in a single proceeding, there can be no doubt that "error most certainly has occurred."

In the civil context, that type of error precludes application of the estoppel doctrine. For example, courts may decline to afford preclusive effect to a verdict that "was the result of compromise" rather than a rational application of the jury instructions and the law. So too in the criminal context, collateral estoppel is "predicated on the assumption that the jury acted rationally and found certain facts in reaching its verdict." Because that assumption does not hold when a jury's decision to acquit is inconsistent with its decision to convict, collateral estoppel cannot apply.

The rule that collateral estoppel is inapplicable when a court lacks confidence in the correctness of the original adjudication carries particular force in the criminal context given the government's inability to appeal from an erroneous acquittal. "It is of course true that verdicts induced by passion and prejudice are not unknown in civil suits," but "post-trial motions and appellate review provide an aggrieved litigant a remedy." And a civil litigant who was deprived of the right to obtain review of the judgment may avoid collateral estoppel on that basis alone. Although the absence of appellate review of acquittals does not prevent the application of collateral estoppel in a criminal case, it heightens the need to "refuse the protection" of the doctrine when its premise "that a criminal jury has acted in a rational manner" is demonstrably refuted by inconsistent verdicts.

3. Applying these principles here, petitioners cannot carry their burden of demonstrating that the jury in the first trial—which convicted them of violating Section 666—necessarily determined that they did not violate Section 666.

Petitioners contend that the jury must have found that they "did not commit the predicate Section 666 offense" when it declined to convict them of conspiring and traveling to violate Section 666. But if the jury necessarily determined that petitioners were not guilty of a Section 666 offense, it could not rationally have convicted them of that offense. "The jury was offered the same theories of Section 666 liability as to every count involving Section 666," yet the same 12 jurors who unanimously voted to convict on a standalone Section 666 crime unanimously voted to acquit on the offenses involving Section 666 as a predicate. As the court of appeals analyzed at length, and as petitioners no longer dispute, those verdicts are irreconcilably inconsistent. In light of that inconsistency, "the most that can be said" about the jury's verdicts in this case is that "either in the acquittals or the convictions the jury did not speak their real conclusions, but that does not show that they were not convinced of petitioners' guilt."

Petitioners' argument to the contrary "necessarily assumes that the acquittals" on offenses involving Section 666 as a predicate "were proper—the ones the jury 'really meant.'" But it is at least "equally possible"—if not far more likely—that the jury "properly reached" the conclusion that petitioners were guilty of a Section 666 violation and acquitted on the related charges "through mistake, compromise, or lenity." Petitioners' contention that the jury necessarily found that they were not guilty of violating Section 666 thus rests on "pure speculation"—which does not suffice to carry their burden of showing that the jury resolved the issue in their favor. The inconsistent verdicts make it impossible to know what the jury actually decided, and "principles of collateral estoppel—which are predicated on the assumption that the jury acted rationally and found certain facts in reaching its verdict"—therefore "are no longer useful."

B. Courts Need not Disregard Convictions that Have Been Vacated in Determining What the Jury that Returned those Convictions Necessarily Decided

Petitioners urge the Court to ignore the inconsistent verdicts in their prior trial because the jury's determination that they were guilty beyond a reasonable doubt of violating Section 666 was vacated for instructional error. Although that error applied equally to all offenses involving Section 666 and so does nothing to resolve the inconsistency in the jury's verdicts or restore confidence that the jury acted rationally in acquitting, petitioners contend that courts must automatically disregard a conviction that has been vacated when assessing what an acquittal in conflict with that conviction necessarily decided. That argument lacks merit.

1. Petitioners' reliance on *Yeager* is misplaced

Petitioners principally rest their argument on *Yeager*, which they contend held that "acquittals retain their preclusive effect under *Ashe* even if the jury acted inconsistently in hanging on other counts." But petitioners misread the case. *Yeager* concluded that hung counts cannot be inconsistent with jury verdicts—and so cannot undermine the presumption of jury rationality—because they do not constitute jury decisions at all. Because hung counts are fundamentally different from vacated convictions in that respect, *Yeager*'s analysis has no application here.

a. In *Yeager*, the defendant faced trial on various charges of fraud and insider trading based on allegations that he had made false and misleading statements about his company and sold stock while in possession of material, non-public information. The jury acquitted him of the fraud charges, which the court of appeals there determined must have reflected a finding that he "did not have any insider information that contradicted what was presented to the public." But the jury was unable to reach a verdict on the insider trading counts, and the government accordingly sought to retry the defendant on those hung counts. Applying *Ashe*, this Court held that, under the collateral estoppel component of the Double Jeopardy Clause, "if the possession of insider information was a critical issue of ultimate fact in all of the charges against the defendant, a jury verdict that necessarily decided that issue in his favor protects him from prosecution for any charge for which that is an essential element."

In concluding that collateral estoppel applied, *Yeager* rejected the argument that the jury had acted irrationally by failing to reach a verdict—rather than also acquitting—on the insider trading counts. Whereas "a jury's verdict of acquittal represents the community's collective judgment regarding all the evidence and arguments presented to it," the Court observed that "there is no way to decipher what a hung count represents." The Court accordingly dismissed the notion that "a mistried count can, in context, be evidence of irrationality." "The fact that a jury hangs is evidence of nothing," the Court observed, "other than, of course, that it has failed to decide anything." Thus, "because a jury speaks only through its verdict," the Court held that "its failure to reach a verdict cannot—by negative implication—yield a piece of information that helps put together the trial puzzle."

b. i. Petitioners contend that *Yeager*'s rationale applies equally to convictions that have been vacated because "the jury has not spoken in a way the law recognizes as legitimate and worthy of public respect." That misconstrues *Yeager*'s point.

Yeager emphasized that a jury "speaks only through its verdict" to contrast decisions that can be attributed to the jury as a whole with hung counts, which do not represent the jury's collective view and so shed no light on how all 12 members of the venire evaluated the arguments and evidence in the case. Based on that distinction, *Yeager* concluded that a hung count cannot constitute "evidence of the jury's irrationality," because, by definition, the jury as a whole has failed to agree on anything. In that situation, a court can conclude that the verdict of acquittal is "the one the jury 'really meant,'" because it is the only decision that garnered the jurors' unanimous agreement. As petitioners point out, the government argued in *Yeager* that "a jury that acquits on some counts while inexplicably hanging on others is not rational." But the Court rejected that argument by emphasizing that "courts should scrutinize a jury's decisions, not its failures to decide." A hung count, the Court noted, can be explained by factors such as "exhaustion after a long trial," which would mean not that the jury was irrational, but that it ended deliberations because of fatigue. "To ascribe meaning to a hung count," the Court concluded, "would presume an ability to identify which factor was at play in the jury room," a matter of "guesswork." The only collective action in *Yeager*—and thus the only relevant evidence of what the jury as a whole necessarily decided at trial—was the unanimous acquittal.

Yeager accordingly did not hold, as petitioners assert, that "collateral estoppel applies despite any inconsistency between the hung counts and the acquittals"; rather, it held that a hung count *cannot* be inconsistent with an acquittal because it is not a jury decision at all.

In contrast to a hung count, a jury's decision to convict represents the unanimous judgment of jurors on the merits of the charge. If that decision to convict is irreconcilably inconsistent with the jury's simultaneous decision to acquit on a related count, the conviction is evidence that the jury as a whole has acted irrationally, even if the conviction must subsequently be set aside for unrelated legal error. Here, for example, all 12 jurors voted to convict petitioners of a standalone Section 666 offense, indicating that the entire jury was "convinced that the Government had proven each of the elements of the crime beyond a reasonable doubt." But those same 12 jurors turned around and declined to convict petitioners of the related offenses involving Section 666, suggesting that the entire jury was *not* "convinced that the Government had proven the elements of a Section 666 offense beyond a reasonable doubt." Those jury decisions are indisputably inconsistent. As *Yeager* itself recognized, inconsistent verdicts there- fore present "an entirely different context" than a mix of acquittals and hung counts.

Petitioners accordingly misread *Yeager* in asserting that courts analyzing a collateral estoppel claim must always find that a jury acted rationally, even when the jury's verdicts conclusively demonstrate that it did not. *Yeager* shows that the Court begins with the presumption that the jury was rational, just as the Court ordinarily presumes that a jury has followed its instructions. But when all 12 jurors vote to return irreconcilably inconsistent verdicts, "'error,' in the sense that the jury has not followed the court's instructions, most certainly has occurred." The "assumption that the jury acted rationally and found certain facts in reaching its verdict" of acquittal is therefore overcome.

Petitioners are also wrong to contend that "*Yeager* necessarily presumed that the 'jury verdicts' from which hung counts fundamentally differed were valid and final jury verdicts." The finality of a conviction has no inherent connection to the question whether that conviction provides "evidence of irrationality." In some cases, of course, the existence and nature of a legal error may resolve an apparent inconsistency in the jury's verdicts. If, for example, the judge "orders the jury to return a guilty verdict" on one count but not on another, that error may explain the discrepancy in the verdicts. Or if a jury receives an erroneous instruction on the count of conviction but the correct instruction on the charge on which it acquits, the instructional error may reconcile the verdicts. But as this case illustrates, inconsistent verdicts may be entirely disconnected from any legal error in the proceeding and so not explainable on that ground. Here, the jury received the same flawed jury instructions on all counts involving Section 666, so that instructional error does not explain the inconsistent verdicts or establish what petitioners must show—that the acquittals represent the jury's "real conclusions."

ii. Petitioners repeat their error by relying on *Yeager*'s observation that "there is no way to decipher what a hung count represents." *Yeager* focused on whether a court could "ascribe meaning to a hung count" to determine whether it could, "in context, be evidence of irrationality." Because "the fact that a jury hangs is evidence of nothing—other than, of course, that it has failed to decide anything," the Court held that hung counts are too inconclusive to create a true inconsistency with "a unanimous verdict that the jurors did return." But as just noted, convictions *are* evidence of something because they represent the collective decision of the jury as a whole. Because convictions signal the unanimous vote of all 12 jurors to find guilt beyond a reasonable doubt, no "guess-work" or "conjecture" is required to decipher their meaning. Thus, in contrast to hung counts, convictions can be "logically inconsistent" with accompanying acquittals "on their face."

Petitioners raise a red herring by observing that the instructional error in this case makes it impossible to determine whether the jury believed petitioners were guilty of an exchange or a gratuity when the jury convicted them of violating Section 666. That is beside the point because it does nothing to eliminate the inconsistency in the jury's verdicts. The erroneous instructions applied to all of the Section 666-based offenses, and a rational jury therefore could not have reached conflicting conclusions on petitioners' guilt of those offenses. The convictions accordingly reveal the jury's inconsistency—which is the relevant issue here—even if they do not reveal which theory of liability jurors relied upon in reaching those inconsistent verdicts.

Petitioners' example proves the point. Petitioners speculate—with no basis in the record—that "all 12 jurors might have thought petitioners guilty of a gratuity, while none thought them guilty of an exchange." But if that is what all 12 jurors thought, then the jury should have convicted petitioners of conspiring and traveling in interstate commerce to violate Section 666, because they were told that a gratuity theory sufficed for liability on those offenses as well. The instructional error does not make sense of the jury's failure to convict, nor does it provide any clue about what motivated the jury to reach inconsistent determinations. Petitioners accordingly cannot rely on the instructional error as a basis to ignore the inconsistency when determining which facts the jury necessarily found in reaching its verdicts.

Petitioners' argument ultimately reduces to a claim that collateral estoppel applies because the government cannot show that the jury necessarily resolved the bribery issue *against* them when it unanimously voted to convict. But that turns the *Ashe* inquiry on its head. It is petitioners who bear the burden of unequivocally showing that the jury necessarily decided the bribery issue *in their favor*. Because the jury returned inconsistent verdicts, they cannot meet that burden here.

iii. Petitioners further misread *Yeager* by contending that it adopted a rule that events occurring at trial that do not terminate jeopardy must be disregarded when conducting *Ashe*'s collateral estoppel inquiry. As petitioners observe, "it has long been settled that the Double Jeopardy Clause's general prohibition against successive prosecutions does not prevent the government from retrying a defendant who succeeds in getting his first conviction set aside, through direct appeal or collateral attack, because of some error in the proceedings leading to conviction." The Court has treated a second trial as a continuation of the original jeopardy, recognizing that the defendant "has a strong interest in obtaining a fair readjudication of his guilt free from error, just as society maintains a valid concern for insuring that the guilty are punished." Petitioners assert that, because a vacated conviction is "a nonevent for the double jeopardy purpose" of terminating jeopardy, it is "equally irrelevant to the *Ashe* analysis."

That argument conflates two distinct components of the Double Jeopardy Clause, which focus on different issues, serve different purposes, and arise under different portions of the Clause's text. The continuing jeopardy principle implicates the defendant's "interest in avoiding multiple trials" and requires a determination of whether he has been "put in jeopardy 'twice.'" The collateral estoppel principle serves a separate "interest in preserving the finality of the jury's judgment" and trains on the distinct question whether "it is appropriate to treat" two crimes as "the 'same offence'" within the meaning of the Clause. Petitioners' effort to blur together those separate double jeopardy doctrines has no grounding in the Clause's text or function.

Nor does petitioners' argument make sense as a matter of logic. Any number of events may occur at trial that fail to terminate jeopardy yet help illuminate the basis of a jury's verdict for purposes of applying collateral estoppel. Jeopardy does not terminate the moment an indictment issues, but the charging document can help to determine what a jury has necessarily decided. Jeopardy does not terminate when the trial court instructs the jury, but those instructions can clarify the basis for the jury's decision. Jeopardy does not terminate when witnesses testify, but that evidence may reveal what issues were in dispute and thus necessarily resolved by the jury. Jeopardy likewise does not terminate when a conviction is vacated for legal error on appeal, but the vacated conviction may nevertheless be relevant when considering what the jury that unanimously voted to return that conviction necessarily decided.

It does not matter that, for purposes of continuing jeopardy, a vacated conviction has been "wholly nullified and the slate wiped clean." That "conceptual abstraction" explains why a retrial does not transgress the double jeopardy "protect[ion] against a second prosecution for the same offense after conviction." But the Court's recognition that a vacated conviction is nullified for purposes of permitting retrial neither changes the historical fact that the jury in the first trial returned that verdict nor alters what that jury necessarily decided.

Yeager cannot reasonably be read to support petitioners' argument. As petitioners note, *Yeager* referred to a hung count as a "nonevent" both in describing why retrial generally is permitted when the jury fails to reach a verdict and in concluding that hung counts are not relevant to a collateral estoppel analysis because they do not constitute jury decisions. But while *Yeager* observed that a mistrial is not "an event of significance" in either of those distinct double jeopardy contexts, it did not draw a causal link between them. For purposes of the *Ashe* inquiry, *Yeager* made clear, a hung count is a "nonevent" not because it fails to terminate jeopardy but because "a jury speaks only through its verdict" and "the fact that a jury hangs is evidence of nothing— other than, of course, that it has failed to decide anything." For the reasons described above, a conviction that reflects the jurors' unanimous agreement and collective judgment on the merits of the charge cannot be characterized as a "nonevent" in the way *Yeager* deemed relevant, even if that verdict must be set aside on appeal for legal error.

Petitioners are also wrong to rely on *Yeager*'s rejection of the government's separate argument in that case that collateral estoppel does not apply when a defendant remains in continuing jeopardy because a retrial does not qualify as a successive prosecution. *Yeager* clarified that collateral estoppel and continuing jeopardy are distinct doctrines. Because collateral estoppel is an independent component of the Double Jeopardy Clause, it can preclude relitigation of issues that were necessarily decided in a prior proceeding, even if the defendant's original jeopardy did not terminate. By treating continuing jeopardy and collateral estoppel as intrinsically linked, petitioners press the very line of reasoning that *Yeager* rejected.

2. Principles of finality and respect for the jury's verdict do not require courts to disregard a jury's inconsistency when applying collateral estoppel

Petitioners contend that courts should ignore a jury's inconsistent verdicts when determining what that jury necessarily decided to show "respect for the finality" of the acquittal. Although they rest that argument on *Powell*, the Court's analysis in *Powell* squarely forecloses their claim.

a. To recap, *Powell* reaffirmed a long line of cases holding that a criminal defendant may not obtain reversal of a conviction on grounds that it is inconsistent with a verdict of acquittal returned by the same jury. In that situation, the Court reasoned, the basis of the jury's inconsistent determinations is unknowable. The Court further deemed it "imprudent and unworkable" to interpret the inconsistent verdicts case by case, noting that "courts have always resisted inquiring into a jury's thought processes." "Through this deference," the Court reasoned, "the jury brings to the criminal process, in addition to the collective judgment of the community, an element of needed finality." Thus, while the defendant in *Powell* "was given the benefit of her acquittal on the counts on which she was acquitted," the Court observed that "it is neither irrational nor illogical to require her to accept the burden of conviction on the counts on which the jury convicted."

In reaching that conclusion, the Court specifically rejected the defendant's argument that the conviction should be set aside based on principles of collateral estoppel. That argument, the Court explained, "simply misunderstands the nature of the inconsistent verdict problem." The defendant wanted the Court to look at the acquittal in isolation and assume that it necessarily resolved facts in her favor. She could not make that showing, however, in light of the inconsistent conviction, which indicated that the jury had resolved facts against her. "The problem is that the same jury reached inconsistent results," the Court concluded, and "once that is established principles of collateral estoppel—which are predicated on the assumption that the jury acted rationally and found certain facts in reaching its verdict—are no longer useful."

b. Petitioners are wrong to assert that *Powell* "commands the conclusion" that an acquittal that is inconsistent with a conviction must nevertheless be given preclusive effect to avoid "impugning" the jury's judgment.

i. Petitioners' reading of *Powell* contradicts this Court's whole point that it is impossible to say that the acquittal resolved facts in the defendant's favor when the jury returns inconsistent verdicts. There can be no ambiguity about *Powell*'s rationale; the Court made the point again and again. Thus, the Court observed that "inconsistent verdicts should not necessarily be interpreted as a windfall to the Government at the defendant's expense" because it is "equally possible" that "the inconsistent verdicts may favor the criminal defendant." Or in other words: "It is unclear whose ox has been gored." Or in still other words: It "is not necessarily correct" that "the acquittal is proper—the one the jury 'really meant'" because "all we know is that the verdicts are inconsistent." And again: "The most that can be said is that the verdict shows that either in the acquittal or the conviction the jury did not speak their real conclusions, but that does not show that they were not convinced of the defendant's guilt."

ii. Nothing about *Powell*'s rationale changes when the inconsistent conviction is vacated for legal error (putting aside those errors that themselves explain the inconsistency). An unrelated legal error does not clarify which facts the jury found in reaching inconsistent verdicts. Nor does the error erase the historical fact that the jury as a collective unit acted irrationally. For purposes of applying collateral estoppel, therefore, the error does not alleviate—and should not excuse—the defendant's inability to carry his burden of showing that the jury necessarily decided facts in his favor.

Petitioners emphasize *Yeager*'s observation that *Powell* "declined to use a clearly inconsistent verdict to second-guess the soundness of another verdict" and instead concluded that "respect for the jury's verdicts counseled giving each verdict full effect, however inconsistent."

But those descriptions merely reflect *Powell*'s holding that a defendant may not rely on the jury's inconsistency to obtain reversal of her otherwise-valid conviction. *Yeager* did not purport to overrule the rationale underlying that holding—namely, that courts should not infer from the acquittal that the jury necessarily found the defendant not guilty in light of the jury's irreconcilably inconsistent finding of guilt beyond a reasonable doubt.

iii. Petitioners likewise fail to establish that *Powell*'s rationale is inapplicable in "the context of a re-prosecution." If inconsistent jury verdicts make it impossible to know that the jury necessarily decided facts in the defendant's favor at the conclusion of the first trial, as *Powell* held, then it is equally impossible to know that the jury necessarily decided facts in the defendant's favor for purposes of applying collateral estoppel in a second trial. In that situation, as this Court has previously recognized, the "inconsistency is reason, in itself, for not giving preclusive effect to the acquittals."

Indeed, *Powell* contemplated that the acquittals in that case would not have preclusive effect to foreclose retrial on the counts of conviction if the convictions were set aside. The court of appeals in *Powell* had reversed the convictions based on the inconsistency, thereby preventing re-prosecution on those counts. In this Court, the government argued that the "outright reversal" was improper because, even if the convictions were invalidated, "the inconsistency in the verdict" meant that "the basis of the jury's acquittal cannot satisfactorily be determined" and "the doctrine of collateral estoppel would not preclude a new trial." Although *Powell* ultimately held that the inconsistent convictions need not be overturned, the Court appeared to agree that a contrary ruling would mean that "the defendant would receive a new trial on the convictions"—rather than reversal—"as a matter of course."

iv. Nor can petitioners escape *Powell*'s rationale by observing that "an acquittal is the most sacrosanct verdict of all under the Double Jeopardy Clause." There is no dispute that a verdict of acquittal is final and unassailable. An acquittal accordingly cannot be invalidated even if it is inconsistent with a conviction and therefore "likely to be the result of mistake, or lenity." In that manner, the verdict of acquittal is given "full effect."

But as *Powell* recognized, an acquittal's special status does not make it any easier to determine what a jury has necessarily decided when the jury issues inconsistent verdicts. And petitioners' observation that an acquittal is a "sacrosanct, final judgment, immune from any subsequent impeachment" in fact "strongly militates against giving an acquittal preclusive effect" because the government lacks an "avenue to correct errors" in that judgment. The government's inability to appeal an erroneous acquittal makes it all the more important to hold petitioners to their burden of demonstrating that the prerequisites for applying collateral estoppel are satisfied.

v. In all events, petitioners' invocation of respect for the jury's verdict rings hollow given that they ask this Court to ignore the jury's unanimous decision that they were guilty of violating Section 666 and instead conclude from an inconsistent part of the verdict that the jury necessarily found that they were *not* guilty of violating Section 666.

As petitioners point out, their Section 666 convictions had to be vacated for instructional error, so the jury did not necessarily find them guilty of an exchange theory of bribery. But the jury instructions included the exchange theory, and the government presented sufficient evidence to support conviction on a proper quid pro quo theory. Accordingly, all 12 jurors may well have found that petitioners committed bribery in violation of Section 666 under a valid theory when they unanimously voted to convict. Principles of respect for and deference to the jury do not warrant transforming that conviction into an acquittal that the jury itself declined to return.

3. Vacated convictions are a relevant part of the trial record when determining what a jury necessarily decided

Petitioners further urge the Court to disregard the jury's inconsistent verdicts by adopting a "categorical rule" that a "vacated conviction may not be used to the defendant's detriment." Petitioners assert that, "to their knowledge, this Court has never held that a vacated conviction can be used against a defendant for any purpose." But, in fact, this Court and lower courts have recognized in a variety of contexts that vacated convictions may illuminate what the jury necessarily decided or provide other relevant evidence admissible in a subsequent prosecution.

a. i. Petitioners' suggestion that unconstitutional convictions may not be relied upon for any purpose contravenes this Court's decision in *Morris* v. *Mathews*. In *Morris*, a defendant who had been convicted of aggravated robbery was subsequently tried and convicted of aggravated murder based on the same incident. As the case came to this Court, it was clear that the successive prosecution for aggravated murder, which required proof of aggravated robbery, violated the Double Jeopardy Clause. The resulting conviction therefore was unconstitutional and could not stand. But it was also clear that a prosecution for the lesser-included offense of simple murder would not violate double jeopardy. The State accordingly sought to reduce the jeopardy-barred aggravated murder conviction to a conviction for murder. The defendant, in contrast, argued that he was entitled to a new trial, reasoning that "because the trial for aggravated murder should never have occurred, the Double Jeopardy Clause barred the State from taking advantage of the jeopardy-barred conviction by converting it into a conviction for the lesser crime of murder."

In analyzing the parties' arguments, this Court observed that it was "clear that the jury necessarily found that the defendant's conduct satisfied the elements of the lesser included offense" of murder when it convicted him of aggravated murder. Thus, although that conviction was unconstitutional, the Court relied on it to determine what the jury had necessarily decided. And reliance on the invalid conviction worked to the defendant's detriment, because the Court concluded that it was appropriate to enter a conviction on the lesser-included offense of murder that the jury had necessarily found rather than grant the defendant a new trial, unless he could demonstrate that "but for the improper inclusion of the jeopardy-barred charge, the result of the proceeding probably would have been different."

Lower courts, too, have recognized that convictions that have been vacated may provide relevant information about what the jury necessarily decided. In *United States* v. *Christensen*, for example, the court vacated the defendant's convictions for violating the Computer Fraud and Abuse Act of 1986 (CFAA), based on instructional error. The court then considered whether to vacate the defendant's convictions for identity theft, which required the jury to find criminal intent under either the CFAA or a parallel state-law statute. To resolve that question, the court considered what the vacated CFAA convictions revealed about the jury's factfinding. "Even though those convictions must be set aside," the court observed, "the facts that the jury necessarily found in returning those guilty verdicts clearly evince intent under" the state statute. Thus, because the vacated convictions demonstrated that the jury necessarily found facts that would establish a violation of the state statute, the court affirmed the identity theft convictions.

The Third Circuit relied on a vacated conviction for a similar purpose in *United States* v. *Velasquez*—and in that case it benefitted the defendant. The defendant in *Velasquez* was convicted of conspiracy, which could have been based on a jury finding that she conspired with a co-defendant or with other unnamed individuals. If the jury had convicted her of conspiring with the co-defendant, the conviction would need to be reversed because there was insufficient evidence that the co-defendant had joined the conspiracy. But if the jury found that she had conspired with other unnamed individuals, the conviction could stand. To help clarify the basis of the conviction, the court noted that the same jury had also convicted the co-defendant of conspiracy. Although that conviction had been vacated for insufficient evidence, the court considered it a relevant part of the record because it showed "a substantial likelihood that the jury's verdict finding the defendant guilty of conspiracy was based on an impermissible determination that she conspired with the co-defendant." Thus, the court relied on the co-defendant's vacated conviction to help illuminate the basis of a separate verdict returned by the same jury.

ii. Courts have also recognized that vacated convictions can have "relevance" in subsequent proceedings in the sense that they have the "tendency" to make a material fact "more or less probable than it would be without" the convictions. For example, this Court has held that the existence of a vacated conviction may defeat an action for malicious prosecution because the conviction, although it has been set aside, provides evidence that there was probable cause for the prosecution.

In addition, courts have concluded that vacated convictions may be relevant, admissible evidence in a subsequent proceeding to prove facts such as a defendant's motive, intent, or plan, or to establish the conviction's effect on the victim's state of mind. For example, the Ninth Circuit concluded that a defendant's prior rape conviction, which had been reversed for instructional error, was properly admitted in a later rape prosecution to show the defendant's intent and plan, where the two crimes were committed in a similar manner. Similarly, the Fifth Circuit rejected a defendant's challenge to the admission of a vacated robbery conviction at his murder trial, reasoning that the vacated conviction was admitted "only for the purpose of showing motive" to kill the victim, who was a witness against the defendant in the robbery prosecution.

And the Eleventh Circuit approved the admission of a vacated murder conviction in a subsequent prosecution of the defendant for violating the Hobbs Act, because the vacated conviction "was relevant to the victim's state of mind" by showing that he reasonably feared the defendant.

Other examples abound.

A vacated conviction that is inconsistent with an acquittal is similarly relevant to a collateral estoppel inquiry because it makes the existence of a material fact—that the jury necessarily decided issues in the defendant's favor—"less probable." The "government's theory" is not, as petitioners assert, "that the vacated convictions embody a factual finding of guilt." Rather, the theory is that petitioners cannot meet *their* burden of establishing that the acquittals necessarily embody a factual finding of innocence because, as a matter of historical fact, the jury returned inconsistent verdicts. In deeming vacated convictions a relevant part of the record for that limited purpose, the court of appeals acted well within precedent.

a. More fundamentally, petitioners' suggestion that courts must automatically ignore vacated convictions when assessing what a jury necessarily decided contradicts *Ashe*. As the Court emphasized in that case, "the rule of collateral estoppel in criminal cases" must be applied "with realism and rationality," taking into account "all the circumstances of the proceedings." Errors that occur at trial are themselves a relevant circumstance of the proceeding that may help to establish what the jury necessarily decided. For example, if a jury is improperly instructed on the elements of a crime, those erroneous instructions may establish that a particular issue was not even submitted to the jury for resolution—let alone necessarily decided by the jury's verdict. A court conducting the "practical" inquiry commanded by *Ashe*, similarly need not disregard a conviction that demonstrates that the jury returned inconsistent verdicts, even if the conviction is set aside for unrelated legal error. After all, *Ashe* underscored that collateral estoppel applies to facts found by "a rational jury"—and focusing on what a rational jury has done makes sense only if the jury has, in fact, acted rationally.

Ashe further emphasized that courts must evaluate the record of the prior proceedings with "realism" and not strain to hypothesize conceivable bases for the jury's decision that lack footing in the on-the-ground facts of the proceeding. Thus, courts should not conclude that "the jury may have disbelieved substantial and uncontradicted evidence of the prosecution on a point the defendant did not contest" so as to deny preclusive effect to an acquittal on the theory that it did not necessarily resolve the sole issue in dispute. But that practical inquiry works both ways. It would be equally improper here to look at the acquittals in isolation and pretend that the jury necessarily found that petitioners were not guilty of violating Section 666 when the same jury simultaneously returned a conviction finding them guilty of that very offense.

A. Petitioners' Policy Arguments Do not Justify Ignoring the Inconsistency in a Jury's Verdicts When Conducting a Collateral Estoppel Inquiry

Petitioners contend that courts should ignore a jury's inconsistent verdicts when determining whether collateral estoppel applies in order to deter prosecutors from "overcharging cases and pushing far-reaching interpretations of criminal statutes." Those policy arguments lack merit and provide no basis for applying collateral estoppel when its essential predicate—the ability to say what a jury necessarily determined in its acquittal—is missing.

1. At the outset, petitioners cite no persuasive evidence that prosecutors routinely overcharge cases or urge unwarranted interpretations of criminal offenses in hopes of obtaining inconsistent verdicts so that they can avoid the application of collateral estoppel in a subsequent prosecution. Indeed, it is fanciful to suggest that prosecutors craft their indictments and statutory arguments in anticipation of a possible *retrial* in a case. A prosecutor who pursues unnecessary and duplicative charges or who urges an indefensible interpretation of a statute risks confusing jurors and increasing the likelihood that they will use their unreviewable ability to acquit out of lenity "as a check against arbitrary or oppressive exercises of power by the Executive Branch." And a prosecutor who gambles on obtaining a retrial faces the risk that "the passage of time may make it difficult or impossible for the Government to carry its burden" of proving guilt beyond a reasonable doubt. Prosecutors are not likely to take those risks and strategically overreach simply to try to obtain an inconsistent verdict and thereby avoid collateral estoppel in any retrial.

In that respect, this case bears no resemblance to the prosecution in *Ashe* that prompted this Court to hold that the Double Jeopardy Clause incorporates the principle of collateral estoppel. In *Ashe*, the State sequentially prosecuted the defendant for robbing multiple victims in a single criminal incident, going to trial first on only one count involving one victim and then, when that trial ended in an acquittal, pressing forward with a second trial for robbing another victim. In the process, the State deliberately honed its trial strategy to shore up its case in light of the acquittal, "treating the first trial as no more than a dry run for the second prosecution." This Court recognized that collateral estoppel should apply to curb that kind of "unfair and abusive reprosecution." Here, in contrast, the government brought all its charges in a single prosecution, with no indication that prosecutors strategically sought "multiple bites at the apple." Petitioners' policy arguments do not warrant distorting the doctrine of collateral estoppel by ignoring inconsistent verdicts that demonstrate that it should not apply.

2. Petitioners' policy arguments further ignore the weighty interests in permitting retrial when a defendant succeeds in having his conviction set aside for legal error.

3. "Reversal for trial error, as distinguished from evidentiary insufficiency, does not constitute a decision to the effect that the government has failed to prove its case." The Court has recognized that "it would be a high price indeed for society to pay were every accused granted immunity from punishment because of any defect sufficient to constitute reversible error in the proceedings leading to conviction." Indeed, it is "at least doubtful that appellate courts would be as zealous as they now are in protecting against the effects of improprieties at the trial or pretrial stage if they knew that reversal of a conviction would put the accused irrevocably beyond the reach of further prosecution." The rule that retrial is permitted after a conviction is vacated for legal error thus has important "implications for the sound administration of justice."

Petitioners accordingly start from the wrong baseline in asserting that "the government should never benefit from having obtained an unlawful conviction" and that retrial would be "antithetical to a fair system of criminal justice." Vacatur of petitioners' convictions for instructional error does not "immunize them from punishment," but rather entitles them only to be tried on a narrower theory. A retrial following vacatur based on instructional error is therefore the default rule—part of the "one full and fair opportunity" prosecutors should have to obtain a conviction of those who have violated the law. There is no injustice in applying that rule here, where the evidence at trial supported conviction on a valid bribery theory, the jury returned a conviction for bribery, and petitioners have not carried their burden of showing that the acquittals necessarily reflect a factual determination that they were not guilty of bribery.[4]

Conclusion

The judgment of the court of appeals should be affirmed.

Notes

References to citations, transcripts, footnotes, and some authorities omitted for sake of clarity.

Brief No. 1: *Dalmazzi v. United States*, Nos. 16-961, 16-1017, and 16-1423.

Brief No. 2: *Byrd v. United States*, No. 16-1371.

Brief No. 3: *Hernández v. United States*, No. 15-118.

Brief No. 4: *Bravo-Fernandez, et al. v. United States*, No. 15-537.

ABOUT THE AUTHOR

Cecil C. Kuhne III is a litigator in the Dallas office of Norton Rose Fulbright. He is the author of 17 other books on litigation matters published by the American Bar Association, including *A Litigator's Guide to Expert Witnesses* and *A Litigator's Guide to Convincing the Judge*.

INDEX